edited by peter finch & grahame davies

THE BIG BOOK OF CARDIFF

new writing from europe's youngest capital

seren

Seren is the book imprint of
Poetry Wales Press Ltd
57 Nolton Street, Bridgend, CF31 3AE, Wales
www.seren-books.com

Introduction and Editorial © Peter Finch and Grahame Davies, 2005
For individual contributions see Acknowledgments

ISBN 1-85411-398-4

The publisher works with the financial assistance of
the Welsh Books Council

Printed in Plantin by CPD, Ebbw Vale

Contents

Introduction

HOW DO YOU IMAGINE Cardiff to be? If you're middle-aged and have never been here maybe you think the hills run right to the shoreline and there's coal in the streets. If you're from north-west Wales, maybe it's a colonial outpost of the English empire – governmental, stern, alien, nothing to do with you. If you're from America, where knowledge of the Principality barely exists, it's the town that gave the world Shirley Bassey. If you're from Cardiff, New South Wales, you might know it's the city that steel once came from. If you're a member of the local population you might still imagine it to be part of the West Country. Served originally by television companies based as much in Bristol as they were here and with reception problems best solved by pointing your aerial at the Mendips such geographic schizophrenia is little wonder. Cardiff, the most important place in Wales. English-speaking Cardiff. Cardiff, city of darkness, drizzle and smoke.

Cardiff is all of these things and none of them. It's changed enormously since most of them stuck in the post-war world consciousness. Cardiff is now post-industrial (one rolling mill, couple of scrap yards, factory that makes television screens), re-structured, re-built and re-marketed. Shops, clubs, bars, waterfronts, opera houses, seats of Welsh government, best rugby stadium in the known universe. Binge centre of Britain, a Welsh Faliraki or Ag Nik. The youngest of European capitals and with the energy to match.

The writing collected in this anthology reflects that place. The new Cardiff, the one that's arrived since the 1980s when the decision to redevelop the docklands and rebuild Cardiff's shopping heart were taken. St David's Hall, Cardiff's purpose-built concert hall, opened in 1982; the Cardiff Bay Development Corporation to regenerate the city's collapsed docklands opened for business in 1986; South Glamorgan County Council re-located themselves to a brand-new pagoda-like headquarters at the south end of the abandoned Bute East Dock in 1987. These were the first signs of the boom to come. Things hit full stride when devolution, thanks to a wafer-thin referendum majority – and no thanks to Cardiff's own 'No' vote – became a reality and the National Assembly for Wales was established in 1999.

The work you'll find here needs to stand on its own literary merits but *The Big Book of Cardiff* is no inclusive and certainly no historical anthology of writers from the Capital. Here contemporaneity and content lead. As editors we wanted an anthology which would reflect the city as it is now, in all its stumbling and gaudy glory. To do that we've searched among the poets and the novelists and the fictioneers in both English and Welsh, most of them Cardiff residents of some sort – either still living here or recently moved on. Now and again we've selected pieces from informed visitors – Chris Torrance who writes about his famous *Adventures In Creative Writing* at the University; Ifor ap Glyn, who opens up the thriving Welsh-language evening-class subculture; Gareth Miles with his sceptical take on the Welsh-speaking middle classes; Niall Griffiths who contextualises Cardiff, Welsh capital of the south, with Liverpool, Welsh capital of the north; and Anthony Howell who writes so brilliantly about the flatlands that lie between this city and its eastern rival, Newport. We've let a couple of historical pieces through, simply to place the roaring present on the solid arms of the past. John Williams has extended his essay about the growth of Cardiff Docks, which originally appeared as part of *Bloody Valentine,* his book on the Lynette White murder, to include the present day. Tom Davies hilariously fills in on paddle steaming in the Bristol Channel and Dannie Abse goes back to his old days in Roath.

We've scooped stuff up and extracted it from the great new rush of Cardiff-based novels that London publishers have produced during the past ten years. Sean Burke, Trezza Azzopardi, James Hawes, Bill James, and Duncan Bush can all be read at greater length elsewhere. Theirs is often a fictionalised Cardiff, although the pieces we've used have been selected for their veracity. You can read material written in Cardiff's notorious can-opening accent – check Tôpher Mills and Lloyd Robson. The Welsh-language community – 11% of the city's population and growing faster than anywhere else in Wales – is represented by novelists like the hell-raising Owain Meredith and the thought-provoking Owen Martell, by poets such as the compelling Emyr Lewis and the irreverent Elinor Wyn Reynolds. Apposite new poetry in English comes from Gillian Clarke, Jonathan Brookes, Viki Holmes and others. And you can read new Cardiff fiction specially commissioned for this anthology from some of Wales' best writers: Tessa Hadley, Penny Simpson, Anna Davis, Nia Williams.

Old Cardiff – the Victorian and Edwardian city of coal and ships and steel – written about by some of the best of twentieth-century authors (Jack Jones, Bernice Rubens, Alexander Cordell, Iorwerth C. Peate, Bobi Jones, Glyn Jones, Emyr Humphreys, and John Tripp among them) is captured to perfection in the predecessor to the present anthology, Meic Stephens' 1987 *A Cardiff Anthology*. For the complete picture that book is worth searching out. But the future is in the other direction. Already St David's Two, the flattening of great swathes of the central city in the name of shopping, is under way. The Bay spawns an increasing number of apartment towers. Nearness to water is vital. Buildings crowd like Serengeti wildebeest. The city moves out to the north and to the east. Sucks in wealth. Replicates, grows. *The Even Bigger Book of Cardiff*, that's next.

Peter Finch & Grahame Davies, Cardiff, 2005

Dannie Abse
From Return Ticket to Cardiff

IT WAS A pilot programme for London Weekend Television titled *Friends of John Betjeman*. I could not claim to be a friend of Sir John. I had not previously met him. No matter; here I was in the studio invited to read a few poems of my own and to chat with John Betjeman about verse that he had selected. The technicians were messing about. It would be an hour yet before we'd wear artificial smiles and the programme would begin. "The first poem I've chosen," said Sir John, "is by Hood." He didn't mean Robin Hood. It so happened that I had recently read a strange long poem by Thomas Hood called 'Miss Kilmansegg and Her Precious Leg'. I asked Sir John whether he knew it. He knew it very well. With surprising passion he turned to me as if I had given him something he had wanted all his life. "How *very* good of you to know that poem," he cried out. "Oh, thank you, thank you very much." Suspiciously, I smiled. But John Betjeman was being quite sincere; he was sincerely grateful that another individual had read and liked a poem he knew and cared for. He continued to thank me rhapsodically and his eyes glittered with pleasure as we discussed the merits of Thomas Hood's poetry. "The poem I've chosen of Hood's," said Sir John, "is 'I remember, I remember the house where I was born'. Some may think it sentimental but it isn't, it isn't and I don't care if it is!" Staring straight ahead he chanted those extraordinary lines that, at first, I thought twee until I really listened. Then I realized how the rhythm of the poem lulled me and half disguised the terrible pessimism and depression that engined the remembrances:

> I remember, I remember,
> The house where I was born,
> The little window where the sun
> Came peeping in at morn;
> He never came a wink too soon,

Nor brought too long a day,
But now, I often wish the night
Had borne my breath away!

I couldn't remember the house where I was born. All I knew about 161 Whitchurch Road in Cardiff was that my parents labelled it 'The Smoky House'. That was because the chimney needed sweeping and since we were about to move my mother never bothered to summon the sweep. I don't recall the house being smoky. I do recall (my first memory I think) that I was being looked after by my big brother Wilfred. He is with me and I am somewhere (in a pram?) and looking through railings at green stuff (a park?). Well, Cardiff is a city of pram-filled parks and perhaps anyone born in Cardiff has a similar early memory. What else? I remember, I remember bugger all.

After the programme John Betjeman remarked, "One day you should go back and visit the house where *you* were born." I nodded. Why not? One day I would. I'd knock on the door of the smoky house in Whitchurch Road. "Here I am," I'd say. I would knock on the door of 289 Albany Road too. Audaciously, perhaps, I'd visit all those Cardiff houses we had once lived in. Middle-aged I would breathe in air I had once breathed in. The more I thought about it the more I resolved to go back to my own beginnings. I even fixed a date for that nostalgic mission: Monday, 29 May, the bank holiday. Then if I hadn't changed my mind, if my enthusiasm had not entirely evaporated, I would travel the 23 miles from Ogmore-by-Sea to the Smoky House which, like a hero, I would enter unarmed.

29 May proved to be a rare day, perfect weather. Do you remember what you did on that blue, beautiful bank holiday, 29 May 1978? Remember the mirages on the roads? Perhaps you were in one of those innumerable cars that travelled to Ogmore-by-Sea? If so, I could have passed you as I travelled eastward from Ogmore, where I think I was conceived, to Cardiff where I know I was born.

Frankly, 161 Whitchurch Road, a plain two-storeyed, semi-detached house, would hardly excite anyone, least of all Sir John. I sat in the car in the bank-holiday-empty Whitchurch Road at 10.30 a.m. and gave the Smoky House the eye. It didn't look as if it would last long enough to have that blue plaque on its grey façade: 'Dannie Abse, Cardiff City FC supporter, was born here, poor chap.' I quit the car and approached the front door. There, I was baffled. Two bells! The Smoky House had been turned into two self-contained flats. Which bell to ring, bottom or top? Eeny meeny miney mo – bottom bell. I was lucky: a young, dazzlingly pretty woman with dark, closely cut, curly hair wearing very short tennis shorts opened the door. Yes, I thought, it is worth knocking on doors, banging on bells, being a commercial traveller, a vote canvasser, a Jehovah's witness. I explained my mission and, yes, I could come in and look around providing her flatmate agreed. Would I excuse her while she consulted her flatmate? Her flatmate, another young woman in her twenties, appeared and I smiled at her, my teeth cleaned. Hesitatingly, the other young lady agreed. Perhaps I did look like a burglar casing the joint. Three inquisitive cats also materialized, six unblinking yellow eyes. The grate, I noticed, had been converted into an electric fire – no more smoky chimneys. In the front room I loitered, trying to feel something, anything. Here my parents, no doubt, entertained the occasional important visitor and brought out the best crockery or offered him or her a glass of sherry with a dainty slice of Madeira cake? I felt nothing.

The attractive curly-haired girl – her name was Veronica – led me into the bit of a garden in the back where a couple of dozen worn-out bluebells and a dusty lilac tree waited to be appreciated. Vaguely, I wondered whether the tree was older than I (the tree is living yet!), then Veronica opened the back door of the garden. A lane and, immediately the other side of that narrow lane, railings. Railings! Railings of a park! I heard a click in my head and Veronica said, "That's called Maitland Park."

So now I knew the name of my first memory, and appropriately as I stood there a young couple pushed a baby across the grass towards a building with a red-tiled roof. Despite the trees, I could read the words painted meaninglessly – doubtless by some erring kids – across this roof: 'ANDY, PAT, PAUL'. Just that. And I thought, were these names mere graffiti or plaques? And was there any difference?

On the way to 289 Albany Road I stopped the Austin Maxi outside Marlborough Road Elementary School where I had first, wide-eyed and reluctant, begun my so-called education. The school had been bombed during the war but now it looked much the same. It was curiously quiet waiting there in the spreading sunlight – no high, piping, pre-pubertal voices sang 'Ash Grove' or 'Men of Harlech'. And then visions, visions, clear, not even behind glass! Those boys there, playing with coloured glass alleys in the gutter, well, one of them was me and it was almost half a century ago.

"Swap you three of these for your blood alley!" said Philip Griffiths.

And of course that vision faded as soon as it had appeared, leaving me with that sense of vertigo that any grown man may experience when he contemplates Time Past or No Time At All. The uneasiness such as one might feel on staring at a night sky and apprehending infinity. But the sky was blue, blue, blue, and the two streets were empty that were called Marlborough Road and Agincourt Road. When a woman came out of one of the houses she smiled at me knowingly as if she knew why I was there. I didn't have to say to her, "I went to school here, you know. George Thomas who's now the Speaker in the House of Commons used to teach me – though that's not why I'm so ignorant!"

As a matter of fact, Mr Thomas was particularly kind to me. "Order, Order," Mr Thomas now shouts in the House of Commons at all those squealing MPs and "Order, Order," shouted the same Mr Thomas, sir, when I first started in the Big Boys.

Before I reached 289 Albany Road I stopped the car again, this time outside St Margaret's Church. Gosh, I was tall enough to look over the graveyard wall. And I had always thought of it as so high, higher than the walls of Troy. Still I could only *just* see over it: if someone had spotted me from the churchyard he would have only seen the top of my head, my forehead, eyebrows and my eyes, that's all. And, of course, underneath, the appropriate caption, 'Wot, no ghosts?'

Nobody was about. I walked though the gate, across the pathway strewn with multicoloured confetti, then on the turf towards the dark high cedar tree. Where were all the stone angels, stone tablets behind which I had once played hide and seek? As the song goes, where had all the flowers gone? There were a few graves, not many. Most of the daisy-spotted turf lay back, tidy, unmarked. I read one tilting stone visiting card:

In memory of Sig Thomas John of this Parish formerly of the 43rd Reg. He fought under Generals Moore and Wellington through all the late war in the Spanish Peninsula. He was also engaged at Waterloo. Died October 10, 1864, aged 83 years.

"Thomas John," I said, "You're dead."

"Absent, sir," he replied.

There were only fifteen graves left in St Margaret's Church. Who had taken the rest away? Who had selected those to remain behind to play for St Margaret's Dead First XV? Here perhaps was the hooker:

In memory of John Roberts of the Town of Cardiff who died March 11th, 1851.

Before I could say, "Heel, John," a telephone sounded from inside the shut church. It rang and rang. Nobody answered. I watched two butterflies the same colour as the daisies crookedly float beyond the cypress tree further and further until they disappeared over the wall from no-man's-land into the District of Roath. Soon I, too, quit St Margaret's Churchyard.

I was disappointed to find nobody in at 289 Albany Road. I banged the knocker, rang the bell, uselessly. All the blinds were ominously drawn upstairs and downstairs. In an empty milk bottle a rolled note read, 'No milk today.' A note so peremptory, so curt. Why? Had the owners of 289 gone away for the bank holiday, or had there been a death in the street? Those drawn curtains, those blinds baldly down.

In the thirties, when there had been a death they blinded the windows of the house. I remember, I remember, when next-door Jumbo Thomas's father died. Yes, the blinds had been drawn then and six black horses had pulled a black hearse away leaving nothing behind, not even manure. Again I felt the edges of panic as I remembered. This surely is what the slow movements of all those quartets, Mozart, Beethoven, Schubert, are about: loss. The sound of loss.

Odd to return to where one was born, to visit a graveyard with most of the graves gone and now a house that seemed to proclaim it was mourning for someone. Not for me, surely, not for the boy I was? But I felt the grey hair on my head rise when I noticed across the road (where there used to be, behind a white wall, handsome Roath Court House) a bold sign: 'ROATH COURT FUNERAL HOME'. This was too apt. *Home*. What a word to use. I fled. No point in visiting any of the other houses I once had lived in, that had once been home. Nothing around here remains the same, I thought, except – there beyond St Margaret's Church – the secret minnow-smelling brook in Waterloo Gardens moving in the old direction.

From *A Strong Dose of Myself*

Dannie Abse
The Story of Lazarus

After the war he settled in kindly Cardiff
his English uncertain, his Welsh not at all.
For three years a clerk who hardly said a word.
Then, accusingly, he showed us the number
on his arm, spoke of how he had survived
in his chemistry, the sudden sound of
his heartbeat. Each stark detail. We were shocked.

Week after week this man's monstrous story
heard in Whitchurch, Llandaf, Canton, Cathays,
in pubs and clubs – The Three Elms, The Conway,
The Golden Shark, the Post House, the Moat House;
told even to Cardiff's patient statues:
John Batchelor, Lloyd George, Nye Bevan.

We closed our eyes till we, too, became stone.

So he whispered his dark story to our children
and years later to our children's children.
Soon they merely nodded, eager to join
the procession banging its way outside
to the Firework Display above Roath Park,
the oompha, oompha, down the street fading.

Ifor ap Glyn
Light in the Twilight

(The following five poems are taken from a 14-poem sequence, partly set in Cardiff, which voices the experiences of a group of adult Welsh learners, and their teacher, Elfyn. They are the 'light' in the linguistic 'twilight' but learning a language is never easy, and the poems attempt to convey some of the difficulties and prejudices they come up against, as well as the new pleasures.)

Shaving in front of my son
(Dave: Tremorfa, Cardiff)

I dropped my razor and saw,
as I picked it up suddenly,
my boy in the brass doorknob,
his hands supplicant like two suns,
his fingers, streaming sunbeams.

In his elastic world
he sees no need for shaving,
just the ants on my face;
changing countries
is just learning a new song,
changing languages
like wearing his morning vest.
He, unlike me, needs no Ulpan course
to change his vest...

But in the brass door knob
I too, can attain Nirvana,
forget the frazzle of language learning
and my halting Welsh
becomes a pair of rubber arms
that embrace my boy...
and at the edge of the shaving sink,
the drops of stray lather
are full of sloughed off ants...

The Welsh language in Cardiff
(Elfyn: Park Place, Cardiff)

It's a plant with leaves as fat as butter
that hasn't put its roots down deep
despite the constant forking-in
of bonemeal from the heartlands,
where the Bibles are carried out of closed chapels,
where conversations become museums
where sentences fall fallow,
and where life,
like the language,
is increasingly lean...

Un-learning
(Julie: Penylan, Cardiff)

I learnt my mutations, then learnt to forget them;
I learnt "blwch llwch", but "ash tray"'s just as cool;
but despite my "un-learning",
I'm still a "learner"
and the label
makes me feel like a fool...

Crossing over
(Dave: Tremorfa, Cardiff)

It happened today,
this afternoon in the pressing plant
with the girl from Llanelli
who asks how my lessons are going.
Something special happened,
like the arrival of a biriani,

all trolley and trimmings
and starched white tablecloth;
I understood the spice in her speech,
tasted it for the first time,
as we lovingly co-spooned
from one dish instead of two;

it happened today,
and a linguistic firework display
lit up the night,
scintillating our discussion
as we walked back from the pub
to her house.

Half empty or half full?
(Elfyn: Royal Oak, Cardiff)

Half empty or half full?

The crisis of faith hits home mid-pint
after my daily dealings
with the learners in Park Place.

Half empty or half full?
Is the whole enterprise as guileless
and pointless
as the two year old boy
fetching the sellotape
to mend the crack in his biscuit?
Half empty or half full?

I sway in my uncertainty;
should I drain this and go?
or seek another pintsworth
of that impenetrable mystery?

Thought is the father of the deed,
and the empty glass
pleads at the bar on my behalf.

Half empty or half full?

Much is possible in a city like this...
and when I recall the time I was phone-canvassing
the only white face
in a roomful of black and Asian fellow-travellers
phoning their fellow Welsh
to urge a "yes" vote,

then I submit most emphatically
that we are half **full**
and **not** half empty!

From The Three Disastrous Poetry Readings of the Island of Britain

No.1: Cardiff 1989

Chapter 1989,
an arts centre
in Wales' capital city,
and I discovered that I was
part of an *inter*-national evening,
one of the 'other' cultures
and in my own country,
sharing the right-on clapping and cheering
with some Romanian bard from London,
Bogdan ap Glyn or something...
And so I was part of an exotic experience
which put cling film between me and the audience,

either to keep me fresh
or to stop the smell of Welsh
from tainting the rest of the fridge.

It was like going into your back garden
and finding a bus-load of tourists
digging up your spuds for souvenirs.

    – y'all wanna talk some Welsh at us here bo'?
    – Play us some rug-bee!
    – Show us yore teeth!
    *– Say! Can y'all juggle with **fahve** pieces of bayra breeth?*
    *– Show us how y'all make them thar **traditional** shawls*
    – outa chicken wool!
    *– Shee-it! Ah didn' even know chickens **had** wool!*
    – Sgynnon nhw ddim
    –What you say bo?
    – They haven't any
    – Thelma! Git back on the bus!!

But back in Chapter I was facing an audience,
a Welsh one, an' all, by virtue of residence,
who saw other cultures like picnic tables,
though eating from them was not one of their foibles,
but hell! They're so handy, whether laden or unladen,
for this lot, like cattle, to scratch their arses against them.
so... International, Schmintenational,
Welsh is just normal.

Warning – Welsh Assembly!

(Performed with a live band at the concert to celebrate the opening of the Welsh Assembly in May 1999)

When a third of our people
turn their aerials to the east,
here's a warning –
the Assembly will not lead
to the final fall of Western civilisation;
farmers' land will not be nationalised
nor planted with windmills or furry gonks
and as well as the much-vaunted
"voice in Europe"
we'll have a choir of voices
thundering in the name of justice
down in Cardiff.

Warning – Assembly

People in Cardiff and the Valleys
will not be rounded up and forced to listen
to Welsh language phone-ins, hymn singing
and other bastions of our indigenous culture.

Warning – Assembly

People in Gwynedd
will not be forced to form kazoo bands,
nor drink pints of laver bread in their pubs.

Warning – Assembly

Newspaper columnists
will not be allowed to persist with their habit
of spelling North and South Wales
with a capital N and S

as in North and South Korea, or Vietnam,
because it's not the 49th parallel or the DMZ
that divides us,
but a crap road,
people who say "sietin"*
and the three-legged sheep
of the Brecon Beacons

so, Warning – Assembly
it will change our way of thinking

Warning – Assembly
leave your prejudice by the door

Warning – Assembly
it will make us part of the answer
instead of being part of the problem...

Warning – Assembly...

*Mid-Wales word for "hedge"

Trezza Azzopardi
Cardiff Glowed

CARDIFF GLOWED beneath a painful light. A bank of clouds boiled up orange in the lowering sun, and there was the saturated clarity of air after rain. I was unprepared for such colour. It used to be a place of grey; a dull pearl sheen, leaden buildings, the stink of the Dowlais like charcoal on the wind. There were pin-sharp moments – trips to the pierhead to watch a ship come in, once to the circus, too often to the hospital – and tingling tram rides in the night to Carlotta's house, sitting in a stunned row and watching my mother argue over the fares. There were people my mother had to avoid, the hiding places in arcades and alleyways where she would look down at me with her finger pressed to her lips. Still and close, we waited until the threat had passed. All the rest was under the gauze of time.

But now the city was busy, set and full of purpose. At the front of the taxi queue, a woman pushed me out of the way. I stood on the pavement, waiting for some recognition of what she'd done to me, as if my grown-up self had come unstuck and fled back to Nottingham and safety.

Never get a cab if you stands there! Come yer, love!

A mini-cab driver, poaching for business, shouted at me from across the road. He wore a tartan cap and a white vest two sizes too small, a motif of a cowboy boot emblazoned across the front. Under the thin cotton, a mass of curly chest-hair lay flattened like the stuffing from an old sofa. Frowning and smiling at the same time, he sat me in the back of the car.

Where you takin' me? he joked.

I told him where I wanted to go.

Are you sure? It's all been brought down, that bit.

My mother still lives there, I said.

He consulted on his radio.

We'll get as close as we can, he said.

We stop-started through the traffic, edging the length of St Mary's Street. Spying a gap, he turned a half-circle into an empty stretch of wide new road. From the window I could see fresh black tar, vivid white markings, a ribbon of traffic cones wending into the distance. Saplings had been planted on the embankment, shivering in the evening light. The driver pointed out the sights through his window, The Retail Park's over there on the right, look ... in a minute you'll see the Bute Dock? It's brilliant what they've done. Exchange Building there – really smart now!

I wound my window down as far as it would go, let in a smell of ash, and then a drift of something else – salt. A scent I'd forgotten I knew: the smell of the foreshore, of a lover's licked skin. A mechanical digger in the distance juddered like a wind-up toy, bright yellow against the glint of the mudflats. Minute gulls rose and fell like shreds of blown paper: something was being unearthed.

We left the roadworks to enter a dense block of streets, then another and another until the tang of salt had vanished and there was only the pressure of brick bearing down. The sky between the rooftops fell heavy here. The cab slowed to a crawl.

All this yer's condemned, he said.

I scanned the houses for people. Two young girls stood side by side on the corner with their hands tucked up their sleeves; a pale child, naked apart from a red pullover, ran out of the black hole of his front door, chased by the cry of another inside. The driver pulled into the kerb.

Can't get you no closer – unless we go all round the 'ouses.

This'll be fine, I said. But it wasn't fine; I was thinking of who might still be here after all this time: Eva, the Next-Door Rileys, the Jacksons. Perhaps the taxi driver was right and everything would be rubble and dust. He took one strap of my bag and swung it up off the floor of the car. He held out a card – Carl's Cabs – and smiled.

Give us a bell when you're wanting out, he said.

It started to drizzle, a dirty, familiar mist, greasing the pavement.

From The Hiding Place

Leonora Brito
Digging for Victory

WHEN MR CHURCHILL'S warship sailed into Cardiff Docks in the spring of 1955, I was seventeen years old and working at my first job, as a clerk in the Ministry of Labour, right on the corner of Custom House Street and Canal Parade.

Of course I loved it there, though that time of year can be very blowy, with the March winds coming in off the sea and roaring around us. Like a great sea-lion, I used to think, grey and submerged, then rearing up to poke cold blue eyes in the sky. In the evenings the winds would die down and the sky was often chemically pink. Then warm sea breezes would bring the smell of fish from around the corner in Mill Lane, and I'd walk home, happy to have done a good day's work for a good day's pay.

I was proud to have a job up town. Stepping over Canal Parade Bridge into town made me different. Teeny said it made me stuck up. "Miss High and Mighty" she'd say, looking down at the brass buttons on my navy coat. "Miss Piss-pot, who you thinks you are I'm sure I doan know."

Teeny was only fifteen and she worked with all the other coloured girls down Oram's, making lavatory brushes in the winter and artificial Christmas trees in the summer. I mean, she *did* work there, for a time, clamping the wire twists and dipping the bristles into the vats of green dye, to make them into Christmas trees. She left after less than a year though, claiming that the tips of her fingers were turning indelible green.

I felt I had to say something that Friday night, after she'd waltzed into the room and thrown her wage packet on the table. "Teeny," I said quietly, "are you quite sure you want to work?"

"Of course I wanna work," she said, taking a bottle of nail varnish from her handbag and bracing her feet against the arm of the settee. "I just doan fancy getting poisoned, that's all."

"Teeny," my voice was patient, "green doesn't necessarily mean gangrene, poisoning that is. Have you tried using half a lemon?"

But she was busy painting her toe-nails scarlet and didn't even bother to raise her head. In the event, she was only out of work for a fortnight, not long enough to claim U.A.B., thank goodness, when Mrs Cheng offered her a job in the steam-room of the Chinese laundry. So she went down there to 'slave' as she put it, almost on the dockside, next to the sea.

I think about Teeny as I stand in the kitchen, ironing my white blouse ready for work, and listening to Mr Churchill's voice on the wireless. He is talking about "this island race" and the "dawning of the second age of Elizabeth". Mr Churchill says we are the new Elizabethans, we English-speaking peoples, bound by the crimson thread of kinship. "The crimson thread of kinship" stays in my mind. I think about its meaning as Teeny flounces into the kitchen, way late for work and wrapped in mother's paradise blue kimono. A present sent by father from sea.

"Aren't you going in then?" I ask, careful not to look up, concentrating on smoothing the creases from the sleeve of my blouse. "Mrs Cheng will dock you an hour, won't she, if you're more than ten minutes late?" Instead of answering, she marches straight to the dresser and starts to fiddle with the dial on the wireless. Mr Churchill's voice is drowned in a crackle of static. "Teeny!" I say sharply, "I was listening to that! It's the Prime Minister, talking to us."

"Us!" she says, flapping the silken arms of the kimono and mooching around the table with her eyes closed. Music from the American Forces Network fills the air.

"Turn that down, please."

"What?" She looks at me with pitying eyes. Enviously I see how the darkness of her skin kills the gaudy blue of the kimono. Of the two of us, Teeny is the one who most resembles father.

I walk to work on my own. Half-way across the bridge I slow down and look over the side. The water in the canal is opaque, it is impossible to see in. My eyes trail the line of chickweed and dead grass up the canal bank and into the first of the bombed out houses. A small tree has forced its way up through the floorboards of a wall-papered room. Someone has propped a newspaper placard beneath its flourishing umbrella of dark green leaves: 'Cardiff prepares for G.O.M.'. G.O.M? I'm half-way down the road before it clicks, Grand Old Man. 'Cardiff prepares for Grand Old Man!'

Inside the office, there is an air of quiet excitement. Edna holds up the front page of her morning paper when we stop for elevenses. "Look at him, Kay, doesn't he look wonderful?"

"He looks marvellous," says Kay, peering over Edna's shoulder. "Have you seen this, Mr Norman?"

Both Kay and Edna are ex-Land Army, while Mr Norman saw service in North Africa. Now he ambles over and stands between them moving his lips as he reads down the column inches.

"Interesting, that," he says, taking out his pipe. "Interesting. I know for a fact that Mr Churchill's nanny was a lady named Everest, Nurse Everest. And look at this now", Mr Norman taps the page with the stem of his pipe, "it says here that the great man is being looked after in his *entourage*, by a nurse call McAlpine. Only a little thing but –"

Everyone exclaims at the coincidence, then Mr Norman looks up at the skylight. "Oh-oh, ladies! Here comes some of your favourite liquid again." He means that it's starting to rain. There is a pause as we listen to the rain falling on the skylight. Then Edna blows her nose. "Our climate is chang-ing," she says slowly, "there can be no doubt about that." I meet her glance with a cheery smile. "Ah well", she scrapes back her chair. "This won't buy baby a new pair of shoes, will it? Now then Kay, what are you having with your tea, buttered bun?"

The war-ship pulled into Cardiff dock just before mid-day. At tea-time, sitting in the kitchen at home, Teeny said the girls in work had stacked bales of laundry in front of the high windows, then they'd taken it in turns to climb up and look out. I asked if they'd seen the Prime Minister? No. First, they saw the flowers, she said. Trail after trail of hot house pinks and giant orchids. Then there were the animals, some feathered, and some furred – and silver buckets of ice. Oh, and live red lobsters, ready for the pot. All trundled up the gang plank by Malayan sailors in dazzling white sailor-suits.

"Have you left anything out?" asked mother kindly; and Teeny laughed. She said the Prime Minister had to have his food killed fresh, it was doctor's orders. "You didn't see Mr Churchill at all then?" I was highly suspicious. Teeny said she'd caught a glimpse. They brought him up on deck for a short while. A fattish figure, lying in a basket-chair with a black silk cloth over his face.

"That was how he used to take a nap during the war," said mother, "with a black silk cloth over his face."

Teeny said she'd thought he was deado, until the cloth fell off and she saw his eyes, looking up at her. But a nurse had bent down, and covered his face again.

That evening after supper, the three of us took a walk as far as the esplanade wall, and stood with crowds of other people, watching. There was no sign of the Prime Minister, but the ship beamed its searchlights over the black waters of the estuary, and we could hear music coming from the portholes on the far side. Mother held a hand up to her ear and nudged us both. "*Eldorado Man*," she whispered, "by Harry James and his Orchestra." At nine o'clock it began to rain; and the people standing in front of us opened their umbrellas very slowly, as if they were in a dream. As we turned to go, we caught the scent of something rotting on the wind and wondered what it was.

Coming down for work the next morning, I was surprised to see mother turn from the front doorstep with an anxious look on her face. A large car was moving down our street, slow as a hearse, and a voice was blaring out. I recognised the voice immediately. "What's he doing here?" I cried, running to the door and looking out. Mother told me to hush, and I realised the car was empty, apart from the chauffeur. Mr

Churchill's voice was coming from a kind of loud-hailer, shaped like an enormous gramophone-horn and attached to the roof of the car. Up and down our street, people were standing on their doorsteps, listening anxiously.

The Prime Minister's voice was tremulous, but unmistakable. His recorded message was brief. The war-ship had collided with the inner gates of the old sea-lock during the night. The gates had collapsed and the canal waters had emptied into the sea. He was calling on all able-bodied persons to offer their services in what was shaping up to be a great task of reclamation. "A task which might prove to be of immense importance in the trying times ahead... This is a test of our national character... Our resolve... You should come prepared to toil, sweat..." His voice continued to echo in the streets around us, right up as far as the green domed mosque in Sophia Street, where the words came out in Arabic. Then there was silence.

We came in and closed the door, wondering what to do for the best. Mother said she couldn't afford to give up her office cleaning, she was late enough as it was. I was unsure as to how best to proceed though I recognised the nature of what was being asked. "Go in to work first," said mother, "that way you'll get paid whatever happens."

Teeny was sitting on a stool in the back kitchen, straightening her hair with the hot-iron straightening comb. She looked up when I told her what had happened. Then she opened her mouth wide like a cat, and yawned. She asked if I had any hair grips she could borrow so she could pin back the sides and roll what was left into a bang.

I remember the trouble I had trying to get into work, that morning. Crowds of people swept past me as I reached Canal Parade Bridge. Most of them carried gardening implements: rakes and shovels, picks and hoes. They all strode past, like a shabby, but purposeful, army. Then I saw Mr Norman standing under the railway arch with Kay and Edna. The three of them were wearing military looking duffle coats, the colour of wet sand, with red plaid lining in the hoods. Mr Norman was carrying a pair of binoculars, which he raised to his eyes every now and then, carefully surveying the crowds. Before the binoculars reached me, I turned, as if in a dream, and joined the flow.

By mid-morning, a system of sorts had been set up, and by the early afternoon the task of reclamation was well under way. The canal looked like a huge valley, its sloping sides crowded with wellingtoned figures sifting through the soft greenish black mud. The water had gone, emptied violently into the sea, and the violence of its going had transformed the area into an enormous excavation site, leaving a tangle of objects half exposed to the light. I remember water wheels and iron wheels and cast iron plate. And heavy, rusted chains endlessly uncurling out of the mud, like snakes being stirred from hibernation. Other things, more minuscule in size, grew into oxidised hills as nails and rivets, nuts and bolts, were salvaged by the bucketful and heaped. It was an exhumation of the industrial past. Layer by layer.

As a government employee, it was my duty to identify and record all findings. It was tedious and dirty unpleasant work, but it had to be done. Everything had to be listed, then taken away for deposition in the huge bins marked 'reclamation'. The biggest find came towards the end of the afternoon, when a group of business wallahs dug up an enormous set of gear-wheels. They had their picture taken standing by the wheels, smiling proudly, their shirt sleeves rolled up, oblivious of the smells that permeated the air as the sun came out and shone on the black, putrescent muck.

As for me, I experienced a moment of happiness and contentment as I looked about me. Giant loading cranes jutted out against the sky-line like the vertebrae of prehistoric animals. The seagulls dipped and swooped; and the trucks made mournful shunting noises as they rolled up and down the sidings. Here and there I saw coloured people, Docks people like myself, helping with the task in hand. It was just like the war-time, I thought, when Britain would have stood alone, if the Empire hadn't rushed to her aid. Jamaica was the first with the spitfire fund! Our family would always remember that, and father had gloried in it. From one small island to the mother island, it was a gesture that would never be forgotten, father said so.

The operation was wound down gradually. At five o'clock a hooter was sounded and someone threw a stretch of green tarpaulin across the mud. A car drew up and an official from the Department of Public Works got out and made a speech. It was the Dunkirk spirit all over again, he said, and wonderful to see. Wonderful! He raised his arms as if to embrace us. "People of Cardiff, go home now; and take a well earned rest. Thank you and God bless."

I walked over to where Kay and Edna were standing with Mr Norman. Edna was holding something small and heavy in her arms. "Just look what I've found," she hissed, "an iron lion! Try saying that when you've had a few." She glanced towards the official, who was getting into his car and said she'd heard a rumour that Mr Churchill might yet be arriving in person. Edna looked towards the horizon as she spoke, but it remained empty.

"Oh what I wouldn't give to see him," she said. "Or even fox-faced Mr Atlee for that matter." "Or handsome Mr Eden," said Kay, wistfully.

Mr Norman lit his pipe. "Ours is not to reason why."

"Yes I know," said Edna softly "ours is but to – isn't it, Monty?" She nestled her face against the little lion in her arms. "Very appropriate name," said Mr Norman, "very appropriate."

Teeny was unimpressed when I recounted my story to mother, late that night. "The more fool you," she chipped in. "Fancy handing over all the scrap iron. I'd have kept it. You were entitled. It was treasure trove."

"But that's why Mr Churchill made his special appeal, Teeny," I said. "On behalf of the nation. All that stuff was needed. Urgently."

"Needed for what?" she asked nastily. "An iron curtain?"

Even mother had to smile at this, though she told Teeny

that that was enough. She could see I was a bit tired and crestfallen.

A few days later, there were pictures of Mr Churchill on all the front pages, standing at the doorway of Number Ten, waving to the crowds. The hand with the famous cigar was held aloft, and he was wearing pyjamas and a white towelled bathrobe. I thought his eyes looked strangely vacant and subdued. The newspapers said that a common cold had occasioned the Prime Minister's recent absence from the public eye. That was all. Yet by the beginning of April they were announcing his resignation.

The Department of Public Works had the canal filled in and eventually renamed 'Churchill Way' in his honour. As a busy thorough-fare, it has two distinguishing features: a very long traffic island, and a single stunted palm-tree dotting its centre.

From *Dat's Love*

J. Brookes
St Fagans

With one resentful eye a rootling boar
of some antique and noble line
observes another 3b pick its way
with little shrieks and steadying hands
to an Iron Age ideal home. Inside,

a Celt with braided orange hair
and home-made coat, pops half a Kit-Kat
on a beam and clears her throat.
Woodsmoke fills the hut and spiders spin
as 3b crackle smoky-bacon crisps

and look about with thoughtful frowns
at querns, at blackened earthenware
and drinking horns, imagining maybe
their own mums threading needle-bones
and shooing hogs from the settee

or whatever the bench-thing's called.
Outside again, and forty projects underway
entitled Daily Life in Iron Age Wales,
the boys are high on ancient warfare
and whoop away for Wagon-Wheels

and waiting coaches, but the girls
come dawdling down beside the Celt
pushing her Muddy Fox along the lane
and speak of an older sister's braided hair,
a camping break in Tenby when it rained all week.

Caravan Site, St. Mary's Well Bay

The dogs bark, the caravans move on
their moorings in the wind. Gypsy Queen,

Romany and Wanderer, each with its plot
of pansies, something hardy in a pot

by the door, and dustbin at the back.
And walking past, along the track

from Sully Island up to Lavernock
the acres of them waiting under padlock

for flip-flopped summer in its funny hat
to bounce across the field and get

things going again, seem such emphatic
statements of the optimistic

that despite the wind and rain I stop
to take the place in, from the shuttered shop

still advertising Walls, to what looks like
a shower room maybe, or a laundry block,

as though there were some lesson I could learn
from Romany and Wanderer and Gypsy Queen

all going nowhere on their breezeblock wheels
but here, a turnip field beside the sea, in Wales.

Lisvane

My missed train sniggers off into the night
leaving me at Lisvane with a Zippo's light
by which to calculate my half hour wait.
Behind, absorbed into the dark and wet,
the modest, muddy hills I slithered down
to miss, despite the shouts, that train,
here, more sensed than seen, a quiet road
of Beazer homes behind an empty Park & Ride,
and down the line, as cosy as a sock, my flat,
its three small rooms behind the Welcome mat,
its central heating ticking towards "on"
and waiting Tesco Sunday Roast for One.
And so, as yet another Rizla comes apart,
I pace the soaking platform with the thought
that, three years on, the bald facts are
I miss you less now than I miss your car.

Sean Burke
Europe's Most Exciting Waterfront

HARGEST WAS STRIKING A DEAL, so much Farissey
knew as he walked through the town centre. The detective
was under pressure for a swift conviction. Usually, only a
series of prostitute killings would warrant such intense inves-
tigation. Farissey thought of the DRC, the Docklands
Regeneration Corporation. Clearly, it wielded more power
than he had supposed.

Butetowners had reacted with scepticism when, two years
ago, the DRC began promoting 'Cardiff Bay' as a northern
Venice or European Seattle, promising that it would be
'Europe's most exciting waterfront'. Quiet assurances had
been made that the redevelopments would provide employ-
ment for the local people. With the murder of Christina
Villers, however, the DRC was confronting an area which it
presumed was not only hellbent on its own destruction but
that of a corporate city already coming to think of itself as
'the world's youngest capital'. After all, Christina not only
lived in Butetown but was killed there and by its own black
gangsters. Farissey recalled how – last summer – the DRC
began to talk up the proposed bypass as providing 'unmedi-
ated access to the waterfront' which most took to mean that
the mythical tourists would escape the threatening length of
Bute Street, the oppressions of the Loudoun Square tower
block, the maze of little council houses or the raw and loud
street life where Bute Street splintered into Angelina Street
and Mount Stuart Square.

Farissey recalled the promotional photography for
'Cardiff Bay': all sparkling white youth, smiling anaemic
businessmen, sprightly, white old age. The promise of redevelopment seemed less an attempt to rejuvenate than to raze
a community with its own, self-regulating and irregular
forms of justice and peace-keeping. With the murder of
Christina Villers, the authorities were now ready to go into
open war with the creole life of Butetown.

Of course, it had always been that way. Even as the long-romanced Tiger Bay, the area had sat at the southernmost point of the city like a restless and imponderable secret, a primal source of land or fortune whose existence must ever be disowned like a distant forebear who sweated, soiled, risked his life – murdered even – so that successive genera-tions might prosper. Those generations soon fled the living ground of their prosperity and, with the arrival of West Indian and African immigrants after the First World War, the isthmus was not only regarded as a slum but also a warren of evil byways, of sordid sexual encounters, open drug-taking, poisonous ethnic cuisine and darktown atrocity. Inhabitants were shamed into accepting that they lived 'below the bridge', almost as if below a species line.

The Cardiff respectable took no account that they lived 'above': they simply did not think of Butetown, still less pass over into a place where they were assured that knives were freely wielded and black men crouched in alleys or cul-de-sacs ready to pounce for money or worse. By the 1970s, and with the terminal decline of the docks, the descendants of these great migrations and miscegenations found themselves as used up as the abandoned canals and wharfs, the rusting foundries and downscaling steelworks. Redundant as well as disreputable in the post-industrial age, they simply lived on: the spent residue of a dream dreamed by someone else.

The law of the land ends here, Farissey thought as he passed under the heaviness of the Bute Street Bridge which sepa-rated Butetown from the city proper. Long ago, those words were on his father's tongue whenever they returned from some shopping expedition in the city centre.

Farissey was just about old enough to remember those days before the Tiger departed its Bay. He was eleven or twelve when the redevelopments began in 1963, remembered keenly those sheltering streets in the late '50s. He was, then, seven and eight years old and the king of his days. He knew his memory played him false, that the time was glorified by a child's recall of a few scenes, a black man mechanically strumming a guitar, an aura of urban magic.

He remembered how you could see, of a sundown, the Irish warming to their drinking and their cards' 45s in his father's bar; the Chinese outback of their laundries and lost at the end of opium pipes or dicing or marvelling at the fire of numbers in the lottery of paku pu or the ornate and shell-based mysticism of fan-tan. How the Italian women would hang out of windows shouting incomprehensible angers at one another from above ice-cream shops and cafés, just a block away from Somalis slaughtering goats on a street corner. He remembered, too, his father telling him of the fifty or so brothels the police passed by with no more than a discreet sideways glance into those dank and gloomy caverns with their own seas and treacheries for the paid-off seamen who might awake from week-long drunks to be crimped or shanghaied, perhaps in the early scalds of gonorrhoea, and aboard a vessel bound, like as not, for northern Spain or the Ivory Coast.

Farissey was old enough to still have in his ears the spectacular noise, of cockatoos, penny-slot pianos, of hurdy-gurdies, irrepressible Breton onion sellers, West Indian newspaper touts and stentorian fish hawkers. Old enough to have the taste in his nostrils of what he thought was 'tarmac' until he was old enough to say 'tarpaulin' and know that it came from shipping chandlers in a bay and a dock where the flags of a dozen or more nations fluttered with a thousand coastal birds and cooking smells in the sea breezes.

He remembered those severe winter mornings when his father took him to see the leviathan-like ships coming in from the world over to a West Dock often so congested that a trained monkey might cross from one side to the other by swinging on the masts of ships. He'd learned the places of the world from vessels and cargoes, and the world's religions from the Greek Orthodox Church, the mosques of Maria Street and Peel Street, the Norwegian Church with a dome like a witch's hat and the abiding and gruesomely iconic cross of St Mary's Church, where the women who looked like they were in fancy dress would gather with mischief, easy sacrileges and good business sense at eight o'clock of an evening.

A place withal where he'd never been but still a vast circus on this small ghetto whose ghosts still danced and cried and laughed and cried in Farissey's reveries as he now walked past the stone seasons of Loudoun Square and alongside the twelve-foot wall (so grim as to seem penal) that separated the local railway line from the east side of Bute Street.

It all changed in the early 1960s. The town planners determined to clear the slums in a dream of enforced integration. They relocated the ethnic groups on some such principle that sharing a corridor, a landing, a defective lift, an estate park and dismal, steel-shuttered shopping centre was altogether more propitious than melding on an exuberant, rank and impossibly variegated main drag. It was carnival that frightened them, Farissey knew: the sight of a creole community evolving its own way of being, its own ethics of spontaneity, respect and cheerfulness – without need of statute, politician or book – like a city shrived of politics or dignitary and mirthed into its own order by jokers, acrobats and fakirs.

The dead hand got working a quarter of a century ago when the sheltering alleyways of his youth were replaced by tower block and cul-de-sac. Why should anyone care if it looked like some maritime Disneyland in ten years' time, a cultural museum, as without people as walls, its clocks and traffic lights turning the time?

From *Deadwater*

Duncan Bush
Hayes Island

THE TWO GIRLS cross the street, towards the grimy sills and tall windows of the Central Library. Are they going to the open-air café on the Hayes Island?

I used to go there with my wife sometimes when we'd done the Saturday shopping in Fine Fare, and we'd sit at one of the tables under the plane trees and have a cup of tea and a sandwich and the kids would have an orangeade and a rock cake, half of which they'd end up throwing to the pigeons waddling round your feet, I always said it was a waste of money, buy them one cake between the pair of them instead of one apiece, maybe that way they'll actually get to eat what I paid for. If you want to feed the bloody birds, I'd say, bring old bread in a bag, don't give them cake. You don't cut sandwiches to feed the ducks in Roath Park Lake, do you? But she'd always say, O, leave them be, Mandy likes the pigeons, don't you, Mandy? Look at the colours in that one there, the purple and that lovely green. She was soft about things like that. Women always are. They don't have to go out and work to get the money in the first place, that's why. It just gets magically put into their hand each Friday night.

But she always liked it here on the Hayes Island, Carol. The French connection again. Like she said once, This is the life. Pavement society. Rickety iron tables under the trees, and the pigeons, and the down-and-outs. A real whiff of Paris.

And she laughed. And I looked towards the railings of the underground toilets and sniffed the air in deep, like on some azure fucking headland, and let my breath out slow again, with satisfaction.

Ah, I said. Is that what it is? I thought it was the pisser.

Because it was a sweltering summer day, I remember. And you could smell that mix of urine and Dettol you get there sometimes from the toilets when it's hot, I suppose, or the wind's in the right quarter. And it's always worse around the steps down to the Women's, it seems to me. I don't know why that should be. Does a woman's smell ranker than a man's? It might. There's no reason why not. (Let's face it, they're not all Sugar and Spice.)

On the subject of toilets, I remember Carol telling me some of the things scrawled on the walls in the Women's in the College Bar. Really filthy things. Which actually doesn't surprise me in the least, not any more. It probably would have, once. It might even have at the time she told me, to think of not just 'women' but *educated* ones writing things like that on a toilet wall. But it wouldn't fucking surprise me now. I can believe anything of them now. Because anyone who's been around the bitches long enough, let alone married to one, knows better than to think that any of them is as innocent as they like to make out.

Butcher's Window

I HALT AND STARE into a butcher's window. Pinkish pork-chops and bloody beef ranged on the slab, a couple of cock pheasants hanging from an S-hook by their necks. The dark shot-silk green of their heads is the green of that dressing-gown my father brought back for my mother from Japan, and she never wore. Next to them, from another hook, a long hare hangs head-down. His eye is blood.

I'm trying to think where I want to be heading.

(I get these blank spots sometimes, when I forget things. Or rather, I start remembering things and lose track of what I'm doing. Memory is a weird thing.)

Seeing where I am, I realise my footsteps have brought me in a circle, or rather three and a half sides of a square, so that I've been walking back towards the Hayes Island again.

(It's just a kind of fadeout, I suppose. I get it sometimes, when I need to. And not only then but when I'm working in the tyre bay, say, or just driving. Sometimes I'll get to a place and I can't remember driving the last five miles. Or the cassette will click off in the tape machine, and it's as if that little noise wakes me up and I don't even know what it is I've been playing, I haven't heard a note, though all this time I must have been watching the road ahead and braking, changing though the gears and so on. Perhaps I'm even driving better, safer, this way, because it's all being done on pure instinct. I don't know. But anyway, it's like I've been on Daydream Automatic. Perhaps it happens to me like this because I never dream at night. Yeah, okay, I know: everybody dreams. Everybody dreams every single night of their lives, they've run tests on the movement of your eyelids and so on. What I mean is, I don't *remember* my dreams hardly ever. And if you don't remember your dreams, you might just as well not have had them. What the fuck. I know one thing: I'd rather have a nice wet daydream than a nightmare.)

I push the handbag up more, under my jacket. And cross the pedestrian area to the Island itself. I skirt chairs, metal tables, customers (bums and businessmen alike) grouped in dappled afternoon sun. I do a quick trot down the worn stone steps between the railings, passing from the bright lunchtime into the cool of the *Gentlemen,* so cool and dim it's more like underwater here than underground.

White glazed brickwork. Black streaked-marble stalls to stand and piss at. The cavelike trickle of green Victorian plumbing. Mahogany doors. That faint, tidal whiff of Lavernock beach and seaweeded rocks and the old rusty sewage pipe. And overhead, a gridded skylight ceiling of thick pale-greenish glass crossed by foot-soles and dim shadows, all the city's numberless destinations.

Finding an empty cubicle along the row, I go in and shut the door and shoot the brass bolt home. I lower the cracked mahogany seat and sit on it. And here I *know* I'm safe. Inviolate. (If not exactly in violets. Ha. Ha. Ha.)

This was why Instinct brought me here: the peace and security of sitting in a locked toilet. And many's the time, I suppose, over the years, that I've sat underground here in one cubicle or other of the Hayes Island bogs after a good stiff walk and felt a good stiff shit at last ease out of me and slide into the water, looking around the cell as I'm doing now, in perfect Calm and Contentment, beneath the pavements and the crossing feet, myself the still, quietly voiding centre of the hurrying world. Sometimes there can be an almost mystic peace in a toilet, not to mention in having a good shit there. And in fact as far as that goes (like I had occasion to say to Tony Barbecue only the other day, after I'd had to walk rather purposefully from Glossop Terrace to The Locomotive so I could have one) the only thing I know to beat it is a lovely fuck.

The handbag is like a small satchel in design. Good leather. Solid, hardwearing, serviceable, Space and Style for the modern Working Miss. Mushroom, they call it, this greyish beige.

I turn the bag in my hands. Feel it. Weigh it. I don't even want to *open* it for a minute or two. Every stitch and fold and wrinkle in the leather itself is already intimate and erotic, like the creases in the insteps of her white fringed boots would be, or the paler, worn rucking the radiates at the lap of her skintight jeans, creasing from how she sits. I lift the handbag to my nostrils and sniff deeply, it's almost odourless except for the smell of leather itself, though there's the faintest sweetish trace of cosmetics too. For smell boots or jeans would be better, to breathe in from a tall, heeled boot the sweat-darkened inside, that faint pong from cramped toes and crinkled arches. Or jeans, yes, even better, best of all, to put your nose delicately just where the double-stitching runs back under her.

From *Glass Shot*

Gillian Clarke
Letting the Light In

'Well building hath three Conditions:
Commodity, Firmness and Delight.'
Sir Henry Wotton, 1624

A cwtch of a country,
houses hunkered to the hill
in heart-less, one-street towns.
The et cetera of terraces
like paragraphs of longhand
in an old language.

In our town by the sea, we children
were construction workers,
clearing glades in the woods for dens,
tree-houses, bird-hides, lookouts.
We'd ease into hollow trees and, safe as houses,
plotted, whispering in the mushroomy dark.

Till suddenly called by the distant drum of a train
we'd race breathless to the viaduct,
to take the measure of it, to shout,
to touch the train's thunder in the stones,
sound and curve diminishing arch by arch,
the lapsing echoes, loops and ellipses.

It prepared us for the lofty gravity
of Museum, warehouse, galleried arcades,
the Victorian covered market, the library
whispering its multilingual stories,
tea and talk under trees in the open air
at the Hayes Island Snack Bar.

*

In the reimagined nation, let's dream
a waterfront where once the coal ships docked,
leafy squares where sunlight turns, touching
stalls, strollers, street musicians, a woman
at a pavement table, steam from a white cup,
the silver in the fiddler's opened case.

Let's make fine buildings, go sandalfoot
into spaces of shadow and reflections,
see what stone, steel, slate and glass,
can make out of air and water and sunlight.
Let's open the city to the light,
to commodity, firmness, delight.

Grahame Davies
Red
(Pontcanna, Cardiff)

You set the olives down beside the *feta*,
and make sure the *ciabatta*'s looking nice.
You light the perfumed candle for the meeting,
open the red wine, put the white on ice.

A little *antipasti* to begin with;
a French *baguette*, a chunk of Danish blue;
this is the way we meet to save our nation
in CF One in two thousand and two.

I wonder what he'd make of this, your grand-dad,
who risked a prison cell for Stalin's sake,
the one who raised the red flag in the valleys,
the man the hungry thirties couldn't break?

The one who got invited out to Russia
to get the Soviets' thank-you face to face,
and came back with a little bust of Lenin,
that's now an ornament above your fireplace.

The one who earned the local rag's displeasure
for calling meetings to arouse the mass,
I wonder what he'd make of his descendant:
Welsh-speaking, nationalistic, middle-class?

I wonder. But you're still so like your grand-dad:
cut from the same cloth, just by different means,
trying to cure the evils of injustice
by painting all the world in red – or green.

Grey
(Commissioned to commemorate the laying of the foundation
stone for the Wales Millennium Centre in Cardiff Bay)

I think that all the lasting things are grey:
the clouds above the mountains when it's late.
When all around you changes, these things stay.

The lichen where the quarry works decay,
the tides that fill the harbours in the strait.
I think that all the lasting things are grey

The twilight in the cwm at close of day,
the ash the coalfire leaves within the grate.
When all around you changes, these things stay.

The mist that hides the slagheaps' scars away,
the winter rain that shines upon the slate.
I think that all the lasting things are grey

The seagulls wheeling over Cardiff Bay,
the patient sea that bore a nation's freight,
When all around you changes, these things stay.

The home we build with steel and stone today,
and blend our light and darkness to create.
I think that all the lasting things are grey.
When all around you changes, these things stay.

Number 62 Bus

I wondered for a moment if I was disturbing their
                                        conversation,
the young student and the middle-aged man from Africa,
as I sat next to them on the bus to Llandaf,

until I realised that his words were a one-way street,
and that she was gazing past him
as he rambled about Jesus, God and eternity.

The nutter on the bus.
An early-rising one, to be sure,
sharing his visions with the BBC workers
and the girls from Ysgol Glan Taf,
but in companionless garrulity like all his kind.

But as he expected no answer,
it was easy to tune into the flow of his words,
to lose myself in the cadences of Prayer Book and Psalms,
as his accent rolled out
one verse after another
like an endless strip of tickets to eternity.
Whatever havoc had been done by sickness,
drink or chemicals

to the cells of his mind,
the beauty of the words was unimpaired

and when he got up to leave by the cathedral,
chanting softly
*"People not things. People not things.
That's what matters in eternity,"*
I kept the salvation of his words
in the inside pocket of my jacket,
like a return ticket.

Lewis Davies
You Alright?

THE SOIL falls back into the deep hole. It's February, heavy
and cold but the ground remains soft. The men take turns in
shouldering a shovel. I can hear the wood of the coffin, hard
and shiny as it collects the earth. Each man tires quickly,
handing the shovel onto another. They are not used to the
work. A friend of mine is dead in the grave, people he could-
n't have known fill the hole. His father and grandfather
watch, to me they are suddenly old men. I stay on the edge
of the circle, thinking what to think. Someone offers me the
shovel but I shake my head. They have an eagerness to fill the
hole which I can see and hate. None of them knows how to
use the shovel properly. I'm glad I'm not paying the grave-
fillers by the hour.

The start was only three weeks before. Two years away
now. One of those winter colds which everyone gets between
November and February. Sajid had been looking rough, his
walking had become laboured, the strength in his legs
absorbed by the cold. His speech was slower, he faltered
uneasily between Urdu and English, spluttering greetings
and requests. He'd been in hospital before. Another cold, the

previous winter. His mother had adjusted his tablets but his huge frightening fits had increased. The hospital staff liked him. They liked his big broad smile when his mother arrived with spiced dhal and chapatis. He was in three weeks, his cold eased and he was sent home with a new set of tablets. Once home it was just another cold as he was surrounded by the warmth of the house, four sisters and three brothers. Sajid was the oldest of eight. His mother liked having him home again. He sat in his big Social Services chair, drank tea, ate biscuits and played with his board of shapes that he clasped close to his chest.

Four days a week a car arrived from the day service. On a Saturday or Sunday he saw Simon, or Helen or Gill or me. We didn't do much, drove to Penarth for a cup of tea, walked between the benches alongside Roath Park Lake, in the summer we sometimes caught a train to Barry Island or kicked a football around the Rec. How much time do you need to become friends?

Saj always wanted to go out and always wanted to come home. The city was a place of buses, people, children and dogs. His home was always full with brothers and sisters and the occasional aunt on a long-stay holiday visa from Pakistan.

Social Services planned things for him. We just took him out. Everyone got paid for it. How much do you charge your friends?

The cold first caught up with him in November, it lingered, festering over Christmas. By the second week of January he could only just raise himself out of the chair. I suggested hospital to his mother. It had worked the last time.

She rings me on the Thursday morning. It's Llandoc this time, The Heath was full. I see him on Friday afternoon, one of a string of visitors. He's sitting up by the side of the bed in a large bright ward with a view south, over the fields to Barry. He doesn't speak much beyond saying "Hello". As I leave he clasps my hand. He says goodbye and squeezes my fingers.

His mother rings me on Monday. Sajid is very sick. He's

picked up an infection over the weekend. At the hospital they've moved him from the open ward to a small room of his own. He lies on his bed, coughing between fits, eyes open but glazed. It's a coma that will last three weeks. His family stays close now. His eldest sister driving down from university in Manchester. I can see the expectation on their faces, his mother in tears. The doctors do nothing. He can't eat so they insert a tube into his stomach. The tube becomes infected, his coma hardens and he's having trouble breathing. His fits follow each other, fast, only seconds between them, they are dark retching spasms that throw his throat into deep splutters as his brain begins to hide away from the horrible pulses which consume it.

There is no panic or even urgency. His consultant, the man with the notes on his condition and the epilepsy which has consumed him, is on holiday. His case history is brought from The Heath but there is no one to interpret.

On the Monday morning before he dies I argue with two house doctors who try to ignore me. I had retreated the week before, leaving his family to the inevitable vigil. We all thought he would be dead by now. This is not his body but a corpse in waiting. The doctors are vague, uneasy, they are doing everything that is normal. I question his treatment. It ends in a shouting match which I win but they do nothing. At this stage they can't risk further surgery. It will only worsen his condition. He is a twenty five year old man who is dying from a cold and an infection he picked up in hospital. I can see it in their faces: he has a mental handicap. What do you expect us to do? It would be better for his family, wouldn't it?

On the morning of the funeral we meet in a cafe on Crwys Road. Six or seven of us. Old friends from Social Services. The mosque is a converted warehouse at the end of a scruffy street I had never noticed before. There is a respectable turn out for a big burgeoning family. Sajid's father has recently become successful with a mini-cab service. He is an employer now. Sajid's mother leads a prayer group. She is a philosopher of sorts and used to look at me sadly early on Sunday mornings when I arrived, still drunk from the night before, to get her eldest son out of bed. We have talked about God and religion. We both agree that Jesus was a man like Mohammed. Allah is another question. She thinks my body will burn in hell but likes me anyway.

She calls the women in our odd group of Christians and Atheists into a room of their own. The men are segregated into a large hall that reminds me of a gym. It is full but apart from Sajid's brothers, his father and grandfather, I only recognise the people I have come with. The Imam recites a litany. I look at the community, holding each other together in a foreign culture. People on the edge of things, the divide between Pakistan, Manchester and Cardiff. Each generation pushing itself away from the last.

Sajid had known very little of this. He was four and still living in Manchester when a strain of meningitis sent him into a coma for a month. It was a different boy who recovered and moved with his family to Cardiff. The boy who endured ten years of a school system that didn't remember he could walk or go to the toilet. When I first met him he was strapped into a wheelchair with a boxer's sparring helmet wrapped tightly around his head. "Just in case he falls out," I was told. Since he was strapped in, this seemed unlikely. The strapping was to stop him getting out. These were people who looked at Sajid and put walls around him. He was handicapped. He couldn't speak English. He was from Pakistan and his mother couldn't speak English. Only one of these excuses was accurate and that's the problem the people were paid to deal with. The rest were just excuses. I could say I don't blame the teachers and health workers who allowed him a schooling of this. I was a social worker of sorts. A fine, easy job for Cardiff Community Mental Handicap Team. Sajid was sanctioned as a person with high support needs. On leaving school at eighteen he got me and a few others three days a week. For the rest he stayed at home, talked to his mother, swore at the young twin brothers who teased him.

I got on with Sajid. He had an open friendliness that you

encounter rarely. I haven't got it and I don't know many people who have. From childhood we develop defences of reserve to deflect the world and insulate ourselves against other people, they stop us from getting hurt or appearing foolish. His greetings of "You alright?" or "Hello, my friend" were full of smiles. Sajid always assumed you were his friend.

We'd shared a year of work while I finished my contract. He walked more, ate pizza regularly, hated swimming, drew round scribbles at an art class, played skittles at The Airport in Tremorfa.

Sajid had caught the end of a care in the community policy that suited him. There was money around for people who wanted to stay at home. It was just necessary to find out where the money was. I applied to a fund based in Nottingham. They wanted to encourage Independent Living. To prevent people from moving into hostels by bolstering their means of support at home. Money was awarded on a points basis. Sajid had so many points he was off the scale. He received money to help him in the house at the weekend. He didn't want to be in the house at the weekend. He wanted to be out, so we went out.

So this was his life. It's not easy to measure someone else's life. There are hidden parts you cannot possibly know. Interests, joys, secret friendships. Did Sajid have these? I hope so. I cannot know. I remember a woman at a case meeting kissing Sajid with real affection before she left to organise more children for the respite hostel she ran. Steve was another close friend who spent a lot of time with him. They could speak to each other for hours. Steve is the man who rang me to say that Sajid was dead. Sajid's mother had rung him first.

We follow the funeral cars up to the cemetery at Ely. The women stay at the mosque. I can't get the translated words of the Imam out of my head. He praised Sajid's family, the strength they had shown in the long years since his first illness. I can see the eyes of the doctors at the hospital. Thinking that perhaps death would be the best way. I can't get this out of my head. I can't face the thought that I must ask myself. Did I agree with them? Was this the best way for my friend? To die scared and weak?

The Muslim plot is on the far side of the municipal cemetery, beyond the last line of conifers. There is a line of new graves for the winter. The eldest of the first generation are beginning to die here now. The digging starts. I speak to his father for the first time since his death. I don't have much to say. He returns some of my words. Yes, he was a fine boy. I'm surprised to see his tears beyond his glasses.

I leave before they can fill the grave.

From *As I Was a Boy Fishing*

Tom Davies
How Jack London Got Me My First Berth

I PICKED up six 'O' level passes, enough to carry on to the Sixth Form and still saw Sandra occasionally but usually as some sort of favour since she was now washing her hair almost seven nights a week. Quite why people never seem able to say what's on their mind on such issues remains a mystery but that's the nature eternal battle of love, I guess. When in emotional doubt we always lie, lie and lie again.

Everything I had ever cared about was lost now I wasn't seeing her anymore and, judging by the wrenching, hurting hole in my belly, romantic love was all it was cracked it up to be. On some days I thought I would actually lie down and die of grief and I simply could not conceive of how anyone might ever take Sandra's place; did not even believe that I would ever find someone who could jive as well as her unless someone sent me one of Pan's People in the post and I could not see that happening somehow.

My friend Ray was still around and we might get drunk in some pub in the city, if we had enough money, but for most of the time I sat in my bedroom, together with Hitler's unexploded bomb, where I began reading any interesting books I could dig out of the local library. Although an aspiring writer I had thus far barely read any books at all and it might have been a good career move if I'd tried to write a few paragraphs of prose too. But I had simply been too busy with the multiple problems of being young.

John Steinbeck was one of the first authors I ever took to and I read almost all his work. Ernest 'Muscles' Hemingway also helped me in my dejected loneliness since many of his heroes were undone or somehow disfigured by love. F. Scott Fitzgerald told me much about the capricious and transitory nature of love which also helped a bit. Where the real world had failed me I found another with fun, depth and a sadness with which I could identify.

We never think we are influenced by books – we have never really understood the process – but those books were already making deep changes in my ideas and world view. Every book I have ever read – particularly in those tender days – affected me in some way, I realise now even if I didn't then. My horizons were expanded with each book; they were giving me new ideas and I was being shown that there were other people out there who were often wrestling with something far more important and significant than why their girlfriend had gone and run off with someone called Mike the Worm.

There was one book in particular which turned me around at that time: *Martin Eden* by the American socialist writer Jack London. That novel spoke to me in ways I needed to hear; it went straight to the heart of my badly floundering condition and, in no time at all, I was up and running in a new direction.

Martin Eden is the story of a sailor who determines to educate himself and become a great writer who will then have access to upper class society and the hand of the elegant and beautiful Ruth Morse who had earlier rejected him as a failure and a 'notorious' socialist. Using the library as a tool Martin works on the ship by day and studies at night, sometimes only taking two or three hours sleep to get where he wants to be. He does become a successful writer and wins back Ruth's hand and heart only to reject her when he realises that she is only interested in his new fame and recognition. Martin returns to being a seaman and a final tragedy in the South China Seas.

Based on parts of Jack London's real life this book chimed with me on a number of levels, mainly in the single-minded way he became a successful writer and got the girl. If I could become a successful writer maybe Sandra would soon realise the folly of her choices and come crawling back to me. Maybe I would also make a lot of money when I hit the top of the American bestsellers and I could wait for her outside her hairdressers in my new Ferrari with Frankie Vaughan singing his new hit on the radio. Maybe I would also then have the option of throwing her over, because she was only interested in my fame and money, to see how she liked it. Maybe, maybe, maybe…

Such absurd fantasies have probably motivated far more writers than any of them would ever care to admit. There can't be any other sensible reason why anyone ever gets caught up with the inherent madness of writing.

Martin Eden also explored the deep romantic notion of running away to sea and putting your problems way behind you. This was very attractive at the time so, the very day after I had finished reading the book, I went down to the Pier Head in Cardiff where I couldn't find a windjammer going to the South China Seas but did manage to get a berth as an officer steward on the Britannia, one of a fleet of six paddle steamers, owned by P. and A. Campbell, which plied their trade up an down the Bristol Channel, calling at Bristol, Portishead, Clevedon, Weston-Super-Mare, Ilfracombe, Lundy, Tenby, Swansea and back to the main base in Cardiff.

For most of the day and much of the night these paddle steamers criss-crossed the channel tirelessly, packed with passengers on sunny days and almost deserted on wet and stormy ones, those great paddles thrashing the water rhythmically and churning the sea into a huge, foaming wake over which seagulls constantly hovered and called out for food.

The steamers never hung around, in and out of the ports and piers within minutes, often reaching speeds of nineteen knots which, for any ship, is very fast indeed. The captains were said to only ever know three speeds: full ahead, full astern and stop and the sight of those ships hurrying across the horizon with black smoke belching out of their distinctive white funnels became a regular feature of all our seaside summers in South Wales.

Such days were always incident-packed for us working onboard since, with the rip tides of the Bristol Channel, the second highest and fastest in the world, we always seemed to be getting stuck on mud banks or else making some spirited effort to knock down – or at least put a good dent in – an old Edwardian pier. Had anyone ever known how those ships were run they would never have set foot on those decks so eagerly and cheerfully. There was no radar on most of them and, given the chief officers' enthusiasm for alcohol, it was often a wonder we reached anywhere at all in one piece. If we weren't smacking into Birnbeck Pier in Weston-Super-Mare our steering might get jammed and we'd end up broken down and lost in some impenetrable fog around Lundy Island. We were always getting stuck on the mud banks in the River Avon leading up to Bristol, sometimes sitting there for half the night waiting for the tide to come back in and refloat us.

The crew had to throw their lines to someone on the pier, which was easier said than done, often missing the old duffer on Ilfracombe pier, who couldn't catch a cold, and then having to steam out in a full circle and come back to try again. The passengers' joy was unconfined when he did manage to catch the line.

Whenever we did get in anywhere it was always hailed as yet another 'great navigational triumph.' The whole working day was controlled by the speedy ebb and flow of those tides and any delay involved furious, last-minute changes of plan, often meaning that several hundred passengers would be abandoned for the night in Clevedon, who would then have to be bussed home to Cardiff, and all this before the opening of the Severn Bridge.

The weather in the Bristol Channel would often turn nasty in a moment and, largely because of the steamers' flat bottoms, we could roll and pitch like drunken butterflies on the confused seas. Instead of cutting through the waves like conventional ships the flat bottom would ride up over them and come smacking right down on the bows, shaking your belly straight up into your throat. The steamer would also pitch from side to side in stormy conditions with one of the paddles rising up out of the water and whirling around like some great lost Catherine Wheel.

The seas could often get particularly rough off Minehead with almost all the passengers becoming sick and vomit slopping from side to side over the floors of the snack bar lounge which I was supposed to keep clean. Even deep-sea sailors would succumb to sea sickness off Minehead since there was never any steady rhythm about the ship's movement they could fasten onto and get accustomed to. You just never knew how the Channel was going to behave next. A waterspout appeared off Porthcawl in that first summer I was working on the Britannia – a 700ft. spiral whizzing over the waves before disappearing after about twenty minutes. The captain said he had never seen anything like it except for the start of a typhoon in the Caribbean.

The officers, apart from a few drunks, were a conventional and even boring lot but the rest of the crew, particularly the cooks and my fellow stewards, were a pretty wild bunch and it was on those paddle steamers that I first learned about feckless, desperate men making their erratic ways in a hostile world.

They turned up from nowhere on some nights, worked for a while and disappeared again. A lot of them were villains or plain outlaws anxious to escape from something in their backgrounds. You wouldn't call them fabulous or even interesting characters since they were largely a mumbling collection of near-misses who might tattoo themselves badly with a needle and lead blacking if they had a spare half an hour or would chain-smoke all day, even when they were shaving or would always nip their cigarettes halfway through so they always had a pocket full of butts and would never have to run the risk of having to go without a smoke. Every other word was 'fuck' or 'cunt' with some even jammed in the middle of longer words as in: "Where the fuck is the fucking marma-fucking-lade?"

Harry the Shithouse Wallah would never pay any maintenance for his many kids, swore he would die, in fact, rather than pay that "cow" so much as one penny so, at regular intervals, the police would turn up and haul him off to Swansea prison where he could work off his arrears. He always had his bags packed when they came for him on the pontoon, never made so much as one word of complaint about his arrest and, when he'd done his time, he would come back to us and be re-employed gladly because no-one, anywhere, ever kept the lavatories as clean and sparkling as Harry. He took a real pride in his work and, when the weather was rough, he would be right in there by the sides of the suffering passengers, practically telling them where to be sick. Harry had the original iron stomach and a few of us would pay fortunes for him to come and clean up our saloons. But he was a disgusting drunk in truth, always finishing off all the slops, if he was helping to clean up in the bar at the end of the night, and sometimes ending up in a worse state than those who had really been sea-sick.

On my first day on the Britannia they had their usual fun at a newcomer's expense, sending me around the ship asking everyone for the key to the fog room locker. "Ah, no," they'd say. "I did have it yesterday but left it with the bosun." The bosun then said he didn't have it anymore and I should try the purser. Another variation on this game would be to send you looking for the golden rivet.

They were long working days, beginning at around half past six when we would be rousted out of our bunks for the 'beer carry' and had to chain barrels and boxes of beer onto the ship before setting up the tables in the saloon for breakfast, always the same greasy bacon and eggs. As officer steward I would then clean their cabins and make their beds with a change of linen once a week before setting up the tables for their lunch, which was always roast beef, before helping out the other stewards with their passengers who could number several hundred over two or three sittings.

I enjoyed chatting with a lot of the passengers who included a sullen Shirley Bassey, the jazz man Acker Bilk, who gave me my first reefer and the Penarth actor who was the radio voice of Dick Barton, Special Agent. I also met and chatted a lot with a Dr David Erskine, a Harley Street specialist, a somewhat Dickensian character who would become a great benefactor to me when I got into several major pickles later in life when I began roaming the world.

Lunch could take all the way to Lundy Island when we might have a half an hour's break for a nap and a game of cards and then it was dinner all the way back to Cardiff, plaice and chips and salads, which we would keep serving up until nine or ten at night.

We usually got back into Cardiff, tides willing, about half an hour before the pubs shut when we would race up the pontoon and catch the last half hour in The Big Windsor pub, often then drifting off into the Bay nightclubs for a few more. Those nightclubs were really rough, particularly The North Star where, it was often said, they searched you for knives and guns when you went in and, if you didn't have any, they gave you some.

The unwritten rule of the steamers was that you worked hard and played hard but, after waiting on tables for twelve hours on a rolling ship, continually re-positioning your feet to stabilise yourself, you often found that you were out for the count at the end of the day, your legs so stiff and sore you didn't want to go to some nightclub, not even to fight with knives and guns and just wanted to fall straight into your bunk.

My aft cabin, with the bunks next to the anchor chains and constant clanking of the capstan, would have infringed almost every rule of the modern workplace but, by the time I got into mine, I was always far too tired to care about anything, still less the constant thick smell of diesel oil, often climbing in fully clothed and it was Goodnight Vienna when it seemed I woke up almost immediately, shaken and shouted at by the chief steward, Vick Taylor. We all had to get up and start the day's beer carry again, often before it had even got light. Just what did they do with all that beer?

Two stewards from Bristol, brothers Ted and John, would come and help us out on bank holidays and sunny weekends. They were an extremely sharp and busy pair of brothers who would even cheat us in our afternoon card schools, largely by covert hand signals. Nothing was beyond them and, even though I never quite worked out how they did it, they were always counting out monstrous piles of money at the end of each day in the dining saloon, almost three or four times what the rest of us made with our tips.

The chief steward caught them up to something one morning and it lead to a furious row which went on for almost half an hour. The brothers argued that they worked so hard on the ship they were entitled to their fiddles but, when the chief steward wasn't having that, they both rounded on him and told him that, if he didn't shut up and let them get on with whatever it was they were doing, they were going to go to the management and tell them where the chief steward got *his* stores.

This was an absolute revelation. Most of the stores we were handling on the ship had been stolen in Bristol and the two brothers had something to do with it and were merely, they said, just nipping off their share. In that one row I began to see how P. and A. Campbell's were going broke and it was almost nothing to do with continuously repeated mantra on bad weather and falling passenger numbers. They were going broke because everyone was robbing them blind.

One night in Penarth, after a long, busy day, there was a panic in the saloon because a woman had turned up at the end of the pier and was loudly threatening to throw herself into the drink. Naturally we all ran up to the main deck to see for ourselves and found this gaunt figure standing in the moths whirling around the sodium lights of the pier, face pinched, hands in pockets, her body stricken and stiff with pain.

This woman, it soon emerged, was one of John's dumped girlfriends who objected strongly to her new-found status and was pursuing him almost everywhere he went, loudly threatening to do herself in unless he came home to her "where he belonged." Even though John was a part-timer on the ship she had an uncanny knowledge of his movements – or it might have been a simple ability to read a timetable – since she kept bobbing up unexpectedly throughout the Bristol Channel as on one afternoon when we were moored in Ilfracombe and she was on the quay making a fuss and wanting to come aboard and be with him "where she belonged" until he managed to talk her out of it.

Somehow you understood the nature of her problem just by looking at John who was always sharply dressed with a melodious voice which amused even when he wasn't trying to be funny. He was also never short of money, forever producing a wad of notes the size of a bog roll and quietly let it be known that he was also a four-star shag in bed. With so many dull, sexless and penniless men around you could see why that woman was so upset that he had stopped coming home to her "where he belonged." Whatever it was John had it in spades.

I identified completely with that pained wraith on the Penarth pier because I knew *exactly* what she was going through and, albeit to a slightly less melodramatic degree, was acting in much the same way myself. My own pain even seemed to reach up through that moth-dancing, sodium darkness and embrace hers, almost as if they were greeting one another in a comforting fellowship of suffering.

I was still absolutely terrified and wretched by what Sandra had done to me; the loss of her was like carrying around some great stone burden and most of the time I didn't feel up to carrying it; didn't think my wounds would ever heal and, rather like that woman on the pier, I feared I would wander the streets of Cardiff for the rest of my life, going half-mad and becoming a menace to everyone in the pubs as I droned on about how I had once been in love with a girl called Sandra Bond who had left me for a prick called Mike the Worm.

There had been no final row or ultimatum between us, just merely that it had been too rough for the paddle steamer to sail one day and I had been given an unexpected day off. We were still sort of speaking and I went down to wait for her outside the hairdressers when she was due to knock off, buying her a red rose and hoping to give her a nice surprise, when I spotted Mike the Worm sitting in a new sports car in the street, also clearly waiting for her.

It was raining hard and I hung back behind some people in the bus stop on the other side of the road when she came out of the hairdressers, smiled and waved before getting in next to him and kissing him. For ages. Even as they did so I just stood there dropping my red rose with the rain mingling with my tears, not wholly surprised by what I was seeing but still feeling as if I'd been punched hard in the gut, hardly able to believe the fiery intensity of the darts of pain shooting through every part of me. A bus came and its wheels broke into a rain puddle and threw water all over my discarded rose.

I guessed he was fucking her and the very thought of him between her legs made me throw up over a nearby shop window. But I didn't confront him or her in any way, didn't rush over there and try to pull off his windscreen wipers or jump on his flash winkle-pickers because I've always hated any sort of confrontation. Perhaps I was also nursing a lingering hope that, like Martin Eden, I would soon become a successful writer and she would take me back again, weeping and wailing about how we all make mistakes and I should at least forgive her for just this one. The power of fantasy, in the face of all the hard facts, is perhaps always the strongest in the adolescent mind.

But, in all the messy circumstances, I took the worst possible option and began stalking her for weeks and even months, just standing around uselessly outside the hairdressers rather like that poor woman on the Penarth pier, hiding myself away but making myself visible too, imprisoned by my outraged feelings and yet knowing there was absolutely fuck all I could do about anything. On days off I hid myself over the road from her work or got up early in the hope of bumping into her as she went to catch the bus to go to work or even waited in the darkness outside her home for her to come back with Mike the Worm then dying a death of a thousand cuts – oh a fucking milllion cuts – as I watched them kissing and fondling one another in his new fucking sports car.

She must have spotted me often enough and the really insane thing about stalking is that it must also completely destroy whatever residual affection for me that might have lingered in her. Far from being a young man who loved her and was one day going to become a great writer I had turned into a complete pain in the arse who was following her around like some wretched official in a peaked cap who was forever threatening to cut off her electricity. One of the golden rules of the mating game, I now know, is that, if you crowd someone, you lose them. Try pushing them and you always end up pissing on your chips. Real feelings have always got to grow freely and of their own accord and I couldn't have destroyed my relationship with Sandra more completely and certainly had I sat down with a manual on how to get someone to hate you forever. *Everything* I did –

and every step I took – messed it up even more.

All I could do was suffer and hope the next day wouldn't be quite so bad as this, except it always was. Surely Jack London couldn't have gone through all this. How could anyone write a word if they were suffering like this?

The hard physical work on the paddle steamers helped to assuage my grief and a good skinfull of beer or rough cider late at night often did wonders for it too, although this was not always guaranteed since sometimes, deep in my cups and in front of my other shipmates, I might break down and start sobbing uncontrollably.

"Oh don't take any notice of him," Ray, who had joined me on the paddle steamers, would say by way of apology. "He's missing that bloody girl again."

There didn't seem any way out – or release – from it. She stormed through my dreams and figured in my every desire and fantasy. Even a quick wank didn't seem to work any more – not even for a few moments before the guilt set in – and there were those days – those long, long, days – when I was convinced I would never even laugh or smile again.

I fell physically ill because of Sandra and that went on for years too, throwing up all the time and becoming wan, pale and stick-thin. It got so bad I could throw up while walking down the street without even breaking my step. I'm not even sure how I survived that first year after she left me since my belly seemed to be almost permanently seething with acid and all I could ever keep down by way of food were lettuce sandwiches. There are plenty of other pebbles on the beach and time heals everything, my mother used to say, but I never really got over Sandra and I have often bitterly cursed that moment in that damned youth club when I first clapped eyes on her.

So I was right there with that woman threatening to throw herself off Penarth pier because we had both been rejected by the ones we loved. We were both united in our pain which was going to last for an eternity and, just for those few cold moments, our tortured spirits rose up into the sea air and came together and intertwined and comforted one another with a common band of warmth, saying carry on, move forward, there are other pebbles on the beach. Don't just stand there shivering and crying into those empty, unfeeling winds.

Time heals all the pain there is.

Believe.

Anna Davis
Tequila-Bonkers

MY SO-CALLED FRIENDS are giving me sidelong looks and sniggering at my new perm – they've been doing it all evening. I am trying to laugh it off but my scalp still aches from the three billion rollers and my nostrils burn with the hot stench of perming lotion. I have been avoiding mirrors and other shiny surfaces all evening – which is not easy in Chicago's, let me tell you. I am afraid of my own reflection.

The waiter comes over and Sîan orders a Slow Comfortable Screw; a bad idea as her head is almost on the table now. But she's the birthday girl so she gets whatever she wants. She keeps forgetting that she has to pretend it's her nineteenth rather than her sixteenth, and I have to kick her under the table yet again when she lifts her head long enough to blurt out how gutted she is that she never got to have illegal sex. Louise tells her it's still illegal if you take it up the arse and we all explode into giggles. My laughter is forced though: Louise's all-knowing persona is pissing me off something wicked. She thinks she's so mature.

Vanessa orders a White Russian and Louise asks for another Marguerita, which worries me because Tequila makes her go bonkers. I've had enough sickly cocktails so I ask for half a Stella (it's the sort of place where girls don't buy pints) and they all call me a killjoy. Then Madonna's 'Like a Virgin' starts playing and Sîan says "it's my song" and drags Vanessa off to the dancefloor. Louise and I watch them gyrating around with all the sad fucks who hang out in this horrible glitzy club: All those men wearing trousers with ironed-in creases and the women in white stilettos. It's the kind of place where they don't let you wear DMs or trainers or even jeans. We wouldn't be caught dead in here normally – we're into live music, particularly from our favourite band, Citizen Duane; we go to gigs held in pubs and bars filled with *real* people with interesting lives, not townie nightclubs filled with zombies – but we could hardly refuse Sîan on her birthday, could we.

Louise leans across the table conspiratorially. "Lush bloke at nine o'clock – take a peep; see if he's looking over."

I glance across. He's not what I'd call lush but I suppose he's not bad.

Ancient though; must be thirty at least. Round-necked white T-shirt; thin silver chain around his neck. He swallows some lager and I see his Adam's apple move. His hair is almost black; eyes very dark too. Oh shit, he just caught me looking. A hint of a smile... "Bastard's smirking at my perm!"

"Rubbish – you're imagining it."

"He is. He's laughing at me. I'm a fucking poodle, Louise."

Corkscrew curls, that was what I was supposed to end up with. I showed the hairdresser a magazine photo of Susanna Hoffs out of the Bangles and she said it would be no problem. "Classic hair for the Summer of 87," – that was her comment; no word of a lie. Maybe I should go back there tomorrow and make her cut it all off for free.

Louise is twisting around to give the bloke the eye. I don't like the way this evening is developing.

"What do you think you're doing, Lou?"

She rolls her eyes. "Christ, when did you get so boring?"

Shit, he's getting up, coming over. He's jigging in time to the music; Cameo's 'Word Up'.

"Yo, pretty ladies... are you going to buy me a drink or what?"

I've heard some lame opening gambits in my time, but this one...

2.15am on Womanby Street and Louise's new friend, Dave, is bargaining with the fat, ginger doorman at the Dog and Duck (claiming he's an old mate), so that we can get in free. We are standing out in the road finishing our Caroline Street chips and I swear that Louise is raring to get into this guy's pants. She's gone tequila-bonkers. We were all supposed to be staying at Sian's place tonight, but Sian (who spent the last hour at Chicago's slumped over a sink in the Ladies' bogs) has just been bundled into a taxi by Vanessa. Vanessa clearly disapproved of our – or rather Louise's – decision to stay out for a bit with Dave, but that made Louise all the more determined.

I suppose I could just announce that we're going home. She'd have to come with me – if she went back to her place at this time of night her mother would go mental. There's nobody in at my house: My mum and brother Jake are away in Spain on holiday – a holiday I was supposed to go on but got myself out of on the pretext that I couldn't spare the time off my O-level revision. Mum agreed that I could kip one week with Louise and the other with Sian while they were away. What I'm not supposed to be doing is staying at the house on my own, basically because Mum doesn't trust me – but Louise and I have been bending the rules, and 25 Teilo Street, Pontcanna has temporarily become our very own single girls' pad.

"Come on, Louise. We're going home."

Her mouth purses up with anger. "What are you talking about, Jane? You're not going to go all boring on me, are you?"

"Well –" I hate being called boring, and she knows it.

Then she shrugs, flicking back her long curly hair

(natural curls, of course – none of this perming torture for our Lou). "OK, then, pal. You do what you like but I'm staying out. See you around."

The stupid little cow is calling my bluff. Well, we'll see who's bluffing… I glance over at Dave, who's now laughing with the ginger doorman and beckoning to us – and back at Louise, who's scrunching up her greasy chip paper and smoothing her tiny skirt. She has a smear of ketchup on her mouth, a drunken blush in her cheeks. Her eyes are wide open and innocent. And I'm suddenly aware of her vulnerability.

We walk ahead of Dave down the stairs which stink of puke, though I can't actually see any. This is a far-cry from Chicago's with its smart-casual clientele and its cocktails. This place is a sort of spittoon, into which is gobbed – after every other club and bar in town has closed its doors – Cardiff's greenest, yuckiest phlegm.

Nobody here looks like anybody else. The only thing everyone has in common is a sort of visible drink-neediness. Actually, I could do with a drink myself, and I'm not best pleased when Louise announces it's my round. As I wait to be served, I take a closer look at the room's inhabitants: A couple of henna-haired crusties are propping up the bar, deep in conversation with a knobbly rugby boy. Three student types in John Lennon glasses and stonewashed jeans are trying to chat up a blonde Barbie girl in a leopard skin jacket. Over by the door a lone old geezer in a faded brown suit is sneezing over and over. When I look at his face, he doesn't have a nose, just a sort of nostril-less shoot. Makes me shudder.

Walking back to the table where Louise and Dave have planted themselves, and balancing three pints precariously, I'm thinking that Dave looks really at home here.

"Dave's in a band," says Louise, grabbing her pint of SA.

"Oh. Really." I try to make my voice express my boredom clearly.

"We're called The Rubble," says Dave, lighting up a roly held between his yellow fingers. "We gig quite a bit: Sam's Bar, Inn on the River, Clwb Ifor… Heard of us?"

I had but I wasn't going to admit that. "Me and Louise do some backing singing now and again for Citizen Duane," I say it as nonchalantly as possible. I'm expecting him to be impressed but he snorts in contempt.

"You girls waste your time singing for that wanker, Sean Prosser?"

His eyes are so dark you can hardly pick out the pupils.

"Sean's not a wanker." But Louise says it quietly, and is still looking all flirtatious.

"You don't want to bother with that loser," says Dave. "You can come and sing with The Rubble. I'll speak to the boys about it."

"That'd be great, wouldn't it, Jane," says Louise.

I take a long drink from my pint of Hurlimann, and murmur, "Not sure I'd have the time." Louise can be so fickle.

"Well, Lou, you can come along and sing on your own," says Dave, and I can see his arm creeping along the back of the seat behind her. "You can be my Linda."

I screw up my face in disgust. "Your *what*?"

He turns those dark eyes on me. "You know what I mean. She could be Linda to my Paul…" He sighs with impatience at our blank faces. "McCartney."

"Oh… right."

Even Louise isn't sure about that one. "I'm just nipping to the loo," she says, and wriggles out from her seat. He looks at her bum as she gets up.

There's a silence when she's gone, except for Bon Jovi's 'Living on a Prayer', which is booming out over the speakers. I watch Dave give his cheap lighter a shake and then keep flicking it. No flame.

When I speak again, it is in a quiet and measured voice. "I know what you're after, *Dave*, and you're not going to get it. She might be acting like she's interested in you but I know her better than anyone. She's just messing. You'll get nowhere."

"Who says I want to get anywhere with her?" he says,

casually, finally getting a flame and relighting his stub of roly.

"Well, it's a bit bloody obvious."

His gaze shifts and I spot Louise making her way back down the stairs. When I turn back he's looking at me really intently.

"You'd fit me like a glove," he says quietly.

3.30am and my resolve to get Louise home after one pint has totally failed. We've had another pint plus a whisky each. I am smashed and Louise looks like she could vom at any moment. Dave is like some kind of hypnotist or something. When you look into his eyes it's really hard to look away again. I keep getting these weird butterfly sensations and I don't like it. I've been trying to get Louise to come to the toilet with me so I can tell her what he said but she won't move from his side. I have to admit that deep down I feel sort of smug; Louise, with all her curly hair and her big cheek-bones is so sure of herself, so totally used to being fancied, that I don't suppose it's even occurred to her that he might be after *me*. It's like Dave and I have a little secret between us. I've stopped being snappy with him. When I do get up to go to the toilets, I am surprised by my own reflection in the mirror over the sink: After all this drink I'd totally forgotten about the perm. It actually doesn't look so bad.

When I get back to my seat, Dave is downing what looks like a double whisky and rubbing his hands together. "So girls, where are we going now?"

Louise says nothing. Just giggles.

I'm suddenly more sober. "Well, I don't know about you, but we're going home."

Dave looks disappointed. "Where's home, then?"

"That's for us to know and for you not to."

"Girls, girls… you're not going to let me down, are you? Here's me thinking we could have ourselves a little party…"

"Sorry, Dave. It's late." I'm folding my arms, resolute. Louise hiccups but is beyond speech.

His expression changes. He's trying to look innocent. "Oh

well. I guess I'll just have to drive back to Pontypridd then."

"You'll *what*?"

"Didn't I mention that I live in Ponty?" He produces a set of car keys from his pocket.

"Dave, you *can't* drive. Not after all that drink. You could kill someone!"

He shrugs. "Can't see that I have much choice. Don't have enough money left for a cab and there's no other way of getting home at this time of night."

Swearing to myself, I'm searching through my purse for notes but after all those drinks I only have three quid left. Louise ran out of cash hours ago. "Isn't there someone you could call? One of the boys from The Rubble or something?"

A little shake of the head from Dave. "Sorry, Janey, no can do. I'm just going to have to drive."

The clock beside my bed tells me it's 5.20am. I can't sleep for knowing that he's downstairs on the couch in my sleeping bag. His presence here is total sacrilege. The game I played with Louise – that 25 Teilo Street is our single girls' pad – feels well and truly over. Downstairs the kitchen is a mess of takeaway packaging, coffee cups, empty coke cans and cereal bowls that Louise and I have let pile up over three days. Seeing Dave flop down on my mother's couch, feet on the coffee table, smoking roll-ups when nobody ever *ever* smokes in this house – was almost unbearable. Returning to the living room with the coffee and catching him trying to put his hands all over para- lytic and semi-comatose Louise was way too much. And then he had the cheek to ask which bedroom he could sleep in – and still with that look on his face; that bloody sniggering look of his like he's laughing at my perm or something.

It took all the strength I had left to shake Louise awake, half-drag her up the stairs and deposit her in Jake's room. When I finally got between my own sheets in my own bed, alone, the tears just wouldn't stop coming. I wish Mum was here.

What was that? There was a sound outside my door.

Footsteps… No, no, must have imagined it – but, wait – that was definitely a creak of the floorboard.

I can't move and I can't make a sound. My throat feels frozen. My fingers tightly grip the edge of the duvet. The door handle is moving slowly… What the hell could I do if… if…

"Jane, it's me."

Thank God!

Louise tiptoes in and silently closes the door behind her. She's wearing one of Jake's old T-shirts. Her hair is a fuzz. I can't see her face clearly in the dark but I sense that she too has been crying.

"I can hear him moving around," she whispers. "He's pacing about downstairs."

"Come on. It'll be OK." I shift over in the bed to make room for her and she slips in beside me.

I can hear him too now. The sound of his shoes on the quarry tiles in the kitchen. The click of the ignition on the cooker as he presumably lights a roll-up; a thump of cupboard doors as he searches for – what? *Please* don't let him take anything or break anything or –

"Jane, what if he comes upstairs?"

"He won't. He's just pissed off because we wouldn't sleep with him." My voice sounds calm. I wish I could believe what I was saying. "He'll go back to bed in a minute."

We snuggle down together. I put my arms around her and hold her close. 7.16am and I hear the front door bang.

Louise is still asleep. I disentangle myself from her arms and get out of bed.

Putting my dressing gown on, I make my way downstairs. Peeping through the open door to the living room I can see the discarded sleeping bag. On the coffee table is a saucer full of ash and fag ends. No other indications that Dave was ever here.

I go to rub at my sore, aching head and feel the alien curls. Bloody perm. In the kitchen, I take a rubbish bag from the cupboard under the sink.

Then I begin to clean up.

Sonia Edwards
Nude Girl

I'M ENJOYING THE fresh breeze on my cheeks. Walking. The sound of my own feet on the pavement. The sound of cars. A city. Civilisation. The feeling of being free, the rest of the day ahead of me, and a leisurely evening in a hotel to follow. I'll go for a cup of coffee in a minute. Somewhere tasteful where they put a *cafetiere* on the table. And that a little table for one in a quiet corner next to a big green plant. Yes. Why not? I'm going to spoil myself a little.

*

Now, over my black coffee at my lovely little table for one – and yes, there's a green plant next to me – I begin to think more clearly. I've managed to give up smoking now and I'm going to lose weight too. Okay, I'm not the bare-breasted goddess I used to be, and I now depend on a bra somewhat stronger than before in order to defy the force of gravity, but things aren't beyond redemption by a long way. Come on, Mared Wyn, for God's sake. You shouldn't mourn your youth, but rejoice in your new maturity. You've got fewer hang-ups now, older and fatter, than you had as a willowy twenty-year-old. I listen attentively to my own sermon. I should feel proud that I'd inspired an artist. Yes, damn it! That was me! Aphrodite. But everyone gets older. Even the goddess of the waves. And it's high time for this ex-goddess to have a bit of a treat.

The Ann Summers shop. What am I doing here among brides-to-be preparing surprises for their honeymoon that will be over sooner than they think, and suspenders that will be stuffed in the back of the drawer with the first pang of morning sickness? And what do they think I'm doing here? A stripper in a pensioners' nightclub looking for new stage clothes? I should shake myself. I should stop being such an old cynic and stop being so self-centred that I think everyone's looking at me all the time. I should have learned my lesson in that respect in the gallery earlier. I venture a glance around me. Everyone looks amazingly normal. I relax. Decide to enjoy myself. And realise with relief that everything is available in size 14 and above. There's lace and silk around me everywhere and it's not all common old stuff either. Even though the usual tasteless black and red stuff is here, there are pretty things too, and I don't have to buy to please a man. I come out of the shop with a wisp of completely impractically feminine silk. Here I am, overspending on incredible lingerie and I've got no-one to appreciate them. I'd be better off buying big bloomers from Marks to hold my stomach in and a sensible pair of slippers for the winter. But then, why should I please anyone else? I've spent a lifetime doing that. It's my money, and I've got a right to spend it on something pretty. I have a right to that nice feeling of knowing that I've got something transparent and lacy next to my skin and not some old black bloomers with frayed elastic. And if I was knocked down by a lorry on the day I'm wearing my silk knickers as least the ambulancemen would have something to talk about.

The urge to spend doesn't stop in the Ann Summers shop. I go cheerfully down the street and for the first time in my life display the bag with the logo on it proudly. I've just bought sexy underwear and I haven't got an iota of shame.

Not like that nude girl in the picture long ago. She wouldn't have dared be so shameless. I wasn't brave that day when I sat naked for the picture. I wasn't venturesome, daring, filled with self-confidence about my own body. I was in love, that's all. Looking back, I realise with some discomfort that I would have done anything to please Johann Roi. No, that Aphrodite wouldn't be completely at ease carrying an Ann Summers bag through the high-street. But she was me. I had that perfect body. I inspired one of Europe's greatest artists at that time. I'm just getting used to the magnitude of the thing. It's starting to give me a thrill. Awakening something in me. Some primitive, naked urge. And going on a credit-card spree in Cardiff's clothes shops is only the start of it.

The hotel room is quiet. I have chosen to eat comparatively early. A table for one. Something else old Aphrodite years ago would never have felt comfortable doing. But I've got a book. Newspapers. And I enjoy this independence. I order a bottle of Pinot Grigio without having to consult with anyone. Olives to start. Caesar Salad to follow. I skip the dessert – the effect of Johann's picture on me I suppose! – and go straight to the coffee. Divine. I sit back and relax.

There's no rush for the tables here, and the room is only half full. I've got wine left. I feel the cover of my novel, and deliberately forget that I've got my own to finish inside a fortnight.

And I let myself flirt gently with the young Turkish waiter who has come to offer to refill my coffee cup. He's a dish. Buttocks like apples and eyes the same colour as the chocolate I was strong enough to resist. I can resist this too. He's too young. Too nice with all the ladies. And I only want some innocent fun with him anyway. The Ann Summers thong feels tighter somehow, after the meal, and is threatening to split me like a cheesewire. What was I thinking of when I bought it…?

"I'm sorry to interrupt your meal… you're Mared Wyn aren't you?"

He's a tall man, and that's the more obvious because I'm sitting and he's standing. Perhaps he's around fifty. Or a year or two older than that. His smile enlivens his eyes immediately. Blue eyes. A white shirt of expensive material. Because of his height and his broad shoulders, his tendency to carry a bit of a paunch doesn't affect the image at all. To the contrary. He looks commensurate, wears his clothes well. A man with a bit of a grip about him, Mam would have said years ago. There's a touch of grey in the blackness of his hair that hasn't yet touched his moustache. I like the way he's turned up his shirt cuffs untidily to show a silver watch nesting roundly against the dark hair of his wrist, the way he holds his leather jacket over one arm. He's speaking again. A deep, melodious voice. His Welsh is natural, strong. From the north.

"I saw you in the exhibition today – I thought to have a word with you but you disappeared to somewhere."

"Oh?"

A handsome man with mischievous eyes has dropped from heaven right next to my little table. I'm wearing the most daring knickers I've worn for a long time, and the Pinot Grigio has started to go to my head in the nicest way.

Mari Emlyn
Step by Step

I CAME ACROSS a school photograph from the end of the sixties or the beginning of the seventies. There we all were, rows of pupils on the school yard with the headmistress and the staff seated in the middle of us. The red bricks of Bryntaf school were our background. What you could not see on the photograph was the other school opposite our school. Bryntaf shared its playground with a school for non-Welsh-speaking Welsh people, or the "English" as we called them. "Welshies" was their name for us – amongst many others. In order to avoid trouble, it was arranged so that the playtimes of the two schools did not coincide.

Unfortunately, it wasn't the children who were the problem, but the mothers. When I started in the school, the bus would take us children through the Mynachdy council housing estate in Gabalfa down to the iron gates of the school. Before long, there was a protest from the residents in the nearby houses. They were complaining that buses were travelling down their street, but Mei and I knew, after a chat around the dinner table in the evening, that our parents believed this was a protest against Welsh-medium education. The Mynachdy mothers won the battle, and the buses which brought us from every suburb of Cardiff had to drop us half way down the housing estate.

To this day I'm still hopeless at measuring things. During the first years of school we learned to measure in inches, feet, yards, ounces, pounds and gallons. Before the end of my primary school career the headmistress had retired and we had a new headmaster, and by then it was time to measure in millimetres, centimetres, metres, kilometres, grammes, kilogrammes and litres. Both headteachers were superb, and the staff were blameless. It would be very unfair of me to transfer the blame for my own stupidity to their shoulders. But to this day measuring anything is a headache to me. That's why, perhaps, I don't know how much wallpaper to buy, that I'm hopeless at finding my way around a strange place, and make a mess of it when I try to bake a cake. That's why I can't say now exactly how far I had to walk from the bus to the school under the new arrangements, but I'd guess it was some six hundred yards – or six hundred metres! To a small child, though, it was a long way. It was a very long way because a rank of mothers would line the pavements, some staring at us threateningly, others abusing us scornfully all the way down the street. One of the Mynachdy mothers really frightened me. I remember her to this day. She was the chief character in many of my nightmares for years. Her name was Lucy. Lucy was a big, buxom woman with curly, black, greasy hair. Lucy wasn't a woman you would want to cross. She lived in one of the houses closest to the school gates. Every morning and every afternoon Lucy would lean over the gate of her wasteland of a garden and snarl at us terrifyingly as we walked past. A cigarette stump was stuck in the gap in her dirty teeth, and she looked like a smouldering dragon, ready to boil and explode. She'd always be in a pitch black teeshirt with her bra-less breasts pushing boldly through the thin material. I compared her with my mother. Mother had a row of pretty teeth, and I never saw her without a bra – except when she was wearing her nightdress. I was thankful that I had a mother who was pretty and tidy, kind and gentle. That was before

Mei and Dad died and before the drink got hold of her.

Every morning Mr Evans would encourage the nervous ones among us to get off the bus by shouting "Today, not tomorrow!" We all walked apprehensively from the bus down to the school in pairs. Each child had to have an older partner, and I was fortunate that I had an older brother to look after me. One morning, as I walked with my trembling hand squeezing Mei's hand, Lucy, and the army of angry mothers, threw tomatoes and eggs at us children.

I've never been so frightened. Our fast walk became a wild gallop as we ran from the pitiless bombardment into the safety of the school walls. I was so frightened that I did a pee-pee in my knickers. I started to cry, and as soon as we crossed the threshold of the school Meilir took me straight to Mrs Hughes. He explained quietly to her that I had wet myself. Mrs Hughes thanked Meilir and he went straight to his class. The teacher took me to the storeroom and to the box of clean knickers and pants. I wasn't the only child in that troubled period to have to go to the clean underwear box every morning after the attacks of Lucy and her gang. I remember how I begged Mam and Dad to let me stay at home, but the two of them insisted that I had a right to Welsh-medium education. We weren't going to give in to threats like this. At that time I didn't give a damn about my rights or about the Welsh language. All I wanted to do was to be able to sleep without nightmares and not to wet my knickers.

Peter Finch
Entry of Christ Into Cardiff, 2005

Anointed Christos Branch of Myrhh Jesse Jesu
Queen Street Elias Jeremias Ensign Immanuel Emmanuel
Jesus Multitloral Carfit Melchizedek Messiah
ObeWan Nazarene Kenobi Potentate Passover Owl
Rabboni Tortilla Bhoona Jasu Rose of Sharon Scepter
Isa Ibn Maryam al-Salaam Christ Shabazz Bandana
Yasu 'Isa bin Maryam Muslim Spire Eesa Esau Yeheshua
Rough Joshua Rahman Yoghurt Iesous Abd of Allah
Jesus Cassanova Bute Street Sorrow Bethlehem
Llanrumney Passover Kalimatimmin Kalimaatullaah
Mary the Virgin Karate Do Splott Saviour Jesucristo come
                                                              back
Kalimat'Allah (peace be upon him) Adamsdown Rasulullah
Jesu Prajapati Jehovah Lifeboat appeal saturdays
Jesus latterday Cardiff Post Vishnu Ya Ruhullah
Enzikiriza Yaba'ddugavu Eye Nono Black Messiah
Saviour Turban Guru Gobind Singh Chapate handwrench
Blood of Ely glass and Potentate Refuge God Iesu
Diolchwch i Dduw y nefoedd Taff will baptise too late now
Bread of Heaven William Williams Cefn-y-Coed Llandovery
St Johns St Marys St Womanby fill slowly with beer

St Mary Street

THE LIGHTS ARE ON. I'm entering the street of Saint
Mary from the north. I've come out of Wharton Street
squashed between Howells – Cardiff's Harrods – and big
Waterstones where poetry and Wales seem to have turned to
dust. I'm just south of where the Street actually starts at

Guildhall Place. Today it's Christmas. Fairy lights on the lamp posts. Revellers in half dress. Bare midriffs, skin shoulders, bow ties, glitz and glitter. On match days the police cordon off the street to traffic and the roadway fills with rugby's pissed and surging thousands. It's like that now. 7.00 pm. Dry. A slow moving line of mixed traffic strung about with roaring drunks. Ibiza uncovered in the south Wales gloom.

As I move south the sense of moral abandonment increases. Dinner-suited youths piss in doorways. A bare-chested shave head sprawls across the bonnet of a parked Mondeo. A middle-aged white-collar wearing a single earring and his shirt half out of his trousers falls off a traffic island. A girl in a short, sequined dress lies slumped again the window of a sandwich shop. On the back of a road sign is affixed the following notice:

BE DISOBEDIENT – part of a global day of action in solidarity with the Argentinean rebellion. There will be a day of fun, disobedience and truly direct action against corporate bullying and greedy multinationals. Dress as Santa. Stop the traffic. Reclaim the streets. Make subversive success. Meet by the Nye Bevan statue, Queen Street. 21st December.

That's tomorrow. Someone comes up out of the Golate and is copiously sick into the doorway of the Bang & Olufsen showroom. No need. We are disobedient now. In our days of fun. We don't have to reclaim the streets. They've always been ours.

Crossing the junction with Wood Street, where buses bend towards the station and the edge of Riverside hoves into view, is like reaching the frontier. Surging hoards spin around the entrances to Weatherspoons. Black-coated, earphone encrusted bouncers watch from their doorways, overwhelmed. Fast-food boxes from McDonalds mix with cans and broken glass in the gutters. Someone comes out of the bowels of The Square, blinking, face full of blood, jacket smeared and ripped. A rubble of glass litters the floor of the

Philharmonic. A line of shrieking girls with lace and lycra and breasts that pop bear WKD with them as they stagger among the stuttering traffic. Coffee Republic has its shutters up. A fifty-year old with the velvet-collared fawn coat of a lawyer or wide boy lies on the pavement outside La Brasserie. Arriving diners, tanked, middle-aged, loud, cigar smoking, ignore him. Women of a certain age with flashing-Santa earrings and decoration tinsel wound into their hair wahoo in a conga line. Their chubby knees and fleshy shoulders shake in rhythm. An overweight on heels with five plastic carriers full of presents, a French loaf and a box of Sainsbury's crackers leans against the end of the bus shelter, a full large glass of house red in one hand, king size in the other. Music roars out of Walkabout. They are dealing again back of the Philharmonic. Guns'n'Roses. But it's Christmas. They won't go off. The world is going to end soon. We are all going to be there when it happens.

In St Mary Street itself the new millennium drive for oblivion is succeeding. Kitty Flynn's on the corner of Caroline Street, an Irish re-branding of the old Cambrian, is a sea of screaming. Someone has put in the window of Sportsales and BT's new blue Broadband Internet Kiosk has had its aluminium vandal-resistant keyboard covered with regurgitated veg. The Square are advertising £1 off all cocktails and three pints of Fosters for the price of two and the entire of south Cardiff have taken advantage. I look into Le Monde, one of Benigno Martinez's three Franco-Spanish sawdust, fish and steak restaurants that line the east side of the street.

The place is a bedlam of whirling waiters, pink-faced overcoats, tight black dresses and coloured shirts. I consider retreating to Dorothy's Fish Bar in Caroline Street, last resort for all failed diners, but remember the rolling panic occurring on the pavement outside the former Cambrian. Give up. St Mary, tell me about Christmas. A passing gaggle of tinsel-bedecked data typists give me a handful of party-poppers along with a number of invitations which I don't

really fancy following up. There's a star-burst rocket gone off
above the old Canal basin. Someone goes past on a bike with
a four-foot Christmas tree strapped to the back. To the west
there are stars. "It's so quiet now" someone once wrote. Not
any more.

From Real Cardiff Two

Mari George
Wales from the Air

Cardiff area

These days
there's no time
to roll in the sand dunes
to linger at the feet of the castles
or to follow the stepping stones back to yesterday.
No time to remember the legends shattered
in the crafty hands of cliffs
or to search for the invisible treasure of the lost myths.
To wander the cloth of the fields of labour.
To see nature's adventure.
To remember the scent of seaweed in the early hours
while collecting shells.
At that time I owned the sea,
a princess, sandcastle mistress,
challenging the succession of the wild waves.
These days
it's too easy to forget the coal ships
carrying the tough workers' blue-black best
and bringing bread and butter from afar
to the tables of Butetown.

Today we're too busy
making our world smaller.

Working. Working
to make things better...
Life will be easier to enjoy afterwards
– when we have time.

Hopes lifted at the airport,
freedom's airplanes
breaking through the quiet of a Sunday afternoon,
shaking fear into our bones.
A train station, the city's artery,
that's moving, always
moving.

Everything's near,
everything's big. Everything's easy.
A stadium that's a throne to our pride
and our stars...
Competing. Mingling. Singing. One crowd.
Manics rocking the foundations,
and the rumour
that Robbie
had thrown the television
from his hotel.

Heard in a taxi.

Travellers and shoppers carrying tales in their shopping
bags,
busybodying in the Hayes.
Their conversation dwindling to nothing
Like the pigeons' crumbs.

Drivers punching the air
to get there quicker.
Cursing
because the car has halted
and the sun's getting hotter.

We're busy busy
everyone swarming like ants to the shops
and to the docks' nice restaurants
and the wind whipping the boats.
Meeting places
for empty people to discuss food while eating their work.

In Barry once, I heard big talk
being squandered between couples
like the fair's pennies,
children skidding their slang
around the place
and a little man like a grain of sand
saying nothing about the world.
Everyone's going somewhere.
Who knows where?
Once, I asked
the Echo man
but he just
shook his head
Live cartoons of people
weaving into one another,
colourful designs.

But the pattern unravels
because freedom keeps us from uniting.
There's no time to hold hands,
… to share an experience.
All we do is come and go
without belonging.
Like old lovers.

No time to strip off the layers
and remember
the child in us
rolling
on the sand dunes

not caring who comes.
Our world's been made small now,
but the people are further away than ever.

Passing without a word
like boats on the water
or seagulls…
in a man-made bay.

Niall Griffiths
A Kind of Liverpool/Cardiff Thing

1. St David's Hotel

IT'S LIKE A COOLING TOWER or something – a vast cylinder spiralling above ringed with internal balconies over which tiny white distant blobs of faces peer. Big floppy couches on the marble floor roundabout as if dropped from that great height and splatted. If I worked here I'd spend all my time gazing skywards, like I do in cathedrals or forest canopies; the architecture continually scoops the eye upwards, towards a heaven. You don't look at the ground, in such places, unless you're above it.

We check in. Names, address, occupation, car registration number – the knackered 12-year-old Ford Escort parked outside amongst the Beemers and Porsches. We get the key and go up in the lift. Up and up and up in the gleaming low-lit lift. On our floor we lean over the balcony and see the people on the ground so very far below and my heart lurches. I feel sick.

Heights, I don't like. We enter our room and explore it all, the carousel mini-bar and glittering bathroom, the bed alone bigger than some bedsits I've lived in. There's a knock on the door and I answer it, admit the porter in his top-hat and tails with our luggage, two burst rucksacks and two placcy bags. Then we take cold beers from the mini-bar out onto the external balcony, look over to Penarth across the water skimmed by feeding swifts and swallows which behave the same here as they do in the mountains, where I usually see them; their delirious flight, their exhiliration and joy in speed. I could watch them for ever. My girlfriend goes back inside to run a bath and I lean over the railings and regard the dockside far, far below and remember living there when I was horribly poor, how it used to be, scrabbling for money and drugs in the ginnels and mouldering rooming-houses and yellowing, desiccated pubs. I remember it all so clearly but then think no, that *can't* be right because I first visited Cardiff in late 2000 and I had money then; I was put up in good hotels and had all my expenses paid. But it seems that, on the long list of coastal cities I've drifted through confused and craving, the city of Cardiff appears. Yet I really don't know what it's like to be poor, here, in this city, although it seems that I do; that sea-smell, this low, dark sky, the bilge-water whiff and the thin people with the loud voices... I *know* all this. It's a memory within. How strange.

Back in the room with another beer on the waun of the bed I notice a small brown bird outside, on the balcony, beyond the glass door. It is limping badly, lurching as it crosses clumsily the wooden decking. I take a bar of chocolate from the mini-bar (two quid!) and break it open and extract a hazelnut and a raisin and put them outside the sliding door. The bird flies away. But then it returns, takes up the hazelnut and flies away again. I wonder how he hurt his leg?

2. Mulligan's

INTERESTING; a CajunIrish crossover band, below the big screen where I watched the destruction of the World Trade

Centre. They're doing a zydeco version of 'Liverpool Lou' which shouldn't really work but it does. The pub is rammed. I have to approach the bar sidey-ways like a crab and I could really go a Guiness but I don't want to stand cramped and angled like this for the time it takes to pour it so I order a lager instead and take it back to my table. Between songs, there's a kerfuffle; over by the speakers it seems a man has collapsed, through booze or a belt I don't know, but he's folded to the floor and in doing so has dragged an amp and a table with him. There's a mess. A bouncer drags and dumps him outside as the band re-set their equipment, then play 'Jolie Blond' in a Pogues-y manner.

This is a place in which things collapse. Horizontalling occurs in this fugged and huddled pub.

3. Another Pub, One Amongst Many

QUITE DRUNK IN THIS ONE. A couple are arguing in the corner opposite, I can't tell what about because their voices are slurred and so is my hearing. The man has his index finger pointed right into the woman's face but she isn't giving a millimetre, she doesn't flinch or recoil, she just leans forwards on her elbows over the table towards him. She has that glow, that glint that shows she's winning and she's enjoying it, maybe because the man is becoming more and more agitated by her calmness, more stirred by her composure. She seems to be sucking all the poise from him and drawing it into herself.

I get distracted by the talk around my table and when I look over again the man has gone and the woman is alone, leaning back in her chair, scanning the pub. There is a small smile on her face. Her skin and eyes are bright and reflective. She looks like she wants to be nowhere in the world but here, triumphant and unaccompanied in this pub by the castle. A man approaches her. I *knew* it wouldn't take long.

Someone asks if I want another beer and I say yes. With a whiskey chaser.

4. City Blur

A FIGHT in the street tables overturned a man spews in the doorway of Waterstone's a woman beats her man with a handbag some Vodafone shirts are acting the wanker as usual students in stupid outfits cruising cars blasting techno police arrest a man with blood on his shirt. Burberry checks abound as do groups of guys in Ben Sherman pastel colours like tubes of Opal Fruits and women wear very little it's too cold for those scanty things too cold. Polyglot and motley pidgin and patois dockside I am and making everything all one is the smell of the sea.

5. Caroline Street

THE GIRL IN DOROTHY'S gives me a keyring. It has a smiley fish on it. Outside, I sit on the kerbstones and eat my curry chips and at the first taste they enter my private pantheon of Very Good Things. There's a moving coppice of legs roundabout, bare legs and blotchy, besuited legs, legs in jeans and legs in chinos and feet in trainies Pods Timberland highheels platforms black sensible shoes. Light from chipper and kebab shop and fried chicken joint all strobed by these scissoring limbs.

6. Cab

HE'S NOT CONVINCED:
  – The St. David's Hotel?
  – Aye, yeh.
  – The *hotel?*
  – Yeh.
  – Yer sure?
  – Course I'm sure.

He shakes his head. – Yer just gunna do a runner down at the docks.

I'm annoyed here; it's taken me twenty minutes to get this cab.

– Alright well. Fuck yiz an al goan get another one.

He laughs. – Jump in, then.

We do and he pulls away. I'm in the front seat. The driver's handbacks, even his fingers, are blue with tattoos.

– Can't blame me boy, tho, eh?

– What?

– I mean, the St. David's Hotel? Scruffy twat like you?

My turn to laugh. – It's been a long night, lad.

– An a good one, aye?

– Oh yeh. Sound.

We talk as he drives us dockwards, through the Bute area, the place where I did or didn't spend deperate wasted days before gentrification set in. I mean I didn't, but it seems like I did; before the Bay development. Before the St. David's Hotel. That winebar there, it used to be the dingy den where I first sampled crack. I scored some powerful Mexican skag down that alley there, alongside the Italian restaurant. And that posh hotel, it used to be a knocking shop where I spent the night with a whore from Kowloon.

No I didn't. Not here. But yes I did cos I recall it all.

The cabbie, he's like me; Welsh/Irish blood, bit of Romany in the mix. We share stories of warzone-weddings and spooky grandmothers and then turn to football and he flexes his left arm in front of my face, shows me the Bluebird tattoo below the Liver-bird one. He wanted to see the Worthington Cup final he says but had to fucking work. Dropped off some local boys at the station before the game and they were carrying a rolled-up banner and he stayed to watch them unfurl it; in big black letters it read WELCOME TO CARDIFF LIVERPOOL / MAN UTD FUCK OFF HOME.

We both laugh loud at this. He tells me of trips to Liverpool, football matches and drinking sprees; I tell him of the same in Cardiff. We give each other information about illicit drinking dens. He's got stories about Jim Driscoll and Joe Calzaghe and I've got some about John Conteh and Shay Neary. And it's late at night in this supposedly newly-genteel area and shadows still drift jerkily through slanting squares of light that still spills, burns yet. Look at it, he says; some people say it's gone too fucking posh, others say it's still too fucking rough. But yew wanna know something? Yes, I say, and then he tells me something tremendous. But I can't remember what it was.

7. St. David's Hotel, Again

I'M WOKEN up by a knock at the door and I trek across the bed and put some clothes on and answer it, let in the Fillipino maid with the breakfast table. She sets it up by the window; pristine white tablecloth and roses. She sings as she does this. From the hotbox and fridge beneath she produces wonderful food; eggs and toast and tomatoes and mush-rooms and jam and marmalade and honey and Glamorgan sausages and bowls of fruit and yoghurt and croissants and pastries and butter and tea and coffee. Nearby this room I once starved no I didn't. We're not even hungry but we can't wait to dive in which we do after I give the singing maid some money and she goes. Hunger-pangs I once had below this room outside this hotel no I didn't not here. I open the door to the balcony and as we eat the breeze brings up smells; bilgewater, oil, yeasty pub whiff, curries and stews and soup made from bones, all knitted together by the sea-scent itself. Tobacco smoke, ganja smoke. Frying onions and exhaust from old cars. I know these smells. I remember them from when I lived longing in Cardiff amongst several other cities but that can't be because I've never lived penurious in Cardiff. I only began to visit the place when I had money and was put up in smart hotels and had all my expenses paid. But I remember it. I do; I remember moving through these smells, these sounds.

Before we leave, we put some crumbs out on the balcony for the limping bird, croissant and toast. Whether or not he came for them I don't know because we had to leave – check-out time 11 AM.

Tessa Hadley
The Trouble is with Summer

THE TROUBLE IS WITH SUMMER, that if you wake up and see that rim of hot light pressing in around the edges of the curtains, you can feel you're not good enough for it. The world is showing you its pleasuring face, its big smile, its possibility of joy. You haven't any excuse not to smile back. It's better – safer – if you wake inside the grey-green cocoon of rain falling. I used to like that.

The other trouble is that in a street like this the summer weather brings the neighbours out. Nobody knows anybody else, it's a place of people in transit: bedsits, students, housing association lets, first-time buyer flats. But in summer all these separate existences are all of a sudden thrust on top of one another, because even in a street like this people like to sit outdoors when the sun is shining, they have barbecues, they have parties in the gardens. If you can call them gardens. Some of them are just bleak concreted yards with metal gates. Some are sprouting with self-seeded ash saplings and buddleia, little cramped spaces left between the tall terraced backs of the houses and the fire escapes and the ramshackle garages or extensions built where the gardens should have been.

Even so, the people who live here get the urge to socialise outdoors in the summer just like everybody else. And then you lie awake until three or four in the morning, carried resentfully out to sea on a hostile swell of music and voices, the beat like chugging pistons from an engine room. Or you hear a flare of violence in the back lane, sudden and crazy as a dogfight. Or your neighbours open their windows wide to try to get a breeze going round indoors, and you're suddenly sharing in things about their lives you'd really rather not; their taste in music, their smelly cookery, their noisy love-making.

These are big Edwardian houses, you can get four, five, six lets fitted into one of them. The place I'd moved into that summer had been the family home of an old lady who died; her son was hanging on before he sold it because the property market was so buoyant. My room was at the back on the first floor, with a tiny kitchenette he'd put in and a shared bathroom. It was papered in a faded pink and green trellis, the lined silk brocade curtains were so brittle they were crumbling away under my hands, and I could see the lighter shapes on the wallpaper where the old lady's bedroom furniture used to stand.

Once when I was sitting at my table trying to work I heard the cat in the next door flat catch a mouse. I didn't hear the cat, of course; what I heard were the screams of the girl who lived in there. Her name was Leanne; I couldn't put a face to her, but I knew she liked techno a lot more than I did and I knew that at nights sometimes a man climbed over into the back yard from the lane and called her name under her window with a brooding urgency that always hauled me up out of whatever depths of sleep I'd plumbed (sometimes Leanne came down to the back door to let him in, sometimes she didn't). When the cat brought in the mouse she screamed and furniture was turned heavily over and her boyfriend (I couldn't tell if he was the same one who called at night) shouted "Fucking cat" and "Kill the fucking thing" and then "Get its head under the television", and for a few moments I actually thought he meant the cat.

Of course you never know for certain what anyone means, when you're only hearing snatches and fragments of their lives through an open window. I don't know what any of them thought of me. Nothing, most likely. I used to imagine that summer that I might be invisible. I was surprised if anyone actually spoke to me if I met them on the stairs or coming out of the bathroom; I half expected them to walk right through me. I felt as though I'd fallen out of a very intricate piece of machinery which had been my life. I could still hear it whirring and clicking busily somewhere far off; the machinery went on, but I had stopped. I have a really loving and close family, but I didn't let them know where I was staying. My mum would have been round wanting to help me decorate. My sisters would have ganged up to take me clubbing or get me a boyfriend. I texted them every so often just so they knew I was OK. "I'm OK", was all I wrote to them. It wasn't a boyfriend problem.

At least I had my work. It wasn't real work. I'd dropped out of my dental hygiene diploma just before my finals, I'd given up my job serving three evenings a week at one of the bars in town. I didn't want to see anyone. I had the little bit of money my Gran had left me when she died, and I was living on that. What I was working on had to do with Gran, too. When we were turning out the stuff from her house in Fanny Street we'd found an old black musty notebook with its covers hanging off, filled with tiny writing: so tiny you couldn't make it out without a magnifying glass and even then it was difficult because of the old-fashioned curly letters. It wasn't Gran's. The date written on the first page of the book was January 5th 1897. Mum looked at the names which were mentioned in the notebook, and didn't recognise any of them. Gran's grandparents had been dead before gran was even born, anyway, and Mum couldn't remember what they were called, so it might have been them.

When we managed to decode bits of the writing, it wasn't very exciting. "Thursday. Chops for Bert, egg for myself. Mrs. Hitchings called, says there's tableware at a good price come in at Collins. H. brought up the chair as promised. Milk of Magnesia." "Friday. Nice piece of fish. T. slight inflammation of the throat, poultice. Postcard from Ivy (?), having good weather at Porthcawl." "Monday. Bert says the someones (Hardys?) want the work finished more quickly than is possible, unless he takes on another help." ("Yes," said Mum, "he might have been a builder.")

The others got tired of the notebook quickly. They wanted it to have some romance or feelings in, and it didn't. But I brought it with me when I left home, and then I bought myself a notepad and some pens and pulled a little rickety table through from the kitchenette and arranged it like a desk, and if there was nothing to watch on the telly I set to work copying out another section. (I did watch telly for long long hours that summer, and sometimes at the end of the evening I had no idea what I had seen). The more I studied the notebook of course, the better I got at deciphering it, although there were still some bits I had to leave as stars or gaps in my copy. I began to recognise patterns. Bert was the husband surely, and T and E must be the children (they mostly got mentioned when they were ill). The writer had poor digestion ("my old queasiness") and when her husband had a steak or broiled pigeon she often only had an egg or broth or a rice pudding. I wondered whether Nellie was a servant; there was often a note of irritation against her, or otherwise of measured approval ("Nellie fairly crisp raised crust"). I had never imagined anyone in my family (if it was my family) being rich enough to have servants.

Sometimes I got muddled and imagined that the diary belonged to the old lady whose bedroom I lived in. I felt as if she and her furniture and her life in here were the solid presences and I was the ghost. When I copied out some moment of uncharacteristic near-protest at all those hours filled up with domestic importance ("On my feet all day. Sheets to wash etc etc etc"), I imagined she was scrutinising me, my days of idleness, my insubstantial life. I was responsible for nobody. Even the food I ate I didn't cook, only warmed up in the microwave. Everything was the wrong way round: the lost past in the book felt solidly real and my living moment was a dream. Nothing specific had happened to me, to make me feel this awful nothingness. There had been no disaster – only my Gran had been in an accident and died, and somehow because of that I had tripped and fallen through this hole in my life and found myself down at the bottom, in a place where no-one knew me. Not that my Gran had been anything like the woman in the notebook. She was very up-to-date, wearing T-shirts that said funny things and harem pants and using tins of cook-in sauce because she didn't want to spend her life in the kitchen. She'd divorced my grandpa years before when it wasn't as common as it is now. She was on her way to her aromatherapy course when the accident happened.

Some days that summer I went for walks in Roath Park nearby which had tennis courts and a bowling green and flowerbeds and big spreading trees. Once, when it was still hot but the sky was blotted out with thick-looking clouds like dirty snarled-up wool, I was staring down from an ornamental bridge into the stream beneath. In the stifled light the water running shallowly over pebbles looked quite black; and then as I watched I saw in the reflection on the water's surface how the clouds parted for a few moments and the sun showed up in the crack between them like a dark silver penny moving mysteriously across (I suppose that actually it was the clouds that were moving). I felt as if I'd seen something nobody else had; when I looked up the real sky was as cloudy as it had been before. And then not long after that sign in the park there was the night when Leanne locked herself out of her flat somehow and I was roused up out of my sleep to an awareness of noises outside my window. Confusedly, half dreaming still, I thought at first some night creature – a fox? – was trapped in next door's concreted back yard and blundering panickingly around, thundering into the big metal gates in its fear. Or then I thought the man had come again for Leanne and because she wouldn't answer he had broken out in a frustrated rage.

But it was Leanne. I heard her moaning as she threw herself around, louder and louder, deliberately, meaning to be heard by her audience roused from its sleep, invisible, intently listening from behind all those open windows. Obviously she'd been drinking, she was really drunk. Because it was dark (the security light that was supposed to come on at the back of their place was smashed) I couldn't have been sure even if I'd tried to look out just what it was I was hearing: was she pushing the wheelie bin to try and climb on it and get in through her window (it wouldn't have been anything like high enough)? At some point she was battering at the side door with her fists. She was shouting then, howling: "Bastard fuckers. Fuck you all. Fuck you. Everything's ruined now. It's all fucking ruined, because of you." And then she smashed the glass in one of the downstairs windows of the flat that was empty , and finally someone came down to the side door and there were more shouted recriminations ("You fucking silly cow") and then these were swallowed up inside the house.

Sitting silent, listening, propped up on my elbows in bed, I felt such a peculiar mix of things. I was embarrassed for her. I was afraid as well, although I don't know what of: she couldn't get inside my room. Also I was glad. I was glad it was her marauding round out there and it wasn't me. I was glad those things she said were out in the air, ripping around with their wild power to amaze and tear things open. The next day I started writing in my own words in my notebook, at the back. Nothing about unhappiness or being angry. Ordinary things. "Got up. Bought tea bags, milk. Launderette tomorrow." "Decided to buy posters in town and put them up on walls." "Beans on toast. Yoghourt." I was feeling better. I was holding on to a hope that I could build myself back together out of these solid things, make my life real.

Graham Hartill
Cardiff Ghosts
A Drunk Man

THE DRUNK MAN wore a big buckled belt, and his wife was in a wheelchair. They were both drunk all of the time, but whereas his wife looked wasted, the drunk man's face was a twice-used, puffy, crimson balloon. Drunk Man rarely looked actually drunk; he had a tough-guy sneer to his lip and he loved to flex his muscles.

I hadn't seen him with his wife for a while and presumed she was dead. I remembered ten years ago in the Ship and Pilot, Bute Town, when she tried to get me to buy her a beer; she'd misjudged me, I was far too shy and broke. Next time I saw her she had drastically deteriorated, pickled.

CARL DASHES TO THE RESCUE
Policemen assist Mr Sampson After His Fall

WHEN 24-YEAR OLD Carl Lobelin saw a man stumbling along the river-bed of the Taff, he grabbed a length of rope from the nearby Swimming Pool and dashed along the bank to help him.

Mr Michael Sampson of Elizabeth II Apartments, Bute Town, tripped and fell into the water after spending nearly half-an-hour stumbling along the river.

Watched by the inevitable crowd lining the James St. Bridge, Mr Sampson was winched to the top of the 10-metre bank. Afterwards, Mr Sampson said: "I wanted to just cool off. My wife's wheelchair was in the river and I wanted to try to get it out."

In the picture policemen are seen arresting Mr Sampson after his fall.

South Wales Echo

Jesus

Jesus sat on an island in the rain
wearing the last surviving afghan
the buses swirling round him.
A nylon fishing net, green, was hanging down his back.
He sat with his feet on the graveyard wall, guitar head down
and snarled at a passing office girl who broke into a run.

"O, do not build your house on sand,
for I have built my house on stone!"

Then one day he was gone for good,
had walked out to sea maybe.

See

A CAFE. A man with a plate of sandwiches and a mug of
tea. He leaned towards the empty chair opposite him and
looked around.

"You see. They can't see me. They think they can but they
can't. You see, I'M THE INVISIBLE MAN."

Unemployment

A SHORT MAN, he was always dressed in a cheap blue,
waterproof jacket with bushy hair and a parting. You're
bound to have seen him. His mid-thirties.
    You're sitting in the library reference room when he sud-
denly appears at your side. "All right mate?"
    "Yeh thanks. Fine."
    "How long you been out for?"
    "Sorry?"
    "Laid off. I was. And I never been back since."

You're standing in a cafe. Here he comes. And there he goes. Hotfoot, for the bloke who's serving has swung up the counter-top and chased him down the street! You're sitting in The Four Bars pub, and there he goes again, without a word, the barman bawling at him as they hurtle past the window.

"All right mate? It's not a bad day." You're crossing the park and he's walking a line across the grass. A little way behind him is an older man, red in face and obviously a drinker. They've clearly suffered a disagreement.

The Trailing Man's white hair is sticking up around his ears; he's almost walking sideways and he stares at you. His arm is slung in a new white triangle of bandage. Mr Unemployed is striding straight across the grass to nowhere in particular. The Trailing Man, red-faced, is blinking and flexing his mouth.

James Hawes
Artichokes

– DAI, I been thinking think it's time Rich went for it a bit. Time we sent him out beyond Offa's Dyke, to fly the flag.

– Broader canvas for our Rich, is it, Aled?

– I think so, Dai.

– Here he is.

– Well done, Richyboy!

Dai Jones-Hughes and Aled Morris-Evans, respectively the Heads of Drama at S4C (the Welsh Channel 4) and BBC Wales (Welsh Language Section) and coincidentally brothers-in-law, were sitting at the groaning table paid for by BBC Wales (Welsh Language Section) at the eleventh annual Cymru-Wales Oscwr ceremony at the Millennium Stadium in Cardiff. Outside, rain lashed the city as usual, but here, beneath the mighty, tight-closed roof, all was warmth and arc light.

Jones-Hughes and Morris-Evans hitched up their silk-taped trousers under their bellies and tucked in their white shirts as they stood to applaud. The BBC Wales (Welsh Language Section) table was smack bang on the centre spot of the floodlit turf, so their lead was rapidly noted and followed across the ground. For the first time that evening, Jones-Hughes and Morris-Evans glanced across at their colleagues on the BBC Wales (English Language Section) and HTV Wales tables with friendly agreement, for the Oscwr in question was going to Richard Watkin Jenkins, and everyone liked Rich Jenkins.

Jenkins, spotlit from many angles and throwing a dozen shadows, strode to the podium with that curious gait only found in the Valleys: a big-shouldered, short-legged roll, like a chippy and aggressive teddy bear. Upon the stage, backed by the towering video display, bracketed in limelight, he raised his Gucci shades up over his lustrous black fringe, smoothed a fine hand over his large, horsehair sideboards, hitched his clubland trousers up around his balls, and prepared to accept the Cymru-Wales Oscwr for Best Short Film (Welsh Language). In the previous four years he had taken the Cymru-Wales Oscwrs for Best New Comedy Drama (English Language), Best Documentary (Welsh Language) and Best Adaptation From Welsh (English Language). Rich was big. All around him, the stirring tones of the Welsh national anthem blared out for the twenty-seventh time that night.

The delegate from the Serbian Republic State Television Network (she was here under the European Union Potential New Candidate Small Nations Media Programme) took notes rapidly, highly impressed at this well-oiled display of blameless cultural fervour. She leaned over, her auburn mane flowing down from her shoulders, towards the Head of Public Relations at BBC Wales (English Language Section). He had mistakenly interpreted her bizarre, Slavic eye contact and was also unaware that to anyone north-east of the

Adriatic Sea, drinking wine simply does not count as drinking. He now leaned gently, happily forward as he poured for them both, so that he could dwell unseen on her considerable tits. As he did so, he nodded wisely and replied to her questions with that easy volubility that can so quickly overcome a middle-aged man who has had two or three large glasses of 14 per cent Oz red too many and fondly imagines that he is on for a shag with an exotic woman who will certainly never meet his wife.

– This is the greatest young film-maker in your country?

– Yes. Look at him: a charismatic boy, our Rich.

– *Charismatic*. Means what?

– It means men want to drink with him and women want to sleep with him, lovely.

– I see. Like our militia warlords.

– Well, his man loved him, see, and his dad drank with J.P.R., and...

– Jaypeeah?

– Oh, one of our old warlords, lovely, ha ha! Drink up then.

– He defeated the enemies of your nation?

– Aye, love, J.P.R. By Christ, you should have seen him, tearing the English apart, year after wonderful year. He skinned their wingers every time.

– Skinned their wingers? she asked, doubtfully. (Even to a strong girl from the Balkans, actually *flaying* enemy airmen seemed a little excessive.)

– Aye. Tied them up in knots, turned them inside out and skinned the sods alive.

– Alive?

– Buggered them sideways. Great days, great days.

– I see. He is dead now, this Jaypeeah?

– No, he's a doctor.

– Ah, she nodded. – Like our Dr Karadjic.

– No, no, no, he does hips and knees in Bridgend. He was never the same after those bastard All Blacks sliced his cheek off, see?

– Ah, yes, all the bastard blacks. We have Albanians.

– What? Does even Albania play, now? They'd probably beat us, too, these days.

– Leave the Albanians to us, my friend.

– Eh?

– Shh! said someone nearby, for Bryn Terfel's and Bonnie Tyler's pre-recorded duetting voices were fading out, and now the lights dimmed somewhat as Rich Jenkins commenced his acceptance speech. Many cameras, held on the shoulders of fit, scurrying girls or swinging around dizzily on lightweight cranes, closed in to catch his every word and gesture, as well as to record the self-conscious smiles and appreciative nods of his audience: for the proceedings of the Cymru-Wales Oscwr night were being broadcast live, on S4C and BBC2 Wales, to an audience of several thousand. Rich Jenkins spoke. He spoke first in Welsh.

– Why does all people tonight speak first in *this* language, if many people not understand it? demanded the Serbian delegate, surveying the people around her, a good half of whom had quickly assumed an air of pious absent-mindedness, like non-believers during the boring bits of a church wedding.

– Oh, replied the Head of Public Relations indulgently, – everyone who can speak Welsh speaks in Welsh first here, love. In fact, a lot of people who *can't* speak Welsh speak in Welsh first here. Well, we all want promotion and grants and jobs, don't we? Same in Serbia, I bet.

– Perhaps. You are angry?

– Me? No, love. Worse things to do to get promotions and grants and jobs than speaking a little bit of Welsh into a microphone just to show willing on the big night, aren't there? Even Prince bloody Charles does it, doesn't he? But don't worry, Rich'll say it in the real language of his people next.

– The real language of his people?

– The South Walian dialect of American, love. Then the 75 per cent of us and the 100 per cent of everyone else except Patabloodygonians who wouldn't know Welsh from Albanian will have some idea what the hell he's saying.

– I see. You are becoming angry. *You* do not understand this other language?

– Me? Listen, lovely, my family have lived in Cardiff, loading coal, shifting steel and dredging docks, ever since more than a hundred bloody people lived in Cardiff, and none of them ever spoke a word of fucking Welsh.

– Rich just said something about artichokes, said the Head of Public Relations' assistant, loudly, proudly and treacherously. She had just returned from her month's study leave (all BBC Wales staff are entitled by right, and encouraged by self-interest, to take a paid month off work so long as they say they are taking it off to learn Welsh): she had heard her boss grow dangerously talkative, and she wanted everyone within hearing to know that she, unlike him, was *on the right side of the fence, even if she was English.*

–What? snapped he.

– *March-ysgall* is Welsh for artichokes.

–Why the fuck did they teach you about artichokes?

– I took the New Welsh Cuisine option on my course in Aberystwyth. Very interesting. Artichokes grow beautifully on Caerphilly Mountain, apparently. Well, *hwyl fawr*, I think I'll just go and have a word with Gethin Davies ...

She left, tactically. Her boss stared at his wine.

– Christ. Miners, we used to have. Now it's fucking artichokes.

– You have declared artichokes your new National Vegetable?

– No, that's still fucking leeks.

– I see. So why does your Greatest Young Film-Maker speak of artichokes. Perhaps it is your leader's favourite dish?

– Look, lovely: Rich Jenkins writes about mad old farmers in Welsh, so *they* like him, but he also writes about disused mines and rugby in English, so *we* like him. He's the only one we *both* like. So he can talk about artichokes all night long for all anyone cares. If he publically stuffed artichokes up his arse he'd get a grant to film it. In English and Welsh versions.

– I see. You mean he is the favourite of your leaders?

– Well, yes, you could say that. They love him.

– This is most interesting. Who is *we* and who is *they*?

– North-West is *they*, the *Gogs*; South-East is *us*. *They* don't think *we're* really Welsh because we don't speak Welsh and *we* don't see why we should give a toss about *them* because there's hardly any of them and they're all whingeing inbred sods, and anyway the Gogs don't play rugby so what good are they to anyone?

– These Gogs are your ruling clan?

– Yeah, but only because we're still run from England, lovely. The English throw grants at the Gogs just to keep them quiet, that's why. Blow up a pylon and get a job, that was their fucking motto. And it's not even the Gogs who are the worst. They're just *foreign*, it's a four hour drive to Gogland, give them Anglesey and Gwynedd and good fucking luck to them, say I. They can shag each other's cousins all they want and leave the rest of us in peace. The ones I hate are the bastards from godforsaken valleys thirty miles from here, who really are *like* us, except they can walk into any job so long as they got two legs just because they speak Welsh. And they reckon people like me are half bloody English just because we don't speak bloody Welsh. Well? English, am I? Were the Pontypool bloody front row English? Well?

– I think they were not, guessed the Serbian delegate.

– Bloody right they weren't. Ate the fucking English alive, they did.

– They were great warriors?

– They were. And if there's one thing I hate worse than South Welsh Welsh-speakers, it's the Welsh-learning Cardiff middle classes. English-paid traitors to their own fucking working class. Half of them *are* fucking English. As bad as those bourgeois bastard Basques and cunting capitalist Catalonians.

– And Turkish-loving, town-living tradesmen, said she, raising her glass subtly.

– Eh? Whatever. I'm telling you, love, you just wait till

we're *really* fucking independent. The Gogs and their mates and their grants and their jobs will be the first to go.

– You hate many people.

– Only the English and all Welsh speakers. This country will only be truly free when we all gather around the grave of the last fucking native Welsh speaker to sing 'Cwm Rhondda' in Welsh. Like the Irish do it. They got the right idea: everyone *says* they love Gaelic, and no one bothers to pretend they can be arsed to speak it

– …Quiet, you bloody idiot! hissed a passing, secret, hastily departing friend.

The Head of Public Relations came to, removed his mouth from his glass and looked around blearily. He had not noticed that Aled Morris-Evans had come over to shake the hand of Hugh Pritchard, Head of Drama, BBC Wales (English Language Section) for the first time that night, to celebrate National Unity (for once) on the occasion of Rich Jenkins's triumph and to discuss the future of their greatest young film-maker. He caught Morris-Evans's hate-filled, slate-eyed glare and saw Pritchard look down in helpless shame. He knew that although Pritchard agreed with everything he had said, and had even said it himself in late, quiet bars, there was no way, these days, you could say it *out loud* in a place like this. Pritchard was his friend; but his days were numbered. And by tomorrow, everyone in BBC Cymru-Wales would know it.

– Oh fuck my granny pink, said he.

The Serbian delegate had been watching closely. A native of Sarajevo, she had been trained from youth to read the ancient fault lines beneath smiling faces, to feel the dark places where the ebb of vanished empires has left unfathomable swamps of vengeance and hatred.

She nodded softly.

– Yes, now I think I begin to understand your small country.

From *White Powder, Green Light*

105

Viki Holmes
post card #1 (winter wonderland)

THE CITY continues much as it did before you went away. lights sparkle in the trees and it's almost picturesque, you might say. people, there are many people here and every one of them thinks differently, every one occupies their own unique space. it's cold, but not as cold as previous years, just enough to make people's eyes shine. scarves are popular this year, i notice. also fairground rides, chestnuts and painted glass. pottery has fallen off slightly, there are trends even among artisans, although ethnic statues continue to do well. there is much of talk of going skating on the outdoor rink. few follow up on this, although it always seems busy. i walk past on my way home most nights. just knowing it's there is enough. my way back takes me past a place that no longer exists. there used to be a kebab shop called ali baba and the forty tasty dishes. the sign was pink, with a parade of veiled, doe-eyed women. it's gone now, and i don't eat kebabs anyway, but i miss the sign. funny thing is, i can't remember where it used to be, i can't tell what has replaced it. i look at all the shop fronts, all the chippies and dry cleaners and inter-net cafes and i don't know which of them used to be the one i miss now. it's hardly a tragedy of unknown soldier propor-tions. nevertheless, i'd like to know.

do you see how this is not about love? life goes on without you and it is surprisingly compelling. nevertheless, my writing is prosaic, something is missing. i don't know what, but i imagine you might. you usually do. please send answers.

Mererid Hopwood
Beneath the Shadow of John Bachelor
– The Friend of Freedom

The morning's yeast has ventured
through the town, light-footed
through the Hayes, the language of summer
is an impassioned whisper,
calling us to follow –
you and I where it might go.

And through the old Cardiff it takes its way,
through the town that the light of day
doesn't touch, the words of its song
always tell of other streets a little way along.

The town between door and doorway
that knows neither night nor day,
the quiet town of tunnels
known to none but ourselves,
one whose accent's an echo,
whose story's never on show.
The summer sweeping through the Hayes,
rhymes the dust of memories,
in the arcade where relics hide
we find new freedom, pride.

Cardiff Born
(to the first generation of Cardiff's new families
– from wherever, and whenever, they came)

It's October, the leaves drift down,
to the bronze streets of our hometown,
brown leaves whose tune is crunched
on the black pavement by your tread.

Still October, and the golden summer
is still, remote, somewhere
in the rockpools, as open and empty
as mussel shells, out like the sea
at ebb-tide; the town's season
is disillusion – October's come.

Pontiago's empty nowadays.
Now I'm in town, all it says
is memory. No more than a name,
and I've become one of 'them'.

Home indeed? As I go walking
the sun of hiraeth is shining
in Llandaf, on the riverbanks,
and the waters' fluid dance
makes me stop to watch. And I understand –
my native town, my own land.
Tears make it hard to see
each salt mile of the journey
through this Cardiff, this home,
whose streets I claim as my own.
Tonight I'm still debating,
my twofold, torn belonging,
in the tongue known by no-one,
a stranger, an exception.

But not quite lost completely
there's still some small part of me,
some fragment of my nature,
kept in two stories: there, here.

Anthony Howell
A Walker on the Wall

The orange digger can be seen for many miles,
From many pastures and as many lanes,
And from this stationary impermanent car
Parked where the stationing of caravans
Is forbidden, it can be seen disgorging loads.
But in between lie unrelated fields:
Attempting sedges battered by the tempest,
Trousers only dampen at the knees
When brought up sharp at each and every turn
By some canal with hawthorn at its edges.
No way to the sea-wall through these traps,
Unless by sluice-gates, half a mile away,
Or by the church, and that's at least a mile.
My chosen path must renounce its doctrine:
Best to walk away from where the digger sits
Biting on stone-chip, keeping all intact
Against the worst abrasions of the winter.
Back on the road, a lorry splashes past
With a rusted skip for further up the coast.
A heron floats off westwards, while the cows
Shelter by that double line of poplars
Bent above them, buffeted by squalls:
Pellets bounce off leaves, brims, eaves
And rims of things, while tatterdemalion veils
Get pasted onto the sky, making it whiter.
Willows churn like whirlpools on the boil
Or people surging frantic at some barrier.

The sea-wall is a break between two worlds:
Above the dead flat land it constitutes
The absolute horizon line behind
Whatever gets between it and the eye.
Being unable to reach it for a time,
Your view beyond is rendered hypothetical.

Is there a sea at all, is there a storm
On the far side of the wall? Is there a part
That is constantly turned away from us,
Completing us, the far side of our moon?
Walls exist to stop this getting into that,
Forbidding seepage, even through a straw.
You can say that he stonewalled or that she
Was just about as wall-eyed as a goat,
But meanwhile, above a works caravan,
A Water Board bulldozer and a bungalow,
The digger raises an arch between askew
Telephone poles and a bunker, reaches down
The incline, scooping to itself the heaps
Pushed at it by the bulldozer below.
And while the cabin spins to salt its load
Over the wide, flat top to the wall,
Garnishing its surface, flattening
The area with a heavy tooth, the weather
Keeps on flowing through the brakes,
Dribbling onto turquoise rows of kale
And tossing rushes clustered like bamboo.

These then are the fen-like Wentloog Flats
To which I come on Sundays off and on,
Sometimes with my son or with my friend.
The gypsies like it too: they use its sites
And often tether ponies to its verges.
Farms between the mountain and the marsh
Raise Dutch barns on lowlands to the north,
While all the south is given to the estuary.
For dike there is that ridge we call the wall:
A track for tractors runs along its top.
Beneath it moves a filth-tinctured stream
Invisibly, its vivid duckweed film
As stagnant as a moat's beneath a rampart.
Crisp-packs flutter gaily in the meadows
Criss-crossed by these ditches known as reens:

The coast roads run in tandem with their trenches,
Though no one can be certain which began this.
Broken, where the wall surveys the sea,
And left as flotsam shored against its mound,
Lie jerry-cans, the torn hoods off prams
And ruptured tires distorted by their scorching:
Tokens of some drowning on dry land,
The palsied earth itself being every jot
As frail, inconstant, waving as that blot
Beyond the Flats, its closer water slack
In the mud's runnels, isolating tussocks
Where the stakes diminish with the distance.

The tide is out a way. The plovers gleam
And paddle. Somewhere off these barrier stones
A peewit, then the trundling of a train
Faintly moving at speed across the land,
As breeze-blown mares go ankle-deep to graze.
The rocks are piled where tides may rush at us,
Though nettles use their lea-sides with impunity.
Seabirds blot the freighters in the waterlane:
At long distance, people read as dots.
Every footstep starts pips and chortles;
Flocks of pipers fluttering suddenly upwards,
But no shooting where the cows lean
Up the grass bank, and the grey-winged gull
Gets nowhere against the wind but floats
Higher than reach. This is the wind that lifts
The long-feathered wings of the crow before it flaps.
Who knows what you may find on the road
To the watermark pole with its yellow band:
Desolate place of inner tubes and milk-crates;
Canisters rusted and devoid of gas;
Mud cracked all over its crust; tough
Grasses looking accustomed to being submerged.
A backlit sky from the moors at sunset
Beams up searchlight rays between ridges

Of cloud above the black tower of the church
North of the wall; and on its chancel's side
The flood is marked at chin-height by a plaque.

Sixteen-hundred-and-six had just begun:
A sad time, when to sit in a tree was a blessing
Close to a chicken. Others fared far worse
That January, as it pleased God,
When retribution rose up to this brass,
And in the rapid matter of the flood,
Without avail, this parish sadly lost
A good five thousand and an hundred pound,
Besides the twenty-two odd persons tossed
Out of their beds, and then completely drowned
With several thousand others in the parishes
Spoiled by the grievous fury of the sea:
Livestock confounded, hayricks whisked away,
And multitudes of buildings beaten down,
For no greyhound could have run before
The waters as they raced in on the houses.
Then the dead were swept away as well,
While Elphin's coastguards wallowed in carouses.
All the church lay drowned beneath its bell,
The wall in disrepair since Roman time.
And now the churchyard cannot raise a tomb,
For who would care to flounder in their shroud,
Or barge among comestibles and kine,
Brought horribly awake behind the coffin-lid?
Built, flooded, burnt and restored – it took
A fire to dry the rafters – usual history
For churches near a lighthouse on a marsh.

Now, in the yard, a horse bites at its crotch.
Goats bleat from a rainswept field nearby.
Blackberries dot the harried autumn hedges,
Peppered already with hips as well as hoars.
Ivy strives to strangle tangled brambles.

Docks clog the fosse. By Sluice Farm
A house of stone gets coated pebble-and-dash.
Limes pale. Barns accumulate haydrums.
Continually the thistles rub their frowzy heads
Against the hollow stalks, the ghost branches
Of the cow-parsley, while thin grasses
Whistle under concrete steps over the bridge
And up the wall from the caravan park.
Lanes led off the coast road finish here,
Or else at isolated farms, yards for stacked,
And bashed-up cars glimpsed through barricades.
The rushes bluster just as much in summer
As in winter here: rushes dense as bamboo,
Good for murder. I can see that ferret
In his van curse because our damn Cortina
Dawdled down the road on some off-chance
A noticed track would take us to the lighthouse.
Once we walked there from the caravans
To find its lantern smashed to smithereens.
But what a staircase! Curving round the rail
In thirties style; and then there were the rooms
Like grapefruit-sectors, leading off its spine.

That architect we took some other time
Quite fancied you, and sat me in the back
Of his extremely small, unhappy car
– Unhappy when negotiating ruts.
We never made it though, the three of us:
His urban chassis couldn't take the muck,
For things get tricky underneath the wall,
Where nightingales may nest in cathode tubes.
I tell you, on a bend I saw a goose
Ruffling its feathers in a depot once.
Petals thrive on refuse at the sewage-farm.
Rabid vegetation spoils the ditch:
Summer long, it's wet for vetch and nettle.
Martins flick the tarmac near the boarded place.

They raid the cattle. Ponies stand with rears
Too near their fronts; manes slack with damp;
Tails each a wet rope. August storms
Come crashing down, dousing clanks from tractors,
Dampening sacks on rickety farm-trucks,
Tail-boards fastened with raffia. Hammering
Hardens its beat on the roof of the car:
What is straight goes zigzag down the screen.
Poplars hiss Medusas, breast a surge
Which seems to run full sail before the blast.
Water pours off the ribbed sheeting on barns
With every gust, while gulls driven inland
Feed off manure in fields smelling of pigs.

The sea-wall stands between this eerie fen
And marshes which in winter seem Siberian:
Tussocks frost, mud supports your weight;
Shallow reach turns dark, ice sheet,
And wall-walkers muffle up their ears,
The wind being cruelly keen above its edge.
They leave it then to stretch deserted on
Towards the town where men are just as sharp.
One fellow named a time and then a place;
Met her there, or so the judge was told,
Sealed their assignation with a kiss,
Then threw his pregnant woman off the bridge.
But who can blame the wall for what goes on
In disused sheds and alleys near the tracks?
That's beyond its precincts: it's the marsh
It draws its line across, between the towns,
Above the vacant cable-drums like magnified
Reels of cotton, rolled out on the strand:
Below the heavens, under nothing less
Except the steelworks at the river's mouth
Which contribute their vapour to the cumulus.
Having lived here now about a year,
I know the wall, or think I do, and stroll

For several miles on breezy afternoons
Before I meet a soul; though when my friend
Sketches a tree-trunk, up the tree-trunk gets,
Uncoupling the beast which has two backs.

Why do I walk when I can along the green
Ridge of the sea-wall, emphasised by light
Behind my silhouette, as I see others are?
I walk to find some motive, I suppose,
Choosing to plumb this radius of the sky
And scavenge meaning where the sea can barely
Be discerned – the tide has pulled it back
Behind the mud beyond the salty marsh.
Here there's a choice of east or west at least,
Where solid ground is kept from stuff less sure.
I walk at height above proposed alternatives:
Voyager's viscous, variable emoluments
Weighed against landlubber's property
Where the water moves in canals only.
Salt air or manure, you see me hesitate,
Then observe me mooch towards the marsh,
Kick at some sea-smooth twist of driftwood,
Climb the wall, descend towards the reen,
Attracted by some half-submerged contraption.
Veerings these, but not affiliations:
Torn between our countries and careers,
We still may walk, avoiding made-up minds,
Through Sunny showers, the sky diverse in mood,
As if the weather wanted to agree with us.
Across the sea, the hillside fields are bright,
For faintly, after sheets of wet, the ghost
Of a rainbow glows and as swiftly fades.

When spring begins by tagging wool to briars,
After the stile, we run on up the steps
And quickly top this barrow of a wall
Immuring sod from shore. We pause for breath,

Descry the dead armchairs, fractured flower-pots.
No better time for poking through this jumble
Hand in hand. We pick our way past mattresses
And cowpats flies lift off on such a day,
Beneath a pale blue sky trailed by planes.
Here you can walk, and feel as if you ride,
Your head higher than the feed-hoppers on sheds.
Bedraggled calves concede the sea-wall track,
Maundering down its slope, crushing discarded
Egg-boxes as they go, blowing awry the teasels.
Should we thank the gypsies or the waves
For all the odd regurgitations tantamount
To wealth discovered here: the bibs and bobs
Attracting boys and magpies? Hard to say.
Only the skylarks act as if indifferent,
Babbling on, into the cauliflower ear
Of a passing cloud. Later we go by the reen,
Where the roan stallion with the white blaze,
Neat socks and flowing mane wrenches at a bush.
The boy uncovers an ants' nest under a stone.
He chucks the stone into duckweed – more of a plop
Than a splash – but enough to make the creature
Move off with a snort behind the hedge.

It's early for the tortoiseshell, I'd say,
Staggering past my nose upon the breeze,
Concerned with thistles pushing through upheavals
Demolition made when breaking up
Foundations left where something stood; the frame
Torn off its hinges sheds no light on what.
That old gate could do with some repair
Beside the solid crossing for the cattle
Tunnelled by its water-bearing pipe.
It's here the wall runs high across the land.
Cows recline like goddesses on top of it
And chew the cud as if it were our destiny.
Test-pilot ducks engage in flight,

Rolling at low level over Peterstone,
To land among the toppled, Gothic trunks
Of naked trees got-up as unhorsed knights.
Mild surf sounds their litany from afar,
While pathos dribbles from the weeping sluice
Which causes shivers where the film allows
A stretch of rusted water to reflect
The halves of footballs booted out of reach.
Are they balls, or ancient ball-cocks actually,
Abandoned when their cisterns failed to flush?
There is a place in the world then for the junked
Engineering of discharged, the jakes' graveyard,
Where even the porcelain for our waste products
Ends as a shard, fallen apart on the marshes.

Telephone poles and a bunker: this is where
The orange digger back in autumn went
Extending down the ridge to scoop itself
Stuff pushed at it by the bulldozer below.
After we round the watermark pole and decide
Enough is enough, the boy sees an exact
replica of this machine, lying in the debris
On its side beneath us by the bungalow,
Just where the real one mustered chips of stone.
This chance event is form devoid of sense:
Walking around for a year, you get to know
These incidentals conjuring coincidence
Which throw amusing patterns on the void.
Rusted but serviceable still, the toy
Thrown out to erode among those castors.
'Can we have this then?' I ask of the man
In overalls watching us while his Alsatian
Incessantly barks from within the fenced-in yard.
The man's head pulls in and then pokes out again.
'Sure the kid can have it.' What a find!
Past the teasels then, we saunter back,
The acquisition swinging from my hand

Or dangling from the shoulders of the boy.
But now we should hurry past the grey sheep
Sitting still as stones and cross the stile
To reach the coast road. From behind the church
Chimes can be heard from the van selling ice-cream.

Bill James
Big City

THERE WAS AN AGREEMENT. Rhys and Jill had spelled it together. They told each other it was for the sake of the children. Rhys told himself that, too. But he knew it was for his own sake. He must not lose Jill. To keep her he had accepted terms. They would be pals, living together with their family. For passion she would go elsewhere. It was painful, she said, but they must accept change. It could happen in a marriage. Look at most of their Cardiff friends! She suggested people were becoming more sexually independent, confident, and generally "big city," now the London government had given Wales *almost* a Parliament, *almost* independence. The Welsh Assembly, as this cut-price Parliament was called, had housed itself in a waterside building on Cardiff's dockland. Jill said this transformed Wales, made it a *real* country again and brought the city the status of a true, world-scale capital at last. Small-town negativeness, small-town prudishness, narrow moralising, were no longer on. She considered the new attitudes were especially evident in folk from their circle – journalists, politicos, lobbyists: those most in tune with the reborn Wales. She said she still loved Rhys, but was not *in* love with him. She had met someone else.

Although Rhys was hurt, he rejected the difference between love and *in* love. Or, at least, he did not believe that side of it would last. He must wait it out. Nor did he see why political devolution from London should mean rampant adultery, but he let the point go. And so, the agreement. He considered it a workable pact and not necessarily humiliating. Later, looking back, he was sure nobody could have foreseen so much tragedy.

When the arrangement began, Jill used to offer fairly plausible tales beforehand to cover an absence, in case Rhys tried to ring her. She'd say shopping or a drink with Beth Postern. That stopped. It obviously sickened her to lie. She had a wonderful honesty: one of the things he loved her for. Now, she would announce only that she'd be out from midday. He did not ask where. Silence was part of the agreement. He noticed she never put on her smartest outfits for these meetings, nor wore jewellery he'd bought her. This meant she refused to rub his nose in it by festooning herself for someone else. He felt grateful. He could not tell her that, though.

In fact, it was when Rhys and Jill called the babysitter and went out as a couple to a restaurant or party that she dressed up and appeared at her most elegant. A room full of people shone if she was among them, shone *because* she was among them. As her husband, Rhys felt pride. Just as much as emotions and sex, her sparkle was the essence of Jill, and could never be withdrawn from him. This helped Rhys accept the agreement. She remained his: he owned that wondrous social side of Jill. He exulted to read the covetousness in men's faces.

Part of the agreement was that, if he found somebody else, he should be free to go to her. Rhys felt sure he would never want that. This certainty enraged Jill, possibly increasing her sense of guilt. Too bad. He could not change. Jill was the only woman for him. Once – only once – she tried to explain what had drawn her to the other man. Apparently, he relayed nonstop *ferocious* desire for Jill. This was the word she picked, ferocious. Rhys was embarrassed by it, not injured. He felt she sounded quaint. Yet she said this man's passion had left her no choice.

When the arrangement was new, he did not allow himself to think much about where the two of them went, and at that stage he would never have secretly tailed her. Although this was certainly not banned by the agreement, it would have seemed shady. He assumed they generally had an early lunch in a restaurant, and afterwards... Gross to speculate on that, and probably unhealthy. She liked to be home soon after the girls returned from school.

Rhys and Jill still visited restaurants themselves. Looking brilliant, she would talk and radiate at full power, and anyone watching would surely have supposed them alight with joy in each other, perhaps even lovers, not man and wife. It thrilled him. This was Jill as Rhys's, her jewellery very much in place. Occasionally, they bumped into acquaintances at these places and would perhaps make up a four or even push tables together for a party of six or eight. The more the better for Jill.

On one of these evenings, they came across friends and colleagues at the Riverside Cantonese Restaurant, and, while helping rearrange the furniture, he felt the back of a hand, a woman's hand judging by size, pressed for a few seconds very firmly against the inside of his left, upper thigh. Very upper. At first, he thought it an accident amid the little confusions of aperitifed people reshaping the restaurant. Soon, though, he corrected: the contact was too prolonged. He yearned to believe it had been Jill. Was she telling him in a sudden, uncontrollable, almost shy fashion she was his after all; totally his, not just her public self? Perhaps her affair and therefore the idiotic agreement were dead. Time had righted things?

But, he must not dream. Really, he knew Jill was never near enough to touch him as they shifted the tables and chairs. He decided only Beth could have done it; Beth, strapping young wife of busy, inaugural Welsh Assembly member Jeremy Postern. No apology or joke came from her about the contact, though. That seemed to confirm the incident was intentional. Yet she did not attempt to sit next to him for the meal, and when he talked to her and studied her as the evening went on, he found no personal message, no readable explanation in her blue-black eyes for knuckles wilfully nudging his nuts. The incident shook Rhys. It made him realise that the notion of "another woman" could be more than a notion. Perhaps someone else *was* available. To his amazement, this interested him. Was Jill correct, after all, to resent his self-righteous dismissal of the agreement's clause entitling him, also, to sexual liberty? Curiosity about the significance of the act dogged him. Perhaps it was part of the new sophistication: a woman would hint and wait.

Early one evening, when he was having a semi-work drink with Jeremy Postern, other Assembly members, and press friends in the Via Fossa Bar, Rhys went outside briefly and mobiled Beth. She seemed warm, pleased to hear him, unsurprised. He wondered if they might meet one evening, and she thought they might. They fixed a time. Rhys went back to the bar feeling not excited or victorious but, yes, more *wholesome* than for ages, more manly.

Beth and he seemed to need no preliminaries. It was as if they had been waiting for each other. She went halves with him on a bottle of Dubonnet and the charge for a room overnight in the plush St David's Hotel and Spa in Cardiff Bay, though they would be using it only for a few early evening hours. They made fierce, prolonged love. Yes, it was even *ferocious*, prolonged love. Afterwards, while they lay relaxed, he reassured Beth about the care he would take with her reputation, explaining how he had phoned only when certain Jeremy was not at home.

"The smug sod wouldn't care," Beth replied. She sounded defeated. "He's too deep in all the superlative Assembly crap for love life. We go our own ways."

"You don't like that?"

Hurriedly, she turned towards him: "Darling, of course I do. I wouldn't be here with you now, otherwise, would I? Aren't you and Jill permissive with each other, too?"

"Good God, no. I couldn't tolerate the idea of her seeing somebody else, screwing somebody else."

"I adore jealousy in a man," she said vehemently. "It

means he cares. It's what makes you so damn irresistible, Rhys. *You* wouldn't doze through a marriage. God, but Jill's lucky."

This encounter revolutionised Rhys, gave him vision. Jesus, might Jill think he did not care because he showed no rage and put up with the agreement? Was this why she had discarded him sexually? But he *did* care. He must show it. He was not like Jeremy – and like many men Rhys knew: by piffling career obsession and bed coolness they forced a wife to seek fulfilment elsewhere. He decided he must watch Jill discreetly when she went to one of her meetings. Although he still loathed the idea of gumshoeing, he had come to loathe apparent indifference even more. He would annihilate this disgusting, arid agreement. But agreements were only words and sentiments. He wanted something solid to smash. He needed a look at the opposition.

Luckily, he could take time off work as he wished. He was part of the newly hatched lobbying industry around Mount Stuart Square in Cardiff Bay at the docks, and ran his own hot public-relations firm. Surveillance was sure to be difficult, though. Jill would soon notice his Citroen. And so, next time she said she would be out for the afternoon, he took a company Vauxhall and went to wait near their Cowbridge, Vale of Glamorgan, house until she left at around noon.

She drove to a side street in Splott, an undazzling region of Cardiff. She parked. Rhys drove on a bit and also parked, then watched through the mirror. Soon, a Toyota arrived and drew in not far from Jill's VW. At once, Rhys sensed this was Lover Boy and turned in the driving seat now to get a proper look through the back window. He kept his face partially obscured by the head-rest. A middle-height man left the Toyota and walked twenty yards to Jill, opened the VW passenger door, and climbed in. For a few minutes they kissed and talked, all excited smiles, arms locked around each other, as if they'd fought their way across ice floes after years of forced separation. Probably they were here every week.

Lover Boy's hair was grey, but cut in a bristly, young-thruster style. Boy? Palely aglow with the tired beams of Indian summer, he must be at least ten years older than Rhys. It hurt. She could prefer someone this age? He had a round, pushy face with heavy eyebrows. Although he could have had them trimmed, he must have felt they were part of his image, proving verve. Image was vital in this jumped-up metropolis. His face was full now of... Full of what Rhys longed to dismiss as raw, lucky-old-me triumph. This was someone in his fifties at least, all set for a nice afternoon with a beautiful woman of thirty-four. Horrified, though, Rhys found he could not honestly describe what he saw like that. His view was imperfect, but he glimpsed... well, damn it, yes, he glimpsed *love* there – maybe ferocious, maybe just intense, but in any case enough to terrify him. He sensed the power of their relationship, almost admired it, certainly envied him, the spry jerk. God, Beth had it so right and Rhys could switch on the jealousy. He was delighted at how well he hated. He might tell Beth about this whole unpleasant sequence.

The man's clothes were like some 1970s sports commentator's – three-quarter-length sheepskin coat and a crimson scarf. Still, he was presentable. Naturally. To think otherwise would be a rotten insult to Jill. And it would be mad to feel jealous if the rival were pathetic.

The lovers left the VW and began to walk. They turned into the main road. Rhys went after them on foot, staying well back. He saw Jill take the man's arm for a while, as though feeling anonymous in this unfashionable spot. But then she suddenly let go and put a little gap between them. She probably realised that, down-market or not, people who knew her could be driving through. To be observed at all would be bad, but walking arm-in-arm was an utter giveaway. They kept the distance between them until vanishing into a rough-looking eatery. Never would Rhys have taken a woman to such a place, and certainly not a woman like Jill, even in run-of-the-mill clothes. At first, he thought Lover Boy must be short of money. But no, it was clearly part of the cleverness. This pair were unlikely to meet anyone they knew in such a dump, and especially not Jill. Secrecy above hygiene. After about ten minutes, Rhys walked past on the other side of the street and looked in. They were at a table near the window, too bloody tied up in themselves to notice anyone else.

He was sick with distance and rage and helplessness. The agreement came to seem contemptible. Bloodless. He returned to his car intending to wait until they appeared, then drive behind them to their next destination; presumably a room somewhere. But he found he could not face this. The old tenderness towards Jill, the old reluctance to snoop on her, ravaged him, made any further shadowing impossible. Briefly, he contemplated vandalising the Toyota. In the Citroen boot he had a tyre lever which could have made an impression. But he was not driving the Citroen and, in any case, that was a crazy, infantile thought – vehicle-breaking by daylight in a well-peopled street. Instead, he walked to the Toyota and glanced inside. On top of the dashboard was an opened envelope showing a name and address. It seemed Lover Boy must be G. Lowther and lived in the Pontcanna district of the city; this comparatively chic spot was home to many loud people from independent television companies, presently coining it with innumerable worthy films about Welsh identity; Rhys thought this lad looked like a Geraint rather than a Glyn or a Gwyn. He couldn't have said why. Perhaps G. was on the technical side, or Rhys might have recognised him through work.

Rhys went back to the office and, as he sometimes did, stayed late. There were papers to deal with after his spell away. Some routines had to continue. But, obviously, his mind was badly troubled and he did not operate well. Would he ever operate well again if he stuck with the emptiness and degradation of the agreement? He finished, went out to the Citroen in the yard, and decided to drive home via Pontcanna. When he eventually reached Cowbridge, he was surprised to find Jill still up. She seemed desolated.

"Jeremy Postern rang," she said.

"Some sparkling speech he wants puffed? Am I to call him back? At this hour?"

"He rang *me*," she said.

"Oh, yes?"

"Beth told him you and she have an affair going."

"Why the hell would she do that?"

"To make him jealous, I expect. Compel him to want her."

"But he couldn't care less, Jill."

"You fool. He's frantic at the thought of losing Beth. He asked me what we can do about it, he and I."

"Just like Jeremy."

"Maybe. Anyway, I won't tolerate this. Rhys, I'm leaving you. Tonight. Now. For keeps. I've sent the girls by taxi to my mother's."

"But, Jill, darling, why?" he cried. "It was only the agreement."

"The agreement is finished."

"It is?"

She wept. "It's not needed. Gaston and I ended things today; it all came to seem ludicrous, barren, mean. The relationship just dropped dead while we walked to a restaurant. We both sensed it, though neither of us understood why."

"Oh, a restaurant where?" Rhys asked.

"I intended a new start."

"But this is wonderful!"

"Not now. Impossible. It's unfair of me, maybe, but I can't stay since hearing of you and Beth. Unbearable. I'm going." Jill went out to her car. He walked urgently after her, and saw that the VW had suitcases on the rear seat. She climbed in, keyed the ignition, and music sounded from the radio. He stood by the side of the car, the driver's door open. She seemed to remember something and went hurriedly back into the house. She left the engine running, as if to tell him she had not changed her mind. He waited. The music ended and a local news bulletin began on the radio. It reported the discovery of a so-far-unidentified middle-aged man dead on the ground in a Pontcanna street. He had been killed by head wounds. Jill returned with another small case, which she placed in the back. She climbed into the VW again and reached out for the door, which still stood open. She said: "Rhys, how in God's name could you betray me with someone like Beth Postern?"

"But it was Beth who taught me the way to hold on to you, love." Jill pulled the door to and drove off. She did not wave.

T. James Jones
Robert Croft
(On the occasion of the Glamorgan cricketer's admittance to the Gorsedd of Bards)

The cricketer, chaos-creating at the crease
the aimed leather spinning
from his hand like a breeze, flying
to the bat with a bite, twisting.
On the wicket at Sophia,
the bowler, hero of summer,
his billhooked curving ballplay,
iron-willed, turns smiles to dismay
on an opponent's visored face
whose bat swiped at empty space.

Each summer, on the capital's grass
his skill will harvest a mass
of famous wickets. His hostile spins
have ended many innings.
Through the surgery of this one,

Hick, head-down, to the pavilion,
a novice again, took the walk,
his willow untouched by cork.
Gatting too found it grim,
his stumps like dust behind him.

A ball of precisest strength,
a magic one, perfect length.

Give our bowler in Bala,
the Gorsedd's summer honour.
The chief bard of the sportsfield,
in his land's green robes revealed.

His skill deserves poems of praise,
set to the harp; the displays
of his skill with the stitched seams,
make Sophia a field of dreams,
its key set by sleight of hand.
My paean's a poor second!

Question

The Assembly and Stadium – places planned
to ameliorate a millennium
of ill-willed thralldom.

Knowing the pain of yielding – to despair,
to the long dispiriting
depression of our blundering,
our struggle from the marsh to cross a stream, to be greeted
with respect at last is a dream
come true by the bay of our self-esteem.
To be stirred, in case the rolling maul should crush us,

the others too strong, too tall
for our red dragon to fight them all,
and to be empowered by a masterpiece
of a goal or undisputed try
in the name of our liberty.
Here's the conundrum – for my people,
will the Assembly and Stadium
ever be symbols that spring has come?

Here's the worry – no-one yet
knows what answer we'll get.

Emyr Lewis
Freedom

This is the city of lost things, thrown away,
caught in the space between Sunday afternoon
and the rest of time; things that had the stamp
of souls upon them once; but not today.
In gutters, underneath the railway bridge,
and hiding in the borders in the park
safe from memory and significance
are passport photographs, a single shoe,

and whisky bottles now half-filled with dew,
and house keys, left-hand gloves, small change; the grime
drifts over them when dog-day breezes blow,
and rain beats down on them in wintertime.

They've not been buried, not been elegised:
there are no rites for the discarded things,
you may just curse them briefly now and then,
then let them go, don't think of them again.
In the imperfect time when we have the right

to dream a little, in the occasional pause
between obeying the merciless ticking
when we can feel the whole universe singing
its lyrics to us when the stars are bright,
in candle darkness, in the sound of cars,
there comes the night.

The imagination cannot plough up the street
into a fallow place where we can pray,
it cannot pick up the lost discarded things
whose elegy was not sung, imaginings
can't change the way of clocks, and so today
in the salem of our evening, it's sweet
to hide away.

Here is our well-fashioned time, our compromise
between the wild innocence of first loving
and the dust that we have been breathing for years,
London-wise, sophisticated as cities.
Between the trees where the Taff is flowing
we rest a last dance to the night-birds' cries, one fine evening.

Geraint Lewis
Sun Will Come

AROUND THIRTY homeless people had gathered in the
vestry at Bethania that Sunday afternoon. Of all ages too.
Some in their teens, others in their seventies. And only three
helpers: Diane, Efa and myself. It was mainly men there, but
there were about half a dozen women too. One of them, a
Welsh speaker, around fifty years old, in a long dark blue
coat, came up to me.

"You're new here."

"Yes. I'm with Efa."

"You're sleeping with her, you mean."

"No… well…"

"Not yet, is it? You're a filthy pig. I can see it in your eyes."

"No."

"Don't you dare touch me, you pig!" she said, flinching and shying away from me.

"What's wrong, Morfudd?" asked Diane, as she tidied a nearby table.

"This one here, trying to touch me up…"

"I didn't touch her," I exclaimed.

"Liar!" Morfudd shouted.

One or two others had come over by now to see what all the fuss was about. One of them, a big man with a long brown beard, came over to me.

"Is he bothering you, Morfudd?" he said in a strong Irish accent.

Diane whispered in my ear, "Don't worry, she's always like this here. There's no real harm in them. If you prefer, go and wash the dishes with Efa."

As I started off in the direction of the kitchen, some north Walian in his forties came up to me, holding his sandwiches up accusingly, opened like a wound.

"I hate ham," he said pointedly. "Is there chicken or what? I had chicken last time. This is rubbish, isn't it?"

I started to mumble that the sandwiches were all out on the tables before I fled to the kitchen, leaving a stream of northern curses behind me. I grabbed a teatowel and began to dry the cups and plates that Efa was setting on the draining boards.

"God, I can't believe how ungrateful they are. It's incredible! Don't they understand that all this is for free? The cheeky sods!"

Efa smiled, finding my anger towards them funny.

"We don't know about their circumstances," she said sympathetically.

"Of course we do. They sleep out on the street. So what? That doesn't give them the right to be rude, does it? I don't think I've heard one of them say 'thanks' even!"

"That's how they keep going," said Efa. "They don't trust anyone enough to be polite to them. They've been disappointed in the past."

"How do you know that?"

"I've spoken with a lot of them, over the years."

"Years? You've been doing this for *years*?" I asked in amazement, unsure if I should sound pleased or concerned.

"Yes, for around three years," she answered, shaking a few bubbles from her pink rubber gloves. "Living in a city can be very lonely, Bryn. Especially if someone's by themselves."

Then she hesitated a moment before saying, in a dejected voice. "Yes, it can be very painful for them."

As I stole a quick glance at the big Irishman who was still eyeing me in the serving hatch, I thought it wasn't much of a picnic for the helpers, either.

A little later, I ventured out of my hiding place to help Diane put the folding tables away. Once again, not one of them offered any help to put them away. I glanced at some of them, holding their dirty supermarket bags as if they'd just returned from some self-indulgent shopping spree. The only difference was that these poor wretches had all their belongings in their bags, not the superficial contents of their weekly shop. I felt myself staring at them, astonished by the lifelessness in their eyes. Especially the young ones. One of them, a Welsh-speaking lad with a crop of curly red hair, was surely only in his early twenties. The same age as I was when I came to Cardiff for the first time. I tried to remember those feelings when I was full of hopes and dreams as I ventured out on an exciting adventure in my country's capital city. Surely this young man in front of me hadn't thrown in the towel already?

"Everything all right?" I offered.

"Oh yeah. Fuckin' brilliant. Twat."

As I waited on the bridge in Roath Park opposite the light-house, I realised that I was thinking of another exciting new adventure in my country's capital city. The possibility of sleeping with Efa. I ventured to hold her cold hand as we looked across the empty expanse of the lake with the odd duck laughing scornfully at my presumptuousness.

"Do you think Captain Scott knew he wouldn't return?" Efa asked, casting a glance back at the commemorative plaque.

"It's hard to say."

"In what way?"

"Well, he must have known it would be hard over there. After all, he wasn't a penguin, was he?"

Efa laughed, saying: "Thank goodness for that! If he'd been a penguin he'd probably have crashed the boat."

"What I mean is that he wasn't designed to go to Antarctica, was he? Not like the Emperor Penguin for instance. They can lay eggs at a temperature of minus sixty degrees."

Efa laughed again, and I asked what was so funny.

"You," she said. "How do you know stupid facts like that?"

"Oh, just some things I pick up here and there," I said, without telling her that I picked up that bit of information that morning from a five-year-old child. Suddenly, the male duck which was straight in front of us started to flap his feathers and to quack in some laborious slow voice.

I smiled and said; "He's trying to make an impression on us."

"It doesn't look as if he's succeeded to charm anyone very much," said Efa, stifling a yawn.

"No," I said, rather apprehensively, worrying that this was some kind of hidden message from Efa that reflected her reaction to my attempts at courtship. After all, I was wearing my long purple coat with the striking green collar. The same colour as the male duck, I noticed. If I quacked, perhaps I'd have more luck with the female duck.

However, Efa stopped some old man on the bridge and asked him to take our picture with her camera. That's better, I thought. This is the kind of thing that happens in films. I succeeded in holding her arm and smiling at the camera. But the old man was having difficulty. He was trying to guess whether he should press anything to get the flash to work. Efa explained that he didn't need a flash, that there was enough natural light. Then the camera clicked as I pulled Efa nearer to me. My hope was that it would look like a lovers' embrace, the two of us unable to stop ourselves touching one another. But I'm afraid it just looked as if we were trying to keep warm.

*

That night we were all competing in the Cardiff Pub Quiz Cup, playing for a place in the West Cardiff district final. The quiz was held in the Stag and Pheasant in Ely. Our research, which showed that the landlord was fond of ancient history, had proved wrong. He's fond of local history. Very local history as it happens. The history of Ely. There are two whole rounds on the damn subject. This is a disaster for Iwan, Lloyd and I, but a bit of a blessing to Phil, who lived in Ely for years, and who, of course, has a keen interest in history. He knows that the Ely Paper Mill, which closed in 2000, had been established in 1865. That's fair enough, as Phil used to work there for a while. But he also knows, (and expected me, the specialist on things Roman, to know!) that a Roman road used to lead into the west of the city through Ely and Canton. And that the confluence of the rivers Ely and Taff takes place at a location called Cogan Pill. He even knows that the main reason why Ely Racecourse was closed in the end was because the stand caught fire in 1937. We manage to win the quiz with points to spare, but I agree with Iwan – it's clear that Phil has much too much time on his hands these days.

As Phil knows the landlord slightly and has made an impression on him, we have a late lock-in session in the snug bar. Phil's in his element, telling us that forty thousand people used to watch the horseracing in Ely towards the end of the nineteenth century, and that fifty thousand watched the Cardiff Bluebirds in the European Cup at Ninian Park in the sixties. Even though there's a part of me that admires Phil for his enthusiasm, I am still thinking about Efa's sudden departure and the pain in my back.

"He's trying to blame my patio for the pain in his back," says Iwan scornfully, adding, "But the bugger hardly lifted a finger all day!"

Lloyd shakes his head, saying, "The back is a bit of a mystery. It could be hundreds of things. Or, just as easily, it could be nothing at all."

I make a mental note to change my G.P., but I know I won't bother.

"You're my doctor," I protest. "You're supposed to help me, not make me depressed."

"It's not Lloyd who's making you depressed," said Phil, sagacious as ever. "It's that woman, isn't it?"

I nod, saying that she's disappeared off to Birmingham for a couple of weeks. This produces another of Phil's famous theories. This is loosely based on the English proverb, "Absence makes the heart grow fonder." In Phil's opinion, it's a biological phenomenon that's at the root of this. He read something about it in the *New Scientist* magazine, which said that the body creates chemicals over a period of time which create a pain in the part of the chest where the heart is. Lloyd, the only scientist among us, laughs into his beer. In fact, he laughs so much that he coughs some of his beer up, the tears rolling from his eyes.

Iwan wants to know when they'll have the honour of meeting the new woman in my life.

Lloyd asks what her name is. I say Efa. Iwan asks if her surname's Braun. I say no, it's Hughes. Lloyd suddenly becomes serious and I ask him if there's anything wrong.

"Oh, no, nothing. I was just wondering about your back. Why don't you make an appointment? Seriously. If it doesn't get better, it'll get worse."

"But you said that the back was a mystery…"

"I didn't say I wouldn't try to cure you. We can try acupuncture. It's been very effective with some of my other patients."

"Sticking needles into people!" says Iwan incredulously. "Is that what they teach you for seven years? You may as well put a bone through your nose and wear a grass skirt!"

As I walk up the stairs to my flat hoping that I wouldn't need a course of acupuncture, I notice that Jo's door is ajar. It's gone one o'clock in the morning, so I go in quickly, hoping that there's no mad burglar with an axe in his hand lurking in the shadows. If anyone of that kind is there, he's a very cultured sort, because Mozart's Requiem is playing softly in the background. Jo is sitting on her bed and she nods to me as she inhales a deep lungful of dope.

"I saw that the door… was open," I explain.

Jo nods complacently, as if the door is supposed to be open all night. She takes the joint out of her mouth and offers it to me. I don't know what to do. I don't like mixing beer and cannabis too much. It tends to make me feel sick. But Jo makes my mind up for me, pushing the joint into my hand sympathetically and saying it will do my back good. I take a sweetish breath into my mouth, stealing a glance at the screen which separates Jamie from his mother. Even with the music playing softly, I can still hear him snoring contentedly.

I breath the drug in deeply, and feel the smoke warming my bones. To be honest, it hasn't done too much for my back. I give the joint back to Jo.

"If you were Mozart, you'd have died by now," she says cooly.

"If I was Mozart, I wouldn't care if I'd died by now," I answer.

Jo smiles, saying I'm a strange guy. She explains that she's listening to Mozart in order to try to understand what genius is. She knows that Steve, Jamie's father, is a genius of some kind in his own way. Geniuses are often obsessive, she says. Music was Mozart's obsession, and mountains are Steve's obsession. I don't try to stop her attempt to make sense of her relationship with Steve. I look at his photograph, in a tasteful frame on the portable television. On top of Everest he literally looks on top of the world, the feeling of pride at completing such an achievement flashing from his eyes like lasers.

Although, with his long white beard and his red coat he looks a lot like Santa Claus as well. I think he's a selfish sod leaving his lover and their son in a cold little flat for ninety per cent of the year, while he's off climbing some remote bloody peak "because it's there". I don't share this opinion of Steve with Jo, partly because she might actually agree with me.

"Did you win, in the quiz?"

"Yes. We're through to the West Cardiff final now."

"Good," she said, before nodding and then repeating the "good" again.

"Has it helped your back?" she says, giving me what's left of the joint.

I shake my head and Jo gets up and fetches me a chair.

"Sit here and I'll massage your shoulders. Perhaps it's just a knot of tension there, that's all. You should relax more.'

I sit and take some more of the joint. This time it goes straight to my head and I feel myself swimming, enjoying some inner peace that, I'm sure, is doing me good.

Or perhaps it's Jo's long fingers that are responsible, massaging my shoulders slowly and rhythmically. Whatever, in no time I feel an erection in my trousers. With Jo it's inappropriate somehow. She's obviously head over heels in love with Steve. Steve who's never there, of course. And she's the mother of my five-year-old bosom buddy, Jamie. I try to think of cold showers, but the idea of nakedness arouses me even more. I think about ice, which leads me to Steve and the photo. But that doesn't work either. I think there must be a special kind of thrill about sleeping with the lover of a man who's climbed Everest.

But what the hell am I thinking about? This isn't the kind of relationship Jo and I have. I must be losing it. I must be imagining that it's Efa's fingers which are pressing my flesh, massaging, massaging, easing my aching pain. Jo is talking about a show that's on at Chapter Arts Centre that week. A modern version of Ibsen's drama *Doll's House*, by some theatre company from Warsaw. She said she likes Ibsen. She saw a production of *Brand* with Steve some years ago, after she'd persuaded him that it was a drama about climbing. Steve had thought it was complete rubbish, but Jo had liked the comparisons which were drawn in it between climbing a rock which was synonymous with the battle of life itself. Even with a giant erection between my legs, the combination of the soft Mozart and Jamie's steady snoring, along with complicated explanations of Ibsen, was sending me to sleep.

"I'd like to ask you a favour, Bryn."

"Go ahead then," I say, thinking she's going to ask me to look after Jamie, something I've done before and which I'd be perfectly happy to do again.

But that isn't what she had in mind.

"Would you come with me to see *Doll's House* on Friday night?" I straighten, not having expected that at all. Jo takes this as a negative, but persists with her request all the same.

"Look, there's a guy in Chapter who's always going on and on about how he wants to go out with me. It'd be great, you know... well, if I was going out with someone already, as it were."

"Yes, that would be great," she adds, unnecessarily.

I can feel her nodding her head, although I can't see her, as she's behind me.

"What about Jamie?" I say, turning to face her.

"He's fine. I've got a friend from work who'll look after Jamie."

"Right then. That would be great," I say.

Jo looks really glad, nodding repeatedly again.

We get there pretty early for the theatre show, so we can have a drink in the bar before going in. I'd been there a couple of times before, to the cinema. Although I'm fond enough of the place, for some reason I always think it's compulsory to look miserable and wear scruffy clothes. Perhaps it's something to do with the 'artistic' nature, but most of the punters there that night, sitting around the cafe and the bar, made the homeless wretches in Bethania look like power dressers.

Having said that, Jo, who works in the cafe, had dressed up especially for the occasion, in a long blue frock. In fact, I've never noticed her wearing make-up before, and the effect was fitting in a way, making her look like a doll. Little Bo Peep, perhaps. Whatever, it's not long before I realise that this unaccustomed preparation on Jo's part has been carried out for one particular reason. As one of the men who work behind the bar approaches us to clear the table, Jo deliberately cosies up to me, holding my arm.

"*Shwmai* Jo," says the barman. He's in his mid twenties, with spiky dyed blond hair, and he's got four rings in his right eyebrow.

"*Shwmai* Carl," says Jo. Then, smiling and holding my arm tighter, she says. "This is Bryn."

Not even "my friend". Certainly not "my neighbour." Jo doesn't need words. She's telling Carl with her body language that we're a couple. It's a very strange feeling.

"*Shwmai*," says Carl, waving his hand in a big circle as if he's cleaning a window. In case he sees through our 'act', I pull Jo closer with my arm, and nod to Carl. I see from the way he's trying to hide his disappointment at seeing Jo with another man that he must be the one who's been giving her a hard time at work. Jo senses his disappointment as well and nods. I expect her to say any minute that we're living together – which, come to think of it, is at least technically true. But Carl says he has to rush back to his work behind the bar.

"Thanks for that," Jo whispers.

"A pleasure," I say. Which is true. I rather like being part of a couple. Until I see the show. I don't think it's a show for couples. There's a note in the programme saying it's a dance version of a famous play, a dance to free women throughout the world from their oppression. There's a tall man in a top hat and tails having maccaroons stuffed down his throat by his wife, who's dressed like a bird. He almost chokes on several occasions. In part of the show he's tied to a shabby-looking Christmas tree, with three women dancing around him – including his wife, who's not, by this stage, dressed as a bird, but as a mechanical doll, with a huge key in her back. All the women are throwing truffles and oysters at the man. There's a fair amount of opening and closing of doors, which appeals to me in some esoteric way. Then, at the end of the performance, the woman gets rid of the key in her back and saws the head off a little dolly. She follows this with a series of striking cartwheels before slamming one huge door with a bang. The audience (fifteen of them, I counted in the interval) applaud energetically as the cast bow before us at the end of the show.

Unfortunately, Jo is keen to discuss the show in the bar afterwards. I don't have a clue what to say.

"They had a lot of food on stage," I say at last.

"Yes. That was deliberate, I think," says Jo, "to convey materialism. Just because the man had bought chocolates for his wife, that didn't mean she was happy."

After a while I say, "It could have been dangerous."

"What?"

"All that food on the floor. One of the dancers could have slipped easily."

Jo nods and thanks me for coming with her. She looks very thoughtful indeed. Incredibly, it's clear she's still thinking about the show.

"They were very fit weren't they?" I say, stating the obvious.

"Yes."

"But they sweated a lot as well. It's bound to be hot under those lights. And you notice it more."

"You enjoyed it, didn't you, Bryn?"

"Of course, I'd recommend it to anyone."

Jo smiles, pleased, then says. "When I took Steve to *Brand*, he didn't enjoy it at all."

"Oh no. Hell, it was fantastic, really now," I lie.

"Good."

"There's one thing puzzling me, though. The doors at the end. Were they supposed to fall down, or was it a mistake?"

Jo thinks it was entirely intentional. Breaking down doors together on behalf of her sex. Then she phoned Alys, who was babysitting, to make sure that Jamie was all right. He was just fine.

Although apparently he'd insisted that she read all three *Pingu* stories in his book to him.

"He's into penguins, isn't he?"

"Yes, I think that's how he identifies with his father," said Jo, nodding again.

Phil Maillard
The Arm

EVERY DAY, I drive into Cardiff to work. I come over the Mountain. There's a point up on top where you get a view right over the whole city. It's a bowl, really. A big bowl. And down in the bowl, you can see the way everything's laid out. There's the areas of old terraced houses – neat rows of rooves in Splott and Roath, and Cathays, Canton and Grangetown – with a church or a chapel or a pub sticking up every few streets. There's the Castle, and City Hall, and all the shops. Then there's the new stuff. The Millennium Stadium, for instance. I don't know what to make of that. It's striking, alright, but there's something aggressive about it. It looks like a UFO and it's got rocket-launchers sticking out all round it, in case the natives aren't compliant. A bit further over again, and there's the Bay – the new road they're building down there from the centre, and all the new little commercial units where the steel works used to be. Then there's the Barrage, and beyond that, on a clear day, Flatholm and Steepholm floating in the Severn, in front of the Somerset coast. It's interesting, that view. I look at it every day. On winter mornings when it's still dark, with all the lights down below, it's like landing in a plane.

I come from up beyond Ponty way. Despite all this *new prosperity* you keep hearing about in Wales, there's still not much work up in the Valleys. So every day I get in my old van and drive over to Cardiff. It's a trek, and the traffic's bad, particularly the last three or four miles through the suburbs. But there's plenty of building going on there.

Last summer I started on a job in an old pub at the bottom of St Mary Street. It was down by the statue of the Marquess of Bute, a bit south of the main shops and arcades. There's something of a restaurant area grown up down there recently – every type of food you can think of, from Mexican to Japanese. The old pub was being gutted, and reborn as a theme bar. The Victorian façade, which was pretty grand if you took the time to step back and look at it properly, was being cleaned up. It was a narrow, tall building, and the top two floors were being converted into offices.

The first week I was there, I worked downstairs. The idea was to make the place look like a 1920s American speakeasy, called *Luigi's*. The job was more like shopfitting than the usual run of site work. There were six of us carpenters in the gang. As well as the usual fixtures, there were some fancy designer touches. They were aiming for the feel of a Mafia place during Prohibition. The windows were all blacked out, and the front door had a sliding peephole in it. We even had to drill holes in the walls to look like the place had been sprayed with machine-gun bullets. There were photos of gangsters and their molls, and in one corner there was even a bathtub and some old barrels and mason jars, for the bootleg gin. Being a Mafia place, they sold pizza and pasta, of course. Real tough-guy food! They also sold overpriced American lager, and cocktails called *St Valentine's Day Massacre*. I know, because I went there once after it opened.

It was pathetic, really. Nothing's just itself anymore, do you know what I mean? Still, I suppose the gangster aspect was authentic, given the way some things get run round here.

The building company who were making over the speakeasy had the whole building to do. The plasterers had finished on the floors above, so two of the carpenters' gang went upstairs to get on with the offices. I was one of them. The other was a short, grey-haired black man called Jimmy.

I got to know Jimmy pretty well after the first few days. He must have been well into his sixties; he'd been born in Dominica before the war. But he was still wiry, and fit. First off, we set up some workbenches in the large, bare rooms, and made saw stools. Then we started on the second fix – doors, architraves, skirtings. The fittings were all light oak, which made the panel doors heavy to hang. We had the fire doors to do. We were also putting in some storage units round the walls, building the cupboards then fitting veneer boards for sliding doors.

At breaktimes – breakfast and dinner – Jimmy and I would get takeaway coffee and rolls from an Italian cafe – a real Italian cafe – nearby. We'd emerge from the gloom and dust and noise of the speakeasy, out into the daylight. The sun would be warm and bright, and the office girls would be click-clacking down the street. Another world. And Jimmy and I would take a slow walk in the sunshine to the cafe and back.

Then we'd go back upstairs, and sit on the saw stools, eating and chatting. Jimmy was a good carpenter, and very methodical. I can see him now, cutting dado with a fret saw for a corner joint, or bent over a board, carefully ironing on the edging strip. He worked steadily all day, although there were no particular pressures on this job – not for us, anyway. Downstairs the usual panic was going on, as the speakeasy was supposed to open in a couple of weeks. Up above, we hardly saw anyone. We seemed to be distant and isolated, yet there was also something intimate about being cut off in those featureless rooms.

Jimmy lived in Grangetown, where he owned a small

house. At breaktimes, he chatted mostly about ordinary things, like his journey to work. Every day he went a different route, trying to find the best way. And every day he'd tell me the time it took, and the cost.

I walked in this morning, he'd say. *Over the station bridge, you know? But I come up right along the river, instead of going up Corporation Road. I'm sure that Corporation Road is a long way round.*

Another day he might say, *I got the bus up Penarth Road today. Sixty pence. And we got stuck in the traffic. Then I walked over the river and up Canal Wharf, you know?*

Once he even walked over the Clarence Road bridge and got the bus all the way from Butetown. But he only did that once.

Jimmy also told me that he didn't like staying at home during the days, even though he could have retired by now.

Why's that, Jimmy?

You're just thinking and worrying about things when you're at home, you know? I'd rather be at work. You can just get on with what you're doing then. He took another sip of coffee from the plastic cup. *I got a few things I could do at home – I've done a lot of work on my house, new kitchen, new bathroom, new windows. But my wife… Well, she's a hard woman to please, you know?* He grinned. *No matter what I do, or how well I do it, she never praise me for it. If friends come round and admire something, she always say, "Oh, anybody could do that!" But that's the way she is, you know?*

One morning as I was driving in to work, I noticed that the bottom of St Mary Street was closed to traffic. Of course, they've been doing a lot of work down there for a long time, changing the roads around, demolishing buildings and putting in a huge new square on the other side of the railway. More shops, apparently. When Jimmy and I went out to the Italian cafe at breakfast time, we saw some lorries parked around the statue of the Marquess of Bute. It's a big statue. The Second Marquess, larger than life, stands way up on a square plinth, wearing full robes and clutching a sort of shield. When we went back across to the cafe at dinner time, we couldn't believe our eyes. There were men in hard hats on top of the plinth, with heavy cutting gear, and the Marquess's head – his head! – was being swung across by a crane onto a low loader. They'd cut his head off. Decapitated him! I was shocked. The Marquess didn't look too happy about it either. His big face looked stern, but nervous. There was a crowd gathered round, watching all this, so I asked someone what was going on.

Oh, they're moving him, the Marquess.

Where's he going?

Round the corner, behind the station. He's going to that new square they're building. Bute Square.

Generally though, things were quiet. As I've said, we felt cut off up in the offices, apart from our trips to the Italian cafe. We hung the doors, cut and fixed the architraves and skirtings, built the cupboards, and, at breaktimes, we sat on the saw stools and chatted.

By the end of the first week, Jimmy told me something about his background, and his family. He had one big worry, apart from choosing the best route in the mornings. He was very concerned about the direction his grandson's life was taking.

Young people don't want to work now, you know?

Do you think not, Jimmy?

No. Well, maybe that's not a bad thing, but I've worked hard all my life, nothing but work, work, work.

What was the first job you had?

That was back home, in our little village in Dominica. When the war began, I left school and started in the carpenter's shop, just fetching and carrying first off, you know? My mother had five kids to bring up on her own. I had to help with the money. Then I started with the tools. We worked everything by hand; all them tropical woods. Not like all this gear we got here now. Jimmy indicated the power tools on the bench. *Oh yes, we really worked them hardwoods.*

When did you leave Dominica?

I went to Martinique, that's a French place, you know? Fort de France, St Pierre. I went all over. Oui m'sieur, non m'sieur – plenty French there! Then I came over to Cardiff in 1957.

Why Cardiff?

I already knew a few people who'd come earlier. I started on the railway, at Canton, repairing carriages. It wasn't too bad there, easy work, and we had a little place where we could cook and take it easy. But it was dirty work and I was only taking home £6 a week. A friend of mine was working on a building site, and he got £8, maybe £10. He says to me, Come on, Jimmy, I can get you on there, you know? I had my family to look out for then, so I went. But of course, in a few months that came to an end; and I went to another site, and I've been going on like that ever since.

So what's you're grandson up to, that you're so worried about him?

Well, like I say, he don't want to work. Not real work, you know? He's got involved in starting a shop, him and this white boy. It's an antiques shop. Up in Pontcanna. He says to me, Don't worry, it's a good location. There's a fancy restaurant on one side, and some kind of television company on the other. The people will come flocking in, he says. I go up there weekends. Help them fit it out, you know? Make it nice. They got a bit of stuff to sell now, old furniture, pine cupboards. Doors with fancy glass. Old fire-places. Looks like old junk to me. But the prices! It don't seem right, people paying all that. Not right, you know?

One dinnertime, about two weeks after the beheading of the Marquess of Bute, Jimmy and I decided to have a walk over to the new square, to see how the statue was getting on. We ducked out of the speakeasy into the sunshine, and bought rolls and coffee at the Italian cafe. Most of the new square was sealed off behind wire fences. It was a warm day, and we sat down on a low wall opposite the square. There were some paviors working, and there, on the far side of the square, was the Marquess, with his head back on again, on his plinth. They must have been still cleaning or repairing him, because he was boxed in on all sides by scaffolding. There was something familiar about that, but for a moment I couldn't bring it to mind. Then it struck me. A few nights before, I'd caught the end of a television programme about modern art. I don't usually bother with that sort of thing, but it must've been running late, or I'd switched on early. Anyway, they had this painting on, all done in garish colours. It was this chap in fancy robes, who looked like he was encased in this glass box, for some reason, all round, like some specimen in a museum. It was a bit creepy. His mouth was all smeary like he could've been screaming, but you couldn't hear him because he was shut up in the glass box. One of the old popes, apparently, although the painting was quite recent.

The Marquess looked like he'd just been dumped there. As I've said, it's pretty bare round that area now, with the empty square all fenced off, and most of the buildings gone. There used to be little factories and warehouses there, and a couple of pubs. Women used to stand around there at night, waiting for cars to stop. I remember going down there once when I was a teenager, on a night out. I had a mate with me. We were much too shy to approach any of the women, so we just gawped, and then got the last train home. But it's all gone now, the factories and warehouses, and the women.

Ever since they'd moved the Marquess, I'd been thinking about him. Monuments are important things. They attract people's feelings. Their memories, good and bad. Look at all those statues of Stalin in Eastern Europe. As soon as communism collapsed, the people attacked the statues. Smashed them. Beheaded them. I've seen pictures of big heads being loaded onto lorries, just like the Marquess.

As we were sitting there, we saw a man looking at the statue, just like we were. He looked like he was from the Sally Army hostel over the way. He had a big beard, and a long black coat, despite the heat. He came over, and told us, right away, that this shouldn't be called Bute Square at all. That was just some made-up name. This was really St Mary

Square. Always had been, apparently. He also said that the Marquess was facing the wrong way again. As far as I could see, he was facing roughly the same way as he had been at the bottom of St Mary Street, but the man said that originally, the statue had been farther up, in High Street. He'd had his back to the Castle, looking down towards the Docks.

After all, said the man, *the Marquess made the Docks, and the Docks made Cardiff. But now they've put him the wrong way again. Looking towards the shops.* He scoffed. *The shops!*

I'd never thought about it. The only connection I'd ever made between the Marquess's statue and the Docks was seeing seagulls standing on his head. But the man seemed to know what he was talking about. He got up, and walked back towards the hostel. Jimmy looked at his watch.

Time we got back.

The job lasted another couple of weeks. The gang downstairs in the speakeasy finished only a few days late, bathtub, bullet-holes and all. Jimmy and I were fitting the last locks and handles, and screwing the FIRE EXIT signs to the walls.

I was sorry to finish. It wasn't just the hassle of having to find another job. As I've said, working up in the offices had been like being separated off from the world for a while, without any of the usual pressures. I'd enjoyed getting to know Jimmy. Despite his differences with his wife and his grandson, he was a friendly, straightforward sort, and I liked his company. I'd also started to think of him as an example of the ordinary men and women who came from elsewhere – other parts of Britain or Ireland, or the Caribbean, not to mention Italy, Somalia, China, eastern Europe, wherever – all those people who made Cardiff and the Valleys what they are. In case you think I'm getting sentimental, I have to declare a vested interest. My own great-grandfather was one of those people from elsewhere. He was a blacksmith, who came over from Somerset to work in the pits. I only just remember him, but I'd very much like to have known him better. Perhaps I'm getting to that sort of age, where you start thinking about who your ancestors were. All I've got of him is an old photo of a man with a beard and a bowler hat.

Anyway, in my great-grandfather's day, it was the Butes who built it all up. But of course, nothing stays the same. Every now and then the power shifts. The money runs out. And now there's others coming in, moving the monuments, beheading the statues, taking over. And people from elsewhere – people just like my great-grandfather, like Jimmy – come in as well, to do the work. And that includes me. After all, no matter what I might think of the new money that's transforming Cardiff, the quangos and the speculators and the shopping boom, I'm right in there helping them do it. Helping to build up the walls of the latest heavenly city.

However, it wasn't until the last week we were there, up in the offices above the speakeasy, that Jimmy told me the thing I remember about him most, the unique thing. We were just sanding off some rough edges and dismantling the equipment, trying to look busy until we were paid off on the last Friday. At dinnertime we did the usual – got coffee and rolls from the Italian cafe, and sat around on the saw stools chatting. It was then that Jimmy told me a story about his childhood.

When I was just little, back in the village in Dominica, everyone knew everyone, and nobody locked the doors of their shacks. They were all open at night. There weren't no bad folks about then. One night, someone hung a sugar bag up in the room where I used to sleep.

A sugar bag? What, one of those white paper ones?

Jimmy laughed. *No, not one of those little things! Not like a Tate and Lyle bag. We had these big brown bags, you know? Like a sack made of jute, they were. You put the sugar in there ready for the ships to come and take it away. Anyway, someone hung this bag up in my bedroom. I don't know why. Maybe someone in the family thought that would be a good place to keep it. But there it was, that big old bag, hanging from the ceiling, you know? In the night it must have started moving around a little bit in the breeze, I suppose. I woke up. I was only a little kid now, remember. I woke up, and I thought that old sugar sack was a big arm coming down to get me!* Jimmy chuckled loudly. *Yeah, coming right down to get me! Lord, I never forget that! Never!*

I don't know why, but there's something about that story. It showed me a new side of Jimmy. But it also confirmed something in him, a simplicity and directness in that memory he'd carried along with him all those years, in all his travels.

I've had several jobs since that one in St Mary Street, but I'm still driving over to Cardiff every morning. And when I get to that spot on the Mountain, I still look down over the bowl of the city below – the old terraces, the new roads and buildings, the Bay. But now, when I look out to all that water beyond, I think of the Marquess of Bute with his back turned to it. I look at the Somerset shore, and think of my great-grandfather the blacksmith, with his beard and his bowler hat. And I sometimes think of a village a very long way away, a warm summer night before the war, and a slight breeze stirring…

Owen Martell
From Man of the Moment

(In this novel, two lovers, Davies and Anna, live together in Cardiff in a triangular relationship with Davies' childhood friend, Daniel. The following scenes show the first meeting between the three, the moment when Daniel has just been given the news of Davies' death in a car crash, and Anna and Daniel's later reflection on the loss.)

I REMEMBER THINKING at the time that I'd remember this meeting in the future, that it would be significant even if I didn't become friends with this girl. And that's what happened; I remembered, and we did become friends too, so perhaps it was more than just children playing. Perhaps the lesson is that these things happen when you're too young to be able to rationalise against them.

And the significant thing by now is that this all happened without Davies being around. It was I who introduced him to her. It was I who knew her, I who was her friend, and Davies was that chosen person I was introducing. These are the friends I choose.

Forcing myself to be brave, and 'sociable'. I had seen her a couple of times before that, coming out of the library, in one of the arcade cafes in town, just around the place. And wearing the long coat. The thing is to find an excuse to start the conversation, but then I bumped into her one day, and was surprised to hear her speak, a gentle, quiet voice, giving the impression that what was leaving her mouth was a little bit different to what she had intended to say. I bumped into her shoulder – not very hard – but enough to have to apologise. I offered to go for a coffee, 'standard fare' – but it seemed like the 64,000-dollar question. As artless and as awkward as that.

After that it wasn't difficult. And you find people don't look like their characters at all – that girls who appear so completely confident are just as likely to be as shy as you are, or that there's nothing to say that a confident person can't also be tremendously nice. Obvious enough that I liked Anna from the start. I was surprised how obvious it was that she liked me too. And Davies. She's two academic years older than us. A research student, doing an M.Phil in the French Department – a long dissertation on twentieth-century literature. Meaning and existentialism, the primal scream, intellectual chic, beyond us, worlds opening up in front of us. She likes jazz and female vocalists like Nina Simone and Ella Fitzgerald.

The night after I met her, the two of us, Davies and I, went over to her house, the house she shares with two other girls, just behind Cathays Terrace, the main road leading away from the University. It's Friday night, and there's a kind of thrill in walking the opposite direction, away from the direction of town. It's as if the endless flow of people going to the union, or to the pubs in town, are determined to drag us with them. As if they were annoyed we were doing something different, but were envious at the same time.

But we reach the house, and the two of us have been unnaturally quiet all the way over. I look at the other students going past us, trying to imagine about them the things I was trying to imagine about Anna: background, what drives them, how they think about themselves – but not thinking about these things with half the enthusiasm, or the same definite urge to know as I had when I was talking to Anna for the first time. (The majority of them were fundamentally stupid anyway. Snatches of their conversation: stories about champagne and being in girls' rooms late at night, English accents talking about people called Dom or Will.) Davies was walking, just as quietly, at my side. I hadn't got any idea what he was thinking.

And he would never, I don't think, admit that he was impressed in any way, or that this was as new to us as swearing during the rugby games back on the village field. He was always too cool, and I hated it sometimes, that he couldn't just forget about all that when he was in company. (Because at other times, there was no-one who could feel things more than him. He couldn't even look at the news sometimes, without having to leave the room in a mixture of embarrassment and pity for someone who was being interviewed: the valleys man who'd just lost his job, criticising the government in a child's English, and his grammar making you think that even if the government were responsible you couldn't really blame them; stories about disabled children's sports teams, with their smiles like the end of the world. He'd just get up out of his seat and leave, talking to himself, just making any noise to hide the sound of the television.)

The house was like a real house, with real people living in it. The other two were out for the night; Anna was the only one there. And that long coat was the perfect complement to the place. The living room was upstairs, looking over the street, and it was quiet there, the one floor of distance feeling like miles, and years. I went to look through the curtains, and waited there for a moment to see if anyone would look up from the street and see me. There were two lamps illuminating the room, the roof was comparatively high and the light reached three-quarters of the way up the wall. The corners of the ceiling were dark. On the walls, and even on the corridor on the way up the stairs, there were pictures. Everywhere. Black and white prints, bought, cut out of magazines and newspapers; actors, musicians, some of her own photographs too she told us afterwards. Scenes from films – films I'd never seen and which could have been just ordinary scenes in black and white, I didn't know. Davies was looking closely at them, individually and as a collection. He knew some of the scenes, and laughed under his breath now and again, as though he were the only one who understood the reference.

"Anna, this is Davies. Davies, this is Anna."

"Hello."

"*Shwmae 'de.*"

"Haven't you got a firstname?"

"Davies is my first name. I'm American. Davies McCormack the Third."

"Oh, okay."

It was possible to foresee even in the first half minute they meet that two people are going to get on. And just as the two of us, Davies and I, had decided unconsciously between us that he would lead and I would follow (if not quite exactly), I could see the same thing happening here. I could see that Davies would take her for granted, would think she was too serious, and that she sees everything in a *basic* way, and that that's a weakness. And that she couldn't make value-judgements either. But he'd love her. And she'd think about him that he was a bit of a twat, stupid sometimes, immature sometimes, but much more than that too. That he expected, and was waiting, for the whole world. That he was good, and honest, and that she'd love him.

That afternoon Daniel walked around the town in a daze. He felt completely exhausted. He couldn't hear the traffic noise, didn't listen to the snatches of people's talk as they passed by, as he would normally do. He let people push past him without making much effort to get out of their way. If they had looked back at him, as if to ask what was his problem, he hadn't taken any notice, just carried on walking. He walked down St Mary's Street, and looked in the shop windows, his mind not so much absent, but deaf or dumb. He went into the Oxfam Bookshop and looked around but without much purpose. He looked along the rows of romantic novels for a long while until an old woman asked him to move so she could reach a book from the shelf in front of him. He hadn't even felt her presence at his side. He spent half an hour or an hour afterwards just walking along the different arcades. There was something particularly attractive about them that afternoon. Not just that the shops there were all *nice*, and sold attractive, soulless furniture, or that they sustained the different scents so much better than those in the open air – the leather of the coat shop, the musty smell of dried herbs in the expensive food shop, or the little cafes whose doors would open and let a breath of warm air, or coffee steam, out into the corridors – but the light, and the comforting feeling of being outside and yet under cover, of being in the world, and in the midst of all the choices – books, cameras, clothes, the things which excited and changed lives in their own quiet way, and the experience of buying them too, suddenly turned into an art form – but also of being, in addition to that, in a *room*. A frame. A compromise between restriction and space. He would have liked it if it had been raining.

He went into one of the little cafes. His coffee came in a glass cup with a frame and a metal handle. He didn't like those cups. He had asked for a Chelsea bun as well. He sat for a couple of minutes just staring at the table. He tried to imagine how he would sit, and how he would order and drink coffee if he had just heard about an incident which had shattered his world. As if he was too shocked to cope with the world. How he would deal with the young girl who would have brought him his coffee. Would he have thanked her, or have become so absorbed that he wouldn't even have noticed? Then he remembered his own situation. He realised that a situation like he had imagined could really exist. That life's mechanics of politeness were so deep-rooted – deeper even than the most spontaneous of human responses. That falling apart was an act, a choice to a certain degree, but that saying thank-you came before everything.

Daniel had walked and walked. When he reached the house again he had made a circuit of the city. Through Riverside to Canton, up to the fields in Pontcanna, down Cathedral Road, had cut through the park and out by the College of Music and Drama. Through the civic centre then, and he sat on the steps of the museum, as if he was waiting to meet Anna after work. Lingered for a moment on every street-corner. Postponed thinking about going back until the next corner. Up through the university buildings, Cathays Terrace, past the Flora, a new year of students having claimed the place for their own, because they lived two doors down, up then to the traffic lights, the sun had come out by then and reminded him of times which were not quite so sweet in reality as they were in his memory. As he walked, Daniel had been thinking about photographs and about a special project. He would take two photographs a day for a year, with no living person in any of them: paving slabs, close ups, individual letters on posters in shops, car wheels, poor graffiti on walls, house gates, railings, the wires of the phone system or electricity system, meat in a butcher's window, the veins in blue cheese too, but nothing that would give any suggestion of context or of simple recognition. Shapes and colours. And he would become 'friends' with some of the shapes, and some of the colours, and some parts of some of the pictures. He would hang them without too much fuss, each one from a little hook in the ceiling. He was jealous of Anna. She didn't have to try. He was at the bottom of Crwys Road, trying to cross the road. City Road was as dirty as ever. He concentrated on his feet, reaching out in front of him.

How to introduce her then? How to see her now that pity had fallen upon her like a curtain? A series of questions: had any of this crossed her mind? That she would by the time she was thirty, bury the love of her life? When she was a little girl in Cwm Tawe, a young woman walking the streets of the town and then the city by herself for the first time, buying clothes, painting, dreaming, dressing up to go to meet her first boyfriend, leaving her parent's home to go to college? Had there flashed any shadow of this on her brain? And might there not be some *presque vu* of every incident, every situation, like code, in our minds already? And if we reach some point of recognition, of ourselves, perhaps, in silence, what is that but foresight? And that foresight playing a role?

Poor Anna.

The music had stopped. Nothing but the sound of the occasional car on the street outside. The heavy curtains absorbing the waves and only letting the remainder seep into the room like longings, like the recognition that in those cars, on their journeys into the night, there is escape. The comfort of the big open road. Turn the mind off and let the dim light guide you.

"I haven't told Mam yet."

The room is warm – body heat and the heat of not opening the window. Anna is wearing a white long-sleeved top, Daniel is pulling off his jumper and tidying his hair.

"I haven't spoken to anyone... since I phoned you."

She is leaning back, to lie on the floor, and putting her hands behind her head and staring at the ceiling.

"I've been trying to think since then about how to talk to you, you know?"

A pause. Daniel was looking at her and she had raised her head to look at him from between her knees.

"All those times when we used to talk, discuss. I've been trying to practise, yesterday and today. Trying to think how to start."

Then she gets up, straight to her feet, suddenly, without even using her hands to push her body up.

"We'll have a drink, shall we?"

She was a girl you could imagine walking to work through the rain. And the rain would suit her. Her black hair shining and her body, in the long knee-length coat, moving determinedly through the weather. On her face too, droplets like tears, and where everyone else would have arrived with their faces like chalk, on her cheeks would be the very slightest blush and her eyes would be dancing. On occasions like this, Daniel imagined her as a combination of the sensuous and the stoic. He would think of her climbing the big wide steps under the grand pillars and the fine architecture, as though she belonged to another age, or to a black and white photograph where her presence, half way up the steps, would make the image complete.

But it was raining. And he would feel guilty about that, if he stopped to think about it. As though he were, for whatever reason, refusing to allow her to be unambiguously happy, and as though *he* had foreseen everything, had included in *his* own mind, intentionally or unintentionally, everything which was now playing out. And if "for whatever reason" is said of the fact that Daniel thought about her in the rain, and in water, that certainly signified something else, more definite and personal, a set of physical behaviours which continue to express themselves in the two of them – tonight, the first night they have seen one another for months, like the last time and the time before that even. Anna always looked her best when she had just come out of the shower. And not everyone is lucky enough to be able to say that about someone. It's a mystical moment, and Daniel felt that, as an experience to acknowledge and to respect. Every time she happened to be on the stairs at the same time as him, for example, or when he opened the lounge door and saw the back of her towel, and her newly-shaved legs disappearing round the corner upstairs. He would feel like a boy again in his parents' house, when he would run round the house without stopping, everywhere at once, his mother in her room having just come out of the bathroom and trying to dress quickly before he jumped through the door and caught her without her dressing gown.

She had gone to work in the museum straight after leaving college. As a temporary job to start with, when she was still talking about getting a studio, and trying seriously to work on her own paintings. But as always happens, she started to talk less often about herself, more about work, as though she had struck a bargain, unwillingly for sure, but which had, with more and more time, become a bargain she was willing to own. These paintings will be my paintings; these will be the wide vistas of my imagination, the intro-spection of my quiet moments.

Owain Meredith
Totally Mindblowing Day Today

Bloody hell! What a totally mindblowing day! The best day of my life so far – easily. Marc took me over for dinner in the Happy Gathering, which was really decadent, and then we went to the bookies in Cowbridge Road for a bit and lost loads of money. After that the drinking started – Westgate to start with. Then we went to play skittles in the back, but I was so pissed after about an hour that the wooden balls were going everywhere and were missing the skittles completely. God knows who won; I was drawing pictures of happy faces on the scoreboard after twenty minutes.

After getting shitfaced there, we went on to the Miller's Arms on the Taff Embankment, the roughest pub I've ever been in. Two boys from Tudor Road came in and we started playing pool against them for money – and lost the lot. The two of them were such stereotypes of black people with jive talk and fluid movements. The young one came to sit next to me. He was very dark, with a beret on his head and an Aids ribbon on his jacket. I told him about Datsyn and how they were playing in Clwb Ifor, and he told me that he was a music agent and he could take Datsyn far, but I didn't believe him.

Then we walked along Tudor Road, and it was good and I was pissed and happy.

There was some old boy looking up at a window half way down Tudor Road and laughing madly. "He's going to shoot me," he said to us, with his eyes full of happiness. We went into every pub and club in Cardiff, to the Casino, to the Philharmonic, to Rummers, to the Green Parrot, spending a lot of time in the Rat and Carrot in St Mary's Street where Marc tried to chat these girls up by telling them he was a famous television producer, but they didn't believe him.

As we walked past the Angel hotel I found a little child's shoe, a blue suede one by itself and I picked it up. "Marc, this is the magic shoe; I'm going to meet someone special tonight!" I said. We went to the Club for a bit but it was incredibly boring, so we decided to go to Astoria because we hadn't been there before. I've never danced so much in my life. I was going round and round and trying to imitate that guy on *Reservoir Dogs* who's about to cut that policeman's ear off.

By about midnight we decided it was about time we had the company of one of these amazing girls who were walking around with nothing on. So we went round asking them all to dance. "Fuck off" was the cleanest refusal we got. I was about to give up when I noticed Marc talking to a crew of tarty-looking girls and suddenly this pretty girl with dark hair, who couldn't stop laughing, was telling me her name was Alex and started to show me all the things that men had given her that night – including a CD and the inevitable rose. Then she says "Guess what this is," and starts running around wildly, wiggling her hand on her head.

"Urnm, Urnm," I said. "It's Brian the Snail," she said, a bit offended that I hadn't guessed right. "Guess what my job is, it's really unusual," she said then. "Are you a grave digger?' I said, trying my best to stay on my feet. I was still looking into her eyes when Marc came from somewhere and whispered in my ear "She wants your phone number." "No, I don't think so, you know…" And before I could stop him he's asking her. "Will you give Owain your phone number?" "Yeeeeeeeees" she says, obviously trying to remember it.

On the way home we decided to call in the Club Inevitable again. There was hardly anyone left there, but Eleri came from somewhere and dragged us over to Lynda who was lying on one of the red seats mumbling something to herself. Eleri has been obsessed that I should get off with Lynda ever since I told her I was looking for a girl with big breasts after finishing with Angharad, and I've fancied Lynda for years because she's totally gorgeous. So I lay down next to her; I thought she was about to fall asleep so I just carried on saying nice things to her about her ears. "You're just taking pity on me 'cos I'm pissed and sad," she said at long last.

By now, Eleri had started to take an interest in Marc and I was desperate to get back to my house; but I wanted Lynda's company, and so we all landed in Eleri's house. While Eleri was molesting Marc on the sofa, Lynda and I went to the kitchen to make toast and tea, and we were talking in a relaxed way, that strange kind of conversation you get when you know you're going to sleep with someone – intimate, flirtatious, quiet, provocative, affectionate, strange. The excitement dwindled a bit as she took about two hours to take off her make-up, but in the end we put a mattress down in the living room, and made love and slept.

Twm Miall
Dole Queue

IT WAS PISSING DOWN with rain when I opened the curtains at dinner time on Thursday. Damn, damn, damn, I wanted money to go out with Nerys, and I'd have to put the old lady's cheque in my account. I felt my stomach turn over as I realised I'd have to go to the post office in Salisbury Road.

As I walked there, I was hoping that the old bitch of a postmistress had had a heart attack. I looked through the window before I ventured inside. She was standing there like a bum bailey. There wasn't another living soul in the bloody place.

She took my book without saying a word. Damn, so far so good, I said to myself. She isn't going to make a song and dance about it today. But she started off when she opened the book. "I can't accept a cheque," she said. "You can only make a cash deposit."

"What?" I said.

"You can only make a cash deposit. Very sorry."

"Of côrs iw can têc it," I said. "That tshiec is ffrom mai myddar. Ai want the myni and ai want it now."

"I'll have to have a word with my husband about this," she said, and disappeared out the back.

I was standing there drumming my fingers on the counter when there was a devil of a commotion from the direction of the door. Then around twenty young people threw themselves in at the door, and started ripping up posters and forms and things. Two boys with moustaches and leather jackets were masterminding the proceedings. I didn't have a clue who was creating all this mayhem, until they started chanting in Welsh; "WELSH FORMS NOW! WELSH FORMS NOW! WELSH FORMS NOW!..."

Bloody stroll on. It was *Cymdeithas yr Iaith*, the Welsh Language Society! They'd invaded Mrs Hitler's Post Office! She and her husband closed the shutters round the counter and rushed into the back again. I was right in the middle of the battlefield, except I wished I had a hammer or a sledge-hammer so I could do a proper job of it instead of the child's play this lot were doing. I started to look around for something I could smash up, but Cymdeithas yr Iaith had finished the job and had started to sing in Welsh: "Far off I see the coming day when every land shall own the sway, of Jesus Lord of All…The mountain tops rejoice and sing, to see the dawn and greet the King, while darkness flees away."

I heard the siren screaming down the street. Then I remembered that my post book and my cheque were behind the counter. Bloody hell, I had to get them back! I started to bang the shutters and the the glass like a wild thing, and the next minute two big policemen were trying to drag me out of the shop.

"Ai'm not widd ddem," I said. "Ai'm inosent. Ai cêm ffor ddy myni. Ai'f got my *llyfr post* beheind ddy cowntyr."

I managed to get hold of the door handle, and stood my ground pretty well, when some big sergeant with the look of a right hard case on him came up to me and said; "Well, well, what have we got here then? What's the matter, sunshine? Lost our bottle, 'ave we? Worried about what mammy and daddy are going to think about all this? Take him in, men."

"No, no, ai was jesd standing bai ddy cowntyr. Asg ddy wymyn, asg ddy wymyn…"

I got a hell of a kick in my balls which doubled me up, before I was dragged into the cop car. I could see Cymdeithas yr Iaith walking into the vans just as if they were going on a Sunday School trip.

In the car I shut my eyes, and hoped to heaven that I was dreaming. Yes, I'd had a nightmare after worrying too much about meeting that fucking old witch in the Post Office.

But when I opened my eyes, the car was screeching round the corner past the Museum and towards the Central Police Station.

In the blink of an eye I was in my stockinged feet and sharing a cell with two crooks.

I was shitting planks.

"What are you in for, angel face?" said one of them to me.

I went through the story bit by bit. The two of them sat on the wooden bed and shook their heads.

"Fucking toe-rags," one of them said.

"It's a fucking police state," said the other.

They were in their best suits and going up before their betters, if betters they were, that morning.

"You wants to get hold of a tidy solicitor and sue the fuckers," said one. "You could be on a tidy little number here, see. They'll have to pay you compensation."

"Aye," said the other guy, "you're lucky. We're in for a five-year-stretch, we are."

"Shut up, Vic, for Christ's sake," said the other one then.

"Where you from?" Vic asked me.

"North Wêls," I said.

"You a Welsh Nationalist?"

"Wel... y... ies in a we... it dipends... "

"Do you know...Um...wait a minute now. Christ, it's slipped my mind. What was his name, Allan?"

"That bloke – the Commander in Chief of the Free Wales Army."

"O, him. Fuck me, what was his name now, wasn't it Julius or something?"

"Aye, that's it. Do you know him?"

"No," I said.

"Hell of a boy, he was. He could blow this fucking shanty to kingdom come, he could."

One hell of a pity he couldn't blow that bloody Post Office to smithereens.

Two policemen came to the door. "Victor Lawrence Garner. Allan John Davidson. You're up in courtroom number three."

"All the best, Taff," Vic said to me.

"Ai, sêm tw iw, Vic," I replied.

Vic said something to the policeman and pointed at me

before the door was closed and locked behind him. I was afraid now, afraid that the sods would keep me there for ever. I could hear Cymdeithas yr Iaith singing hymns and Dafydd Iwan songs.

When the city clock struck two, the policeman came to fetch me and took me to a room where the fat sergeant was sitting behind a desk.

"Now then, boyo," he said. "Sorry we couldn't lock you up with your mates. Damn nuisance you lot, you always fill the place up. Right, name, address and occupation."

"Lisyn," I said. "It's ôl a big mistêc... "

"No, you listen to me," he said. "I've got a heavy schedule, I've got a wife and kids who are expecting me at home, and I want to get shot of the lot of you as soon as I can. Now, name, address..."

"Ai was jest standing in ddy Post," I said. "Ai'm not widd ddem."

The fat sergeant was about to get up from the table and rush at me when the other policeman whispered something in his ear.

"OK then," said the sergeant, "out with it. What's your story?"

After I had finished telling the story, he started massaging his face as though he was trying to make a loaf out of it. Then the two of them went out and left me there by myself.

They must have gone to ask Cymdeithas yr Iaith. I was sure of one thing, that lot were bound to tell them the truth, and say that I hadn't got anything to do with them, because the majority of them are children of ministers and teachers and what have you.

The fat sergeant came back and offered me a cigarette. "Right then, mister... er... mister... What is your name, by the way?"

"Bleddyn. Bleddyn Williams."

"Right then, Mr Williams. It seems that there's been a bit of a cock-up. We all got a bit excited back there at the Post Office. These language activists are a right pain in the arse. I don't know what all the fuss is about – no-one speaks Welsh in Cardiff…"

"There are a couple, sarge," said the policeman. "There's Jonesy – PC 1783, he speaks Welsh, and the lady who lives next door to me…"

"When I want your opinion, Harding, I'll ask for it," said the sergeant. The policeman dropped his head, and looked at his big feet. "Now then, where was I?" the sergeant said. "Oh yes, as far as I'm concerned it's a complete and utter waste of time and a drain on our resources. I'm very sorry for the inconvenience we may have caused you. Now, if you follow P.C. Harding here, he'll return you all your personal effects. Good day, Mr Williams."

I didn't budge. My legs started to tremble, and my mouth became as dry as a desert.

"Ddat's not gwd inyff," I said. The sergeant looked at the policeman, before saying.

"Sorry? I didn't quite catch that."

"It's not gwd inyff," I said. "I want tw si e solisityr."

He walked up to me, stood above me, and put his big finger right in front of my nose.

"Now listen here, sonny jim," he said. "any more of that kind of talk, and the only person you're likely to see is your maker. Now, start making tracks. I'm counting to ten. One, two…"

"Ai'm demanding tw si e solisityr," I said. "And ai want compynseshion."

"I'm going to plant one on him," he said to the policeman. "I swear to God I'm going to plant one on him."

"Iffiw dw ddat," I said. "Ai'll tel Dafydd Elwyn."

"Tell who?" he said. He was starting to go crazy.

"Dafydd Elwyn. Hi's mai niw M.P."

He jumped for me, but the other policeman got between us. "Take him out," said the fat sergeant. "Take him out before I throttle the little bastard."

"I think you've pushed your luck a bit," the other policeman said to me before locking the door again.

I started to regret that I'd made a row. But then, I thought about Nain, my grandmother, and about Uncle Dic, and Vic and Allan. Yes, I'd done the right thing... why the hell should that sergeant have a free hand to do whatever he wanted? There's a boss above everyone.

The town clock sounded five times. Ta-ta Nerys, ta ta, private viewing. Then a fear gripped me suddenly. Oh, Mam, perhaps they were getting the carpet ready. They were going to wrap me in it and kick me from here to the middle of next week. I put my hands over my balls when the door opened. There was a lump of a bloke with a moustache standing there. He was wearing ordinary clothes. "Follow me," he said. There was a hellish rough look about him. We went down the corridor, turned left, then right, and there in front of me was a big iron grille – like a lion's cage in the circus. "In," the mountain said.

I had just walked down the corridor of the shadow of death, and the coppers had barricaded the paths of righteousness. I was about to get the beating of a lifetime. The table and chairs were bolted to the floor. I would be lucky to get out in one piece, let alone alive. He put a cigarette in my mouth and lit it, and then he sat down and put his feet on the table.

"How's your old man?" he said in Welsh.

I almost had a fit.

"What?" I replied, in Welsh again.

"How is... Harri? You're Harri's boy aren't you?"

"Uh... fine, as far as I know... er... but how do you know who I am?"

"Easy," he said, and he threw my post book onto the table. "The information's all in here, isn't it? A couple of phone calls here and there and Bob's your uncle."

I almost said, "And Harri's mai ffaddyr."

"I used to work with Harri years ago, before I joined the force. You've been in trouble before, haven't you?"

"Um... yes."

"And you've stirred up a bit of a hornets' nest this afternoon."

"It wasn't my fault, it was them…"

"Shut your mouth and listen to me. You've got two choices. I can go and get you a lawyer now, and then you can try to make a case for wrongful arrest against the police. That's up to you. But I'm telling you now that something like that would take months before the case came to court, and perhaps you wouldn't win in the end because you've got a record. Your only other choice is to sign this piece of paper, and we'll send you money. But remember, if you sign this, you can't say a word to anyone ever. You understand?"

"Yes."

"You make damn sure you don't tell anyone, or we'll get you for something else."

I was just dying to get out of the hole. I would have settled for half an ounce of tobacco and a nice little apology. I read the paper, and signed it, and kept the counterfoil.

"Leg it now," the guy said. "I don't want to see you near this place ever again."

"Would you like me to ask the old man to send you a Christmas card?" I said.

"Get out of here now, before you get the toe of my boot up your arse."

There was a touch of a smile on his face.

Gareth Miles
Fireworks Party

(Dewi, a working-class ex-soldier and Northern Ireland veteran from north Wales, works as a private detective in a valley town for Olwen, a middle-class lawyer.)

"How would you like to come to a party?"

"Love to."

"Good. It'll be in my parents house, in Cyncoed, a suburb outside of Cardiff in the direction you'll be coming from. Don't worry, I'll send you a map. There'll be a lot of lawyers there. Useful contacts. I'll introduce you to them."

"I'd better put on my best suit!"

"No way, Dewi! We'll be outside most of the evening – wear something warm. It's a Guto Ffowc party."

"Who's he, Olwen?"

"Guy Fawkes…"

"Ahh…"

A shiver ran through me. She noticed.

"Have you made other arrangements..?"

"I'm supposed to play for the darts team in the Club. I don't know if I can get out of it."

"Do your best. I'll be really disappointed if you don't come."

And I went. And started to regret it when looking for somewhere to park my four-year-old Escort among the BMWs, Mercs, Audis and the brand spanking new harp-Volvos in the wide leafy driveway outside *Afallon*, the home of Eunydd Humphreys QC and his wife Nesta; a quarter of a million's worth – at least – from circa 1935 Home Counties-style mock-Tudor. The old car wasn't at home there, any more than I was.

Tied to some of the old-fashioned street lamps which illuminated the drive were white leaflets with the words 'GUTO FFOWC' on them, and arrows pointing to a path of shining black slabs going round to the back of the house. It was a dry night and October was biting. I breathed in a lungful of pine and followed the signs.

Behind the house the black slabs spread out to form an L-shaped patio between the house itself and a crystal palace of a conservatory. Then a generous lawn and beyond it a little pavilion with a red tiled roof, shadowed by more tall pine trees.

In the middle of the lawn, in what had been a flower bed, there was a blazing bonfire, and around it, standing or sitting at garden tables or benches, were around fifty men and women in smart casuals, chatting, laughing, boozing and eating, and children playing hide-and-seek around the fire and in the shadows.

I'd noticed earlier that the adults divided into two generations – 20-35 and 35-60+. It was the older group who were drinking the heaviest – red wine, pints, shorts. White wine and bottles of Becks seemed to be what the younger ones had gone for. Every so often, twos and threes of them would disappear behind the pavilion and come back happier.

I stood for a while between the corner of the house and a big rhododendron bush, sussing the scene – an instinctive, neurotic habit. Also, I was looking for Olwen Angharad, the only one I'd know, and the only reason for me to have chosen to go into the midst of the Cardiff Welsh-speaking *crachach* rather than earning deafening applause in the Trefabon Non-Pol by leading the darts team to another victory.

My mind began to wander, and my eyes to look for snipers in the trees at the end of the garden.

"Dewi! What are you doing standing here?"

It took me a moment or two to recognise Olwen Angharad, stepping quickly towards me across the lawn. I couldn't remember where I was. She looked so different in a flaming red tracksuit with a little red hat of the same colour, like a Jew's cap, on her head. The Girls' Hockey Team Captain.

"Looking for you, Olwen," I said, and walked over towards her.

"I was afraid you weren't coming," Olwen Angharad said, her tongue rather slurred, and her eyes shining. Come and meet Dadi and Mami. Then we'll find a drink for you, and something to eat."

I'd learned quite a bit about Olwen's family by this time. Eunydd Humphreys QC Head of Chamber of Goldberg & Humphreys, member of any committee which runs anything in Wales – WDA, BBC, University of Wales, National Eisteddfod, etc etc. Nesta, his wife, still worked as a supply teacher in Cardiff Welsh-medium schools even though she could afford to stay at home and help the gardener. Iwan, two years older than Olwen and working in his father's firm (couldn't be in the party as he was dealing with some case in LA) Trystan, three years younger than his sister, a film and television director (on a shoot in Pembrokeshire).

Although Eunydd Humphreys was a short man – a good two inches shorter than his wife – he's not one to belittle. Carrying too much weight, like a middle-aged solicitor, but no softness of character. Agreeable, courteous and in good spirits in the midst of his friends and family – but I wouldn't like to be cross-examined by him in a court of law, innocent or no. A staunch chapel-goer, "not pleased" that his daughter had given up attending the means of grace since she'd moved from home to her house in Pontcanna, and "cross" that she was living tally.

I asked myself what else, apart from the piercing blue eyes, Olwen had inherited from her father.

I made a very favourable impression on E.H. by drinking orange juice, like he was doing. He was a T.T. QC. but very generous with his wine, nonetheless, to anyone who wanted to knock it back.

Nesta, Olwen Angharad's mother, who's a good bit younger than her husband, was originally from Aberdare. She had the same colouring as her daughter. A sensible, natural, very likeable woman. When the talk turned to the Valleys Then and Now and everyone but me had praised how green it was up there now, Mrs H. said that she preferred the place before the pits closed, when the Valleys were full of dirt and life."

After a bit more smalltalk, Olwen took me over to a big trestle table with a buffet on it, and after she had loaded my plate with meat, canapes, cheese, salads and so on, we joined her 'partner', Huw Alford and another couple, Gwilym and Marged Prydderch, around one of the small round cast-iron tables.

I had a warm welcome from the three, especially Huw, who was a much jollier creature in his dark and light blue Cardiff RFC shirt than the fashionable apparition I'd encountered in Olwen's office. He shook hands enthusiastically, as if we'd never seen one another before.

Gwilym Prydderch had just turned 50 at the time, even though he looked ten years older. A pained look on his face all the time – especially when he smiled. I thought Marged was twenty years younger than her husband, but there was scarcely ten years between them. A pretty doll-like face. In the light of the bonfire and the lamps hanging on the bushes and trees, it was hard to decide if she was a bottle blonde or a natural one. A bit of both, most likely. Mr and Mrs Prydderch had one thing in common – His and Hers Scotch plaid golf clothes, red and blue, naff.

Gwilym Prydderch had been a lecturer in the electronics department of the University before 'diversifying' at the end of the 80s. That was why he looked and sounded more like a professor than a business man, and made me feel he'd be more in his element in a library or a laboratory than a party.

After Olwen had introduced me, Huw, trying to pull Gwilym's leg and soft-soap him at the same time, said: "You have the privilege of being in the company of the wealthiest Welsh-speaking Welshman in the world, Dewi!"

"Says you, good boy!"

"Not yet, perhaps. But when Cymrucom is a plc…" said Huw, smiling and turning to me. "There's not another private company in the south that's seen such an increase in turnover, profit and in assets in the last two years, Dewi.

Make sure you buy shares when it goes on the market next year."

"*Boring, boring!*" said Marged. "You promised there'd be no talking shop!"

"Agreed," said Olwen and poured red wine into the glasses of the other three.

"Where have I seen you before, Marged?" I asked, as agreeably as I could manage.

She was delighted.

"*Hei di ho?*"

"Come again."

"*Sigl-di-gwt?*"

None the wiser.

"*Dibyn a Dobyn?*"

"Marged used to present children's programmes," Gwil explained.

"Classics", Huw added, with conviction.

"Like the works of Bach and Beethoven," said Olwen, and let Marged smile shyly for about three beats until throwing the *sucker punch.* "And almost as old!"

"Evergreen, Oli." said Marged, a sweet smile on her lips, poison in her eyes. "I gave up a promising career in the Media, Dewi, in order to marry this here man…"

"This lucky man!" said Huw.

"Hear, hear!" seconded Gwilym.

Marged finished her sentence graciously: "… and to be a full-time mother to Siwan and Llew. I've not regretted it for an instant."

The talk turned to things which were, apart from golf, pretty unfamiliar to me – S4C programmes, the latest gossip from the BBC, the Language, what kind of place the Assembly would be, the prospects of the Welsh rugby team, new places to eat in Cardiff, exotic holidays, money…

Gwilym went off in the direction of the pavilion where the fireworks were flashing and crackling. I went into the house, through the *conservatory*, following a series of arrows, towards the Ty Bach/*Toilet*, which, in a whacking understairs room, was the most cultured lavvy I had ever been in.

Facing you as you went in were two Victorian shelf cupboards, full of Welsh and English books and magazines. On the right-hand side, the white throne, and either side of it, two framed posters – *Beth yw'r ots gennyf fi am Gymru?* – *'What do I care about Wales?'* by T.H. Parry-Williams, and *Cofio* – *'Remembering'*, by Waldo Williams. In front, looking out of a post-Referendum poster at me as I pissed, were Ron Davies, Dafydd Wigley, Rhodri Morgan and other politicians I didn't know.

After I'd finished my business, the fireworks were still resounding at the back of the house. I should have gone home, but I didn't want to offend Olwen Angharad. I crossed the lobby from the toilet to the open door of a room with music coming from it. The same music that could be heard outside, if you could hear it out there.

This was a long room, with subtle lighting. A grey granite fireplace at one end with fake blue and yellow flames playing in it, and a Welsh dresser full of blue-and-white crockery at the other end. Two tall windows five yards apart looking on the garden.

The loose curtains were pulled across enough so you could ignore the flashes but not the bangs and explosions in the garden of *Afallon* and the other gardens in the vicinity. A green room. Green was the main colour of the chairs and the sofa, the carpet, the curtains and the wallpaper. Different shades blending together. Two landscapes of somewhere in Wales on the longest wall and a big Napoleonic portrait of Eunydd Humphreys Q.C. in legal regalia, above the fireplace.

On the mantelpiece, photographs of the family in silver frames. Eunydd and Nesta twenty years younger, and Iwan, Olwen and Trystan twelve, nine and seven. Two pairs of grannies and grand-dads. And on the wall closest to the fire, pictures of the three children in their cap and gowns after graduation; a photo of Olwen Angharad at eleven, in Welsh costume, pretending to play the harp, and, beside that, a

framed certificate she had won for coming first in the Urdd
National Eisteddfod, under 12.

I sat on the velvet sofa and closed my eyes tight. I forced
myself to listen to Mozart or whoever it was, in the hope it
would drown the row from the garden.

Tôpher Mills
NEVUH FUHGET YUH KAAIRDIFF

Fraank Fanaarkaapaanz on duh mitch
inis bestest daps
onis faastest underaang bogey
like uh propuh Beano comic

Mad Motters donkeyin
raaysin froo Grange-end gaardns
korzin uh woppin grate malaarkey
dodgin duh diddykoys

scraamblin kross duh daaffs
kraakin jelly froo duh chewlips
an nuh Paarkeyz frowin uh wobbley
totulley owta duh winda like

"BLUDDY LIDDUL DOWZOWS"
ee yelz all jottld up to is Dodgem
"YEWUL GET SUM GROLLUP YEW ERVA
PAARKS YUR AARS ROWUND YUR AGEN"

Motter mite be beejobulld
buh Fanaakaapaan ees norra dill
iss is dreem wen ee growz up
tuh bee obbuldeeoy tuh duh kween

aan duh Paarkeyz aad uh maajorum
is germojumz gon all maankey
"Faaraawaakin bolluhwoks" ee baars
"iyum orf down duh skin ows"

aark aark duh laark
frum Kaairdiff aarms paark
iyull aav uh Klaarksee pi
aan un aarf aan aarf uh Daark
aa aan
uh baanaanuh jaam saarnwidj

DIS IS JEST TUH SAY LIEK

dat i skoffed
duh sarnee
yoo id in
duh freezuh kumpartmunt

an wat
yooz wuz praps
kraabin
fuh laytuh liek

sorree yuhno
ir wuz jaamtastik
reelee baanaaanaaree
aan reelee baaraaas

(Translated from the American of William Carlos Williams)

174

Sheenagh Pugh

Toast

When I'm old, I'll say *the summer*
they built the stadium. And I won't mean

the council. I'll be hugging the memory
of how, open to sun and the judgement

of passing eyes, young builders lay
golden and melting on hot pavements,

the toast of Cardiff. Each blessed lunchtime
Westgate Street, St John's, the Hayes

were lined with fit bodies; forget
the jokes, these jeans were fuzz stretched tight

over unripe peaches. Sex objects,
and happily up for it. When women

sauntered by, whistling, they'd bask
in warm smiles, browning slowly, loving

the light. Sometimes they'd clock men
looking them over. It made no odds,

they never got mad; it was too heady
being young and fancied and in the sun.

They're gone now, all we have left of them
this vast concrete-and-glass mother-ship

that seems to have landed awkwardly
in our midst. And Westgate's dark

with November rain, but different, as if
the stones retain heat, secret impressions

of shoulder-blades, shallow cups,
as sand would do. The grey façade

of the empty auction house, three storeys
of boarded windows, doesn't look sad,

more like it's closed its eyes, breathing in
the smell of sweat, sunblock, confidence.

Elinor Wyn Reynolds
Nye

He's stood there in bronze for ages,
firm, immovable,
a symbol to us, as we shop on credit,
with his broad shoulders dripping with the droppings of the
                              impertinent south Wales gulls
and the tough city pigeons.
silent Aneurin gleaming white under his burden of crap,
this is our hero riddled with unabashed rheumatism
not turning a hair under rain's oppression and the gale's
                              scorn.

And this giant's not one jot afraid of his sexuality either.
A chunk of man from crown to sole
he hangs around Queen Street
wearing pink marigolds on a Saturday night
after some airhead wag lent them to him,
then he's up to his elbows in the suds of bellowing, beer and
                              brawling

trying to keep the city clean for the ages to come
without throwing the baby out with the bathwater.

Sometimes he wears a bollard at a jaunty angle on his head,
all "Hello Sailor!" showing he can take a joke.
Despite this, he points seriously at the earth of Wales where
                          his feet are rooted –
to the land he came from – but on a frantic Friday
no-one in the city's listening.
He's head and shoulders above people and their dopey,
                          doo-lal, dumb, dull minds,
his oratory is swiped away daily and whipped off on the wind
an old forgotten curse or yesterday's newspaper without the
                          chips.
A rock face scowling at the future
where all will have the right to health and long life, he says,
stiff with the tiredness of all the waiting rooms.
"Get it down, boys," say the people on the pavement in party
                          mood
"You can't take it with you. You've got to live for today."
"It won't do you any harm," wrapping a purple boa round
                          his neck
and tickling without him sneezing.
Tonight Aneurin's celebrating once more.

lloyd robson
a curious pace

at the junction of newport & city roads a bank neon informs
of high street mutation, declares corporate growth, instructs
good welsh boys to colour the times to relieve bleak tones to
unsheathe the steel to bare the blade to shine the light to alle-
viate to necessitate to amalgamate market force the threat of
metal for cashpoint notes the street corner challenge between
scissors, paper, stoned:

> *'lloyd: stab'*

keep the receipt
the 'A' hallucination already absorbed.

~

the A.
the O A.
the old arc.
aid: bread pudding soaking up daytime pints, betting shop
pens give up on wet echoes. a loser backed & a cocked up
crossword.

> *"ya daft a'puth"*
> > *"ya dozy born bastard"*
>
> *"the thing is…"*
> – *"my arse!"*

a right piccalilli.
arguing the toss.
waking up in the night to dance the brains dark trot.

~

the brewery gone. the albert closed. caroline divorced, in
sunder, cleft, rent, hewn, carved, sliced, *chipped* even, fractured & fractionised by the number crunch hosts. frontline

between the brewery quarter & the old alf-n-alf you do the math & i'll pick the bones. dorothy's world famous chicken curry or a soupçon of pretension served on a bed of sweet rocket with a drizzle of balsamic vinaigrette, extra virgin olive oil or fresh basil sauce. hmm, doan sound half bad when yungry. stick one a them in a crusty cob then sweetheart & i'll take it ome. portion a chips an all. & a tub a curry sauce. growing boy see. woan do no arm. no. no.

wrappers booted at passing cabs or spilt on the street. john batchelor doan get to eat no more.

adam street rapists, muggers on black bridge, verbal hurled from the bars of knox road. school kids giggling on gravestones, the smell of wet trees by the magistrates' court. sunday planned & prepared on the dark walk home: a pint in the clifton & listen to elvis, a lamb dinner at tony's, watch football, get stoned. not too bad as weekends go.

~

on broadway, a notice in the car dealer's window declares:

"all mileage must be taken as incorrect".

the old city's death much overblown, its change at a curious pace:

"rising tempo"

sprayed on a railway street wall, joyride through the city in the warmth of a dat sun setting, fading

but not *that* fast though.

jump in luv, we'll give you a lift home.

Penny Simpson
Something for the Weekend

"He's bought the whole bloody tree with him!"

A noisy racket as McNiff dragged the huge branch in under the railway bridge. Dai the Hat jumped up and grabbed a handful of dusty leaves.

"Will it burn, McNiff?"

"Yeah. We can have ourselves a barbie."

McNiff hauled the branch a few yards in and then stopped to take a breather. He had brought the branch all the way from Roath Park and up Penylan Hill, surprised no one had stopped him. At the turning into Ty-Gwyn Road, he had taken a sharp right down the steps that led to the disused railway bridge where he kipped with Dai the Hat, Finn and Hughie. Tonight, they planned to cook some food Dai had been given earlier, as he sat begging outside the Post Office in Albany Road.

"Daft bat. Does she think I got a cooker stashed away in my rucksuck, or what?"

"The kindness of strangers, Dai. Don't knock it."

"Well, they're beef, they are and I'm veggie."

"Beggars can't be choosers."

Dai scrunched up handfuls of leaves and piled them around the thickest part of the branch. He poured a little lighter fuel over the collection and struck a match. The leaves were dry and quickly caught. Hughie leant out of his sleeping bag and watched the fire with his sorrowful eyes. His hooded eyelids looked as if they might fold up any minute, an effect exaggerated by the pills he had taken earlier in the afternoon and had yet to sleep off. Dai ripped open the packet of burgers and speared one on the end of a twig he had ripped from the branch. Within seconds, it was reduced to a cinder.

"Harder than it bloody looks," he muttered, before anyone could mock his culinary efforts.

"Hold the next one higher up," Finn suggested, taking a

swig from a can he kept in his duffel coat pocket.

"Kind of let it smoke itself."

"Can you cook a burger over a ciggie?" Hughie asked.

McNiff cuffed him, but not in an unfriendly manner. He was worried about Hughie.

He had slept most of the morning at the pitch they shared outside the newsagent's, but it didn't show from his appearance. McNiff crouched down by his sleeping bag and rolled him a cigarette.

"You all right, man?"

"Tired, that's all."

"What you take?"

"Something from Monty, that's all."

Monty sold them pills whistled up on forged prescriptions. He dropped by at the bridge several times a week with his rucksack full of goodies, like an out-of-season Santa. Monty was six foot five and always wore white, except for his crocodile leather slip-ons. He wore a gold chain round his neck thick as McNiff's thumbs. He traded them pills that should have alleviated an old age pensioner's sleepless nights, or incontinent mornings.

"I owes him, McNiff," Hughie muttered, his chin buried deep inside his fleece.

"How much?"

"Over a hundred by now. Lost count."

"Out for the count more like."

McNiff ruffled Hughie's hair. He wore it long in a ponytail. A glint of an earring in his left lobe. A sporadic diet had left Hughie thin as a pipecleaner. His cheekbones erupted through his skin.

"You could always take a walk."

"He'll find me wherever."

Hughie waved an arm, too tired to muddle through another sentence. McNiff returned to the camp fire, which was now seriously out of control. The burgers had been reduced to a couple of sooty pebbles. Dai stamped on the leaves, as if doing a complicated war dance. Finn took off his duffel coat and used it to beat out the smaller flames. McNiff joined in. The smoke and the stink inside the tunnel was almost overwhelming, but his biggest worry was that one of the neighbouring houses might raise the alarm. Their kip had served them well and McNiff didn't want an unscheduled call from the emergency services to disrupt things. The flames put out, the trio of rescuers retreated to their respective ends of the tunnel, hungry and irritated.

It was a hot night. Taxis roared over the bridge. A group of straggling clubbers could be heard singing and and swearing in the near distance as they walked home. McNiff sat out on the steps to smoke a last cigarette. He figured he could probably lift enough to pay off Hughie's debt. There were some smart cars parked up on the hill and this time of year people were often careless about what they left on the seat, or the dash. He'd take a stroll and see what was what. McNiff blew smoke rings and watched them circle up towards the road above. A young woman screamed, as she slammed a car door shut. Another Saturday night fracas, he thought, a smile playing across his lips. He stubbed his cigarette out on the heel of his boot and walked up the steps towards the road.

The air was warm on his skin. He flexed his hands and realised how sticky they were – liable to leave marks, if he wasn't careful. He searched his pockets and found his bandana. It would have to do. Gloves in this weather would raise too many eyebrows. He turned right at the top of the steps and started on down the hill. A few lights shone in the windows of houses leading towards the park, but otherwise it was as still as could be hoped. McNiff flicked a practised eye over the first half-dozen cars, but it was a battered old Punto that received his attention, particularly the interesting looking plastic bag left on the passenger seat. He pulled down his jacket sleeve and wrapped the bandana round his fingers. So concentrated on the task in hand, he failed to notice a young woman heading towards him. McNiff froze, but she gave only the briefest of smiles before turning in at the nearest gateway. He turned back to the Punto, braced his arm ready to strike and took a step back to maximise impact.

"Did you drop this?"

An attractive voice, however unwelcome in the circumstances. McNiff was dumbfounded. He turned round and there was the woman he had just seen, close to his heels and holding out a tobacco tin. She smiled again, before putting the tin down on the bonnet of the car.

"It's mine," she added, before turning back in to her gate.

Night as hot as day. People spilt out on to Mill Street, glasses in hand, anxious for the smallest reprieve from the wet stickiness of bar and club. No one wanted to go home; no one wanted to be indoors. Two women with pussy cat ears and fluffy tails tripped and sprawled into Orhan and his friends. One of the cat's tails had been quickly soaked in Orhan's spilt beer.

"Sorry," he offered by way of apology, although it was cat woman's drunken stagger that was the real cause of the disaster .

"Fuck your sorrys, mate. This tail cost me five squid in Hyper-Value."

"Don't even think it," Tariq warned Orhan.

"She's just trying it on."

The beery cat-woman splayed her legs over the bistro table where Orhan sat and waited for his next move. Her off-the-shoulder T-shirt made her look seriously deformed. He was annoyed and not aroused at the sight of her dumpy frame, because it obscured from his view a pretty brunette with cut-off jeans. Orhan had spent the past hour weighing up whether to make an approach, goaded on by Tariq and his other friends, but all schemes had to be put on hold thanks to cat woman's unwelcome arrival.

"What's your name then?" she demanded.

"Orhan?"

"Or – what?"

"It's Turkish."

"Oh, I love Turkey, I do. Went on my holidays there a few

years back. Fell in love, I did. No, tell a lie, it was lust, it was. Must be the heat that brings it on, don't it, Donna? We work in nail extensions. What you do Or-hun?"

"Set design."

"You what?"

"I make scenery for plays."

"Musicals an' that."

"Opera."

"Don't go there, me. All that screaming and wailing. Sounds like they is in pain, or something."

"They often are. Broken hearts."

"Yeah? Well that's me to a T, Orhum. My hen night, tonight, see? And what does the bastard do? He texts me, don't he Donna, just before we gets on the bus and you know what? He dumps me. Four bloody words for each of the years we's been shagging."

"That's awful."

Orhan decided to offer cat woman a drink on the grounds that anything was better than keeping conversation going with the dumpy dumped one. He signalled his intention and cat woman squealed with approval, either that, or she had belatedly discovered the fact that she was sitting in a beer bath. Orhan slipped his way through the throng in front of the table and peered over a few shoulders. No sign of the brunette. Worried, he scanned the crowded street. A man in a tangerine flamenco shirt winked at him; another man stripped to the waist danced to his own rhythm, clutching a Red Bull can. A group of men dressed in John Travolta white suits and Afro wigs saunted past him, sweat pouring down their cheeks, but it didn't stop them acknowledging the cheers and whistles from the surging crowds. Orhan wished he had the guts to steal one of the wigs and hide from cat woman. Preoccupied as he was watching the Saturday night carnival, he failed to notice the mystery brunette materialise at his elbow. His shock at being so unexpectedly close to the object of his affections left him speechless. Dozens of words pinpricked his tongue, but it might as well be weighed down with lead.

Orhan stood staring at the woman's glossy brown hair, desperate for inspiration. Maybe the wigs would sashay back again and he could use that for an excuse to nudge her and make contact? Someone beat him to it, a man in a paisley shirt, with unlinked cuffs that flapped back as he swigged on his glass; a man with a tan and highlights and confidence. Orhan felt as if the lead weight had now bounced down on his head and hammered him into the uneven paving stones. A loud shriek and his misery was made complete. Cat woman had reappeared stage right, her top slipping still further off her shoulder, revealing a tattooed breast; her cat ears were balanced precariously on her nose.

"Oi! Hot to trot, babe, or what?"

The crowd parted and cat woman fell into his waiting arms. It was like a scene from a particularly ugly, day-glo nightmare. He had the lead role, but he wished he was painting the back cloth. Out of the corner of his eye, he saw the brunette wink at him and then turn back to Paisley Shirt.

It was too hot to trot. Too hot to even breath. Lula's apartment was a microwave set at full heat. She picked up her keys, put on her flip flops and headed for the coffee shop in Albany Road where she knew she could find a garden and a decent cappucino. Her head ached – too much gin from the previous night – and she was conscious that she had arranged to meet a complete stranger that evening for a curry. A curry? Obviously, her brain had evaporated, although she did have vague recollections of a blagger in a paisley shirt, surrounded by gyrating Afro wigs, and a ghastly jelly roll of a woman dressed in skewiff cat's ears who had flattened a man in the street.

"Oh, god, how embarrassing for him," Lula thought, circumnavigating a trio of wolf-whistling tarmac spreaders at work in Wellfield Road.

She couldn't help thinking it was getting to be more and more of a circus going out for a drink in town. Lula was hitting thirty and the hoop-la of it all was definitely wearing her out. She wanted to lie in a cold bath and eat Milky Bars, not head off to a curry house and make small chat with someone who was bound to be interested in little else other than what might lie below her recently pierced navel.

"No pants, no pants," Lula chanted triumphantly, as she headed through the cafe door.

When it was this hot, she dispensed with anything that might save on domestic labour. Underwear was the first to go, then she pulled down the wood blinds in her front room to obscure the layers of dust lining every available surface. And so it went on, until she was free to curl up on her duvet-free bed and plot her escape from the travel agent's where she worked. Everyone she told about her job thought it sounded idyllic, but they didn't spend eights hours a day cursing malfunctioning computers, or a stubborn head office undecided over the policy to take on flight delays, unpaid refunds or half-built honeymoon hotels.

Lula collected her mug of frothy coffee from a dishy blue-eyed Aussie serving behind the counter and made a beeline for the cafe's "garden", a backyard decked out with tables and chairs and a wobbly looking BBQ. She pulled a sheaf of Sunday newspapers from her wicker basket and settled in for a good, long read, but it was hot and she was soon distracted. She sat back in her seat and earwigged the conversation between two young lovers smooching at the table under the metal fire escape. Niet doing – Russian, or some other Eastern European language she didn't understand. Lula returned her attention to the colour supplement she had spread out by her coffee. A tortoiseshell butterfly danced its way over the pages and settled on the rim of her cup. It was something startlingly beautiful in the concrete yard. Engrossed in her study of the butterfly's wings, Lula failed to hear someone approach her table. Suddenly, a hand appeared, depositing a tobacco tin on top of her magazine.

"Yours."

Lula looked up. It was the man she had seen on her way

home in the early hours of the morning, hand bandaged and flexed ready to smash her car screen window. He leant forwards and she could clearly see how ill he looked. His eyes were red and filmy. A thin layer of sweat coated his face and collarbones, which stuck out of his fleece jacket. It was not the most appropriate of clothing given the record-breaking temperatures of that summer but Lula realised he probably didn't have any choice when it came to dressing in the mornings.

"Thank you."

She pocketed the tin and carried on staring at the man. He was her age, possibly younger, but it was hard to tell. His skin was grey and taut. There were scabs on his lower lip.

"I don't like to ask but could you stand us a coffee?"

He made his request to her coffee cup, his display of embarrassment quite touching.

"Hold on to my seat and I'll get you one. Milk, sugar?"

"Milk. Lots of sugar."

He settled himself in the chair opposite. Lula picked up her handbag and headed back to the counter to make her order. The Aussie at the bar offered to bring it out to her.

"He's bothering you, I'll ask him to leave," he added.

"No, it's okay. He's a… well, he's my neighbour, actually."

Lula returned to her table. The stranger was still sat in the same place, his attention fixed on the coffee cup – now minus its butterfly.

"One coffee. The sugar comes in sachets. These be enough?"

Lula pulled half-a-dozen sachets from her bag. The stranger emptied them one by one in his cup and then stirred it slowly for several minutes.

"Ta," he said eventually.

"My pleasure. Any chance of finishing my magazine?"

The stranger shifted his cup and Lula made a pretence of studying an article about the latest designs in fishermen's waders. He didn't shift, which surprised her, just began tapping out a melody on the edge of the table with his forefingers.

"Did you want something to eat, as well" Lula asked

"No, not hungry."

A short pause. They held each other's stare.

"I wasn't stealing, right."

"No?"

"Well, I was, but there was a reason."

"And that would make up for the hassle, if I found my car broken into?"

"Probably not. I dunno. Had to do a friend a favour."

"Enough to get yourself caught?"

"I wouldn't have done, if you weren't a dirty stop out."

Lula laughed. The stranger smiled – or maybe he grimaced? His teeth were terrible, rotting away into his head. She recognised him as the man who regularly begged outside the newsagents in Albany Road. He sat for hours on his backpack, which probably contained all he owned in the world. Imagine that, she thought, being able to sit on everything you owned. Downsizing gone mad.

"Are you sure you don't want something to eat?"

"No, ta. I had a BBQ last night. I'm John, by the way."

"And I'm Lula."

"I won't do your car, okay, Lula?"

John gulped down his coffee and stood up. Lula was unsure what to say, or do next. John was ahead of her. He held out his hand for her to shake. She noted the filthy fingernails and the faded letters tattoed on the backs of his fingers. They spelt 'Hate.' She scanned the opposite hand. There was no corresponding lettering spelling out 'Love.' Lula shook the hand offered her.

"Okay, John. It's a deal."

Then he was gone, as quickly as he had arrived. A butterfly man, Lula thought, as she absent-mindedly flicked through the rest of her magazine. Why was it that everything that summer seemed so transient and flyaway, like dust, or gossamer thread? Lula leant back in her chair. Summer time, but the living was far from easy.

Iain Sinclair
Crackerjack

I HAVE NO CLEAR MEMORY of the event, even though I was already two or three days old when it happened. What I do remember is my mother telling her version of the tale. Repeated often enough, these fables become history. Out of an enveloping plain of darkness that absorbed all mere facts, she highlighted a few over-directed and non-linear tableaux.

The ambulance hesitates, runs out of petrol (or coupons) – it's not important – on the rim of a hill overlooking the city of Cardiff. (Premature visions of future horror: driving tests, relatives in sudden and unexplained hospital deaths, poetry readings.) The pregnancy was a tricky one; another baby, a girl, had been lost. Our family journey through the unlit countryside *was* necessary. Certain districts, like Larkin's squares of wheat, were ablaze. The docks had been a target for several nights.

Then, both of us, mother and new soul, suffered a long, painful parenthesis – and I was born: out, present. Roath Park, or thereabouts. (Memories of this lake, water and vegetation, will be transported to London. A lifelong fondness for the spaces of Victoria Park, Hackney.) Cardiff was not where we lived, I was estranged from it, to a degree that might seem overdone: I refused to take a breath. Despite the warmth of the slaps and blows that induct us into the social world, I was stubborn, blue as lead. As a Bluebird (the slow crucifixion of Ninian Park fandom).

It didn't look good.

My father paid a visit, a small pile of paperbacks crooked under his arm. A typically oblique but significant gesture. Entering the heat and nervous closeness of that private cell, he stumbled. A tall man, stiff Highland bones, he dipped dutifully to look into the cot. A single volume dislodged itself, fell through the air and struck the baby on its undefended (still open) skull. Plucked from deep dreams the newborn creature howled, sucked recycled breath into reluctant lungs.

Launched, there was no remission.

Cardiff-born: for life.

On every form, passport, criminal record.

My mother held on to that title, where she confused all others: *Crackerjack*. No author, no publication details. (Subsequent research points the finger at W.B.M. Ferguson, who also penned *Boss of Skeletons*, *Escape from Eternity* and *London Lamb*.) The book must have been lightweight, in wrappers. My father wouldn't have invested in a hardback under such an ad hoc set of circumstances (perhaps a patient left it in the waiting-room, a traveller on the seat of a train). My father was Scottish – which is not to say that he didn't feel at home in Wales. Scottishness is the condition of feeling comfortable everywhere, except within the borders of Scotland.

Crackerjack was my 'Rosebud', Orson Welles moment. I was stuck with it, my fate twinned with some unimaginably obscure pulp novel. In years of combing through book-stalls, junkshops and charity caves, this item has never manifested itself.

I searched my father's library, clearing things up after he died. No trace. My mother had no library. Her books were absorbed into his, or they disappeared. I don't want to know. I share the superstition of the orphan who refuses to confront biological parents. *Crackerjack* is my black spot, my Cardiff plague token. It is waiting for me. One day, when I least expect it, it will arrive. And I will gratefully return to that interrupted dream.

Ifor Thomas
I Told Her I Loved Her a Lot in Splott

I said I'd be sad if
she didn't come to Cardiff

I called her a sensation
when I met her at Cardiff Station

I sang like a lark
when we walked in Roath Park

I said I'd never met anyone finer
in Rhiwbina

I vowed I'd be her man
in Pen-y-lan

I fell at her feet
in Oakfield Street

I told her I loved her a lot
in Splott

I said I like having you
in Western Avenue

But our loved turned sour
over beer in the Glendower

She called me a fool
in the Empire Pool

She broke down and cried
in Riverside

After I'd let her down
in Grangetown

She shouted YOU BRUTE
in Bute.

So we called it a day
in Manor Way

The next time she said
I'll get an A to Z.

Caroline Street

The divide:
Brewery Quarter –
a brash 1/4 quarter
kitted out
in building designer gear
glossed in structural glass
quaint orange rendered panels
windows eyelined in grey steel
balconies jutting
like a young slapper's tits
hey – signature architecture.

This lot looks down on the
clapped out south side –
Dorothy's chip shop,
Tony's kebab, the burger bars –
feeling the sharp elbows
of the new kid in town
> *(Wasn't old man brewery*
> *carted off because the smell of hops*
> *clinging to his coat blistered*
> *Chanel like paint stripper?)*
In the day they skulk, shuffle feet

on cracked paving stones,
it's the daylight – it burns their eyes.

Come Saturday midnight
a tide roars through
strait Caroline.
The old fast food joints
throw chips, gristle and grease
into the gullets of the good timers
a flotsam tide of food wrapping
slops and swirls ankle deep.
The lads take a piss
on the Brewery Quarter wall
hell they know which side of the street
their bread is buttered.
On to Life, Oz, Oxygen, Sams
Cardiff nights fuelled by Caroline Street.

Chris Torrance
The Loneliness of the
Long-Distance Writing Tutor

Down the first ratrun
                    Andrew Place
narrow path under bridge
single rail separates
from angry traffic

                    along Salisbury

past Ramon's   where I used to hang out

then down ratrun two, Lowther Road
another single file pavement
                            lashed by exhaust fumes

cross panicky Richmond
                            bolt down Northcote Street
turn left up City Road by the Roath
                            to the
meeting place of 5 ways

                    ghost haunted

5 brilliant points of light

                    5 burning pits of hell

Teeming narrow pavements
metal girls
navels 'r' us
dark boys
dogs on string

meat turns
in heated window
neon slides
down the glass

secondhand books
never open
army surplus
boots & blades
guns & locks

the human hulk
rests his bulk
behind monitor banks

cuffs & chains
"legitimate restraint"
cash immediately available
no questions asked

                   except for later

the hulk stands, leans forward
to impress the punter

                his paunch

domes out
a snagged grey teeshirt

                love & hate

blue grain by blue grain

trading a shotgun
renting a crossbow

                charging

a door off its hinges

                a preliminary negotiation

a roundhouse-
to get on terms

Class Four

K. beefed about other class members coming in
late, & also time wasted coffee break – when *he*
was a tutor he insisted on strict punctuality in
a class. Well, I dissembled round that by saying
I had had an authoritarian education & too *much*
discipline, so it wasnt part of my style in class.

It strikes me that K. is one of these unrelaxed
people; into "avant garde" or "free" music but
somehow very conservative & rather bullish. Yes,
I *do* run the class on an easy rein: I've never

stressed punctuality or criticised lateness in
25 years – for a lot of people it's better to make
the class late rather than not at all. For some
of them punctuality is not an option.
But it was a bringdown, & I was quickly into
doubting myself again, sludging home next day in
the rain. I try to be fulcrum & hinge for writers,
not lock & key. Drilling my lot would be like
trying to round up ants, or sheep without a dog –
they just wouldn't get the message. Lighten up, K.,
I wanted to say – these people are adults. & the
point is that writing gets done.

★

There is a tension in this
field of creative writing;
a flux between academic/orthodox
& an improvising wild jack,
on-the-hoof, off-the-cuff
practitioner such as myself

a wasp among bees, a palm
wine drunkard drawing dizzy
figures in a frigid zone
of auditors & accountants,
seat-holders & empire builders
– I'm surprised to have lasted
this long.

★

drinks after
at the Goat Major, used to be
the Blue Bell –
navigation mark or buoy?
on the old Taff

its slip of history
accumulation
of mud data, tide tales
within arrowshot
of Roman walls

crying of herbsellers
& fishwives, shouts
of deckies drift
through the open door

Iberian mercenaries
served by the same girl

placing the perfect pint
in front of me in 2001
smiles as she delivers
to shaggy writers

as from the castle enclosure
the stone animals escape
            one by one
spirits of the wild
hyena, destroyer, render
of flesh & bone
great lustrous black-on-amber
eyes

a lion
            fasttrotting, dodging
through traffic

joining the pubbing
clubbing crowds

Carnival
(for Barry & Eve)

Walking over the bodies of the dead
        at Llandaff
ceremonial avenues, a clump of Scots pine
        on an island in the river
a jumble sale in Gabalfa
        a beckoning mound that
skimmed endlessly behind the horizon formed
by an advancing brow of larch
        as we rode gently along in the Morris van

At least your pee looks good & green
in the white enamel bowl
a fit of the horrors
in a bar jammed with piratical scowls
& 5 o'clock shadows at noon
burnt grease stench ramming the air
riot talk thick & nauseous
haunted shagged faces of the night before
stare right down into the bottom of their beer

everyone looks like a murderer
PLATINUM STREET, ZINC STREET, PEARL
STREET, TIN STREET, DIAMOND STREET, IRON
STREET

Cardiff was a dream
as clear & lucid
as rays of sunlight
through a glass of pale ale
the pure Northerly tumbling
big awkward leaves of maple
towards the street of cardealers,
hands in pockets. The open-top Rambler,
retailing at £395, the gas-gobbler

Dodge Coronet at £465
        a buyers market, plenty
of big fat bodies
going to the cruncher these days
strip out all the items of use
then burn the sonofabitch
polluted smoke crowding the sky
turning out a box of
tightly compressed metal to be reintegrated
into the maw of the economic monster

METAL STREET, ORBIT STREET, BUTETOWN,
GRANGETOWN, BESSEMER STREET
        Bessemer inventor of
                the converter
        turning pig iron to steel
        tungsten carbide dumped
        behind rotted boards
                of torn Splottland deserts
        the old dossers simmering over their
        cider bottles below Hayes Island

TOPAZ STREET, LEAD STREET,
  RUBY STREET, EMERALD STREET,
    SAPPHIRE STREET, FOUR ELMS ROAD

We pushed through the door into the
smoke of the Roath, where
grainy-necked men chatted & laughed &
slapped each other

        the velvet bitter
slides down in thoughtful silence
creamy atomic mushroom explosions
trigger dead circuits into charging life
                the talk begins
dreaming skulls nodding atop pineal spires

                    the funny old dear
reading & rereading beermats with
a shredded intensity Weobley Castle &
"a tradition as old
                    as your next pint of Brains"
all tongues jerking ceaselessly frothing &
                    foaming utterance
voiceroar blends into radiophonic mush
shiver exquisitely the orgasm drums,
the power drums, the dance of egos swarming
          the Roath Park a temple
                    to the analgesic hop

COPPER STREET, STAR STREET, MOON STREET,
CONSTELLATION STREET, GOLD STREET,
SILVER STREET, METEOR STREET, PLANET
STREET,
    COMET STREET, ECLIPSE STREET, THE
        ROYAL HAMADRYAD GENERAL & SEAMAN'S
                                        HOSPITAL

          & now in the morning
          I sit here in the window
          not quite sure whether I
          have a hangover or not
          sparrow perching on rosebud sends
          dewdrops plummeting
          how will today fill itself
          with drops of life & death
          the conundrum spouts distrails across the deep

Anna Wigley
In the Castle Grounds

Gaudy as transvestites
the peacocks float

their long torpedoes
of petrol blue,

opera singers eyes
painted for twilight

sightings
from turreted rooms.

Haughty and rapt
as Sitwells in smoking suits,

bold from the pages
of Beardsley and Wilde,

they pace the lawns
like dowagers,

last exhibits of an age
of disdainful indolence,

when their high-strung cries
were thrown like banners

over the ramparts,
and the coffers of their tails

opened idly to amaze
with a sunburst of coins.

Andrew Craig Williams
Rosie's Last Week

IT'S RAINING TIGHT LITTLE LINES on me, as I'm skipping over puddles on Richmond Road. My flares get soaked through every time I'm unsuccessful in my leaping, water and brown leaves sticking fast to my shoes. My toes get wetter, but I keep on jumping, I have to meet Rosie before eight or she'll kill me. She told me she's got something special planned for tonight but she wouldn't say what. I turn quickly on to Newport Road, into the honk and blare of cars ripping through the wet tarmac. I pause under the viaduct to light a fag, and two girls walk past me with a Gucci umbrella held between them,

"You look like you're bleedin' love!" says one of them. I look down at my red t-shirt, and the large drops of water make the red even darker like I've just escaped a psycho killer in a slasher movie. I smile as they pass by giggling and flicking their hair like manes; one brown, one pink.

Rosie told me to meet her at the clock on Queen Street, just like we used to back when the food hall was still open in Capitol. Every Wednesday afternoon would see us sipping coffee at The Continental clutching Poppy Z or Phillip Larkin, eyeliner and attitude, dark, dyed hair and bright smiles. I'm running now, trying to get there before her. Scruffy pigeons fling themselves out of my way casting accusatory glares at me with their reptilian eyes, suddenly I can smell hotdogs and the whiff of engine and for a second, I'm back at the fair.

I can see Rosie ahead of me, she has no coat either and she's wearing her wine-coloured velour top, the one she knows I like because it makes her look sexy. She knows because I make her wear it so often. I try a last burst of speed to reach her and fall headlong into a rivulet caused by the wonky overflow channel in the slabs on Queen Street. I look up into her concerned face, pale skin glowing in the half-light, one eye tracing a mascara line down her cheek, and smile.

"Oh my God, are you alright?" she asks helping me up. I look down at my clothes expecting to see my new black combats ripped to shreds, no rips but I am soaked through, my t-shirt sticks to my body, bloodbath red with the rainwater.

"I'm okay." I reply shivering slightly, "Can we go to a *warm* pub?" Rosie laughs easily, the shock on her face at seeing me fall slowly being replaced with smiles at the funniness of the situation.

"C'mon you." She says putting her arm around me, "I've got something to show you."

"What?" I ask dripping with every step,

"You'll see." She says, still silently shaking with laughter at me.

We head down Queen Street, me protesting that I need to stop and Rosie urging me on and telling my we're going to be late. Nearly every person that sees me stifles a laugh or points and cheers, if I was a different kind of person I would be enjoying the attention, but I'm not. I blush redder than my t-shirt and cringe whenever someone jeers at me.

"Ignore 'em love," she says, but I can't. I feel like a hen weekend drunk, an A-level celebrant, Brynaman park with a flagon of 'Bow.

Rosie and me have only started seeing each other again after nearly two years, this is kind of a renaissance in our friendship, a brand new reel. I've missed having her near me and plan to tell her later when I'm drunk, when the words will come out smoothly, not garbled as I know they would do now.

I'm expecting to get drunk tonight, hopefully sit by a radiator, and talk shit with my best friend. We stop outside Rummers and Rosie hugs me,

"You'll be dry soon." She says and we step inside, I'm dreading the stares and cheers but manage to keep my composure as we make our way to the nearest radiator. I cling my arms around it grateful for the warmth as Rosie goes to the bar to get our drinks. I re-arrange myself so that my back is touching the rad, my eyes close in happiness.

"You're not sleepin' are you?" asks Rosie and I open my eyes with a start.

"Just gettin' warm." I assure her, and then see the girl standing with her. She looks shyly down at me on my seat and smiles, her eyes widen then close as she moves her gaze away from me.

"This is Heledd. Heledd, Geraint. Geraint, Heledd." Rosie introduces us.

"Hi Heledd," I say shaking her hand, a few drops fall from my arm and onto the small table. I notice one drip into my pint, imagine Cardiff pollution slowly spreading into the beer.

Heledd and Rosie sit down and we all reach for our beers. Heledd's big eyes glance up at Rosie who smiles back,

"So Heledd," I begin as brightly as is possible for a soaking wet shy person, "how do you know Rosie."

"Oh, we met when Tarina was DJing at the Kings. I gave Rosie a badge." They both laugh.

Seeing Rosie happy makes me smile and I laugh too.

"Cool, can I see it?" I ask Rosie. She nods yes and reaches for her bag. Pinned to the strap of her way too hippy bag is the badge, it is small and white and has a few words printed in black. It looks punky. I lean closer and read it: FUN 4 U. I smile and raise an eyebrow. Rosie avoids my gaze, so I content myself with waiting until Heledd needs to go for a pee.

"Do you know Tarina?" Heledd asks me, and I explain that I work with her boyfriend Kahu. We talk about Heledd's job in the University's Archaeology department, and she promises to take me on a guided tour. I tell her how excited I am at the prospect of this, she laughs at how eager I am. Our glasses chink and my top gets drier the more we laugh. I tell her how amazing it would be to hold an actual arrow-head from Mesolithic Wales.

"We don't have many human remains though," she tells me, "but plenty of animal ones."

"Oh my God!" I exclaim a bit too loudly, I am starting to feel slightly drunk, "So you mean I could actually hold a sheep's tooth or something, that actually grazed at an Iron Age farm?"

"No problem." she tells me, seeming genuinely pleased that I am so chuffed to bits. I offer to get the next round in and I stand up, Heledd moves her skirt out of my way and her knuckles touch Rosie's hand, which is reaching into her bag. I see the two of them exchange a quick peep at each other. Rosie keeps looking, but Heledd breaks eye contact first. I see this millisecond of action take minutes.

When I return from the bar Rosie and Heledd are laughing out loud, and it kind of saddens me, makes me feel excluded. Not by those two in particular, but like everybody in the pub is happy and content in their places with the people around them, and I've suddenly been thrown in and everyone is too polite to ask me to leave.

The rain has thankfully stopped by the time we leave Rummers, Rosie says she should be in bed already because of work in the morning, I tell her I'm jealous, I have to input eight-digit numbers all day in work on Monday. She laughs sympathetically. I like her. I like the way her greeny eyes clash with all the other colours she's wearing, like she's done it on purpose or something. We walk to the taxi rank to say goodbye to Heledd, the three of us holding hands in a short crocodile. I am feeling really drunk now, my head is doing that falling asleep thing. It falls and then jerks up, awake. I try to say 'goodbye' but my words all slur together.

"I think I'd better take you home." says Rosie.

"Mm." I agree, and together we make our way back down Queen Street, avoiding the puddles, back to my flat.

I drink the cup of tea that Rosie has made me thankfully. My head has stopped spinning and I can concentrate on asking her,

"So what's going on with Heledd then Rosie?" Rosie tries unsuccessfully to hide a smile, and I swear she starts to blush. Rosie *never* blushes, you could march her down

Newport Road naked and she'd *still* look serene.

"Rosie!" I exclaim, "Are you seeing her?" Rosie laughs out loud at this.

"Of course I'm not," she says her eyebrows all crossed, "we're just friends."

"Oh, fair enough then..." I start saying but see her holding back more laughter, blinking to stop the smiling from starting again. "Rosie, tell me!" I shout at her, nearly dropping my tea in my lap.

"Well, we kissed the other night," Rosie relents, "I was wondering how long it would take you to notice."

"I *did* notice, but then I didn't want to say anything just in case I was wrong. I *thought* I saw you two flirtin'." Rosie tries her best to look bashful, but I already know different – I've seen her so stoned she couldn't wipe the dribble off her lips, and just sat there giggling about it. "What about Australia?" I ask her, "Does Heledd know you're leaving next week?"

"Hmm, yeah she does know. We haven't spoken about it much." Rosie's eyes look a little too large, like they're going to fill up until they spill on to her little nose and run down her face.

"C'mon babe," I begin, moving over so I can hug her, "no need for tears."

"I know." Rosie sobs. I can hear the church bells bonging out a sad tune, and the last birds are squawking on their way to bed.

I'm looking at my ceiling, close up because I have a loft bed so I'm quite high up. I can hear the TV making squealing noises and there's bacon in the air. I clamber sloppily out of bed, down my metal ladder and into the living room. Rosie is up already and she's making me breakfast. I can hear her singing in the kitchen over the cartoons on the television. She comes out of the kitchen wearing my yellow apron, cup of tea in one hand and a plate of croissants in the other.

"Morning chicken!" she says happily, "Come and 'ave

some breakfast." I grimace and throw myself down on to the settee.

"Rosie, thanks," is all I can manage to say. I feel crumpled and sticky.

"We've got croissants to start with, and bacon, egg and tomatoes on toast in a minute," she says briskly, putting the croissants down in front of me with a mug of tea. It's the 'I Love Ammanford' mug, I'm not sure if this is a good sign or not. The mug was a present from an ex-boyfriend from Ammanford. I can suddenly feel a stabbing pain in the right side of my head, in the temple. I realise I'm too hungover for omens so I have a sip of my tea instead.

"What time are you working today, love?" I call out to Rosie. She returns from the kitchen with our plates of food and says,

"I'm off today, I *did* tell you last night but you probably can't remember can you?" I shake my head and then stop because it hurts so much.

"What are we up to today then?" I ask Rosie, trying my best to perk myself up. The sunlight sends rays through my net curtains, filtered by my cheeseplant, they make lovely shadows on the floor.

I feel half inclined to dance over them, but know that I can't make myself get up from my settee.

"I thought we might go to the museum. What do you think?" Rosie asks me. I am suddenly a lot better, the world has opened above my head again and the sun is helping to evaporate my headache.

It's nearly two o'clock now, and I'm waiting for Rosie outside a phone box as she calls her Dad. I can hear them having a mini argument so I walk on a bit, motioning to Rosie that I will be over there. I'm looking over at the castle walls, trying to imagine laying siege to it, how difficult it would be to conquer. I read in one of my Mam's history books about all the different ways invaders would try to get over castle walls, I'm thinking none would work on *these* walls: too high, too thick and probably too well guarded. I've never been inside Cardiff castle. I've lived here for nearly six months and I've never been inside. I was in a pub right opposite it last night and I didn't even look over at it. All these years of visiting Cardiff for Christmas presents and tops that no one in Llanelli would own are swilling around me like floodwater. I go back to where Rosie is still on the phone, she hangs up as I walk over there.

"Grr!" she grunts, a tear in each eye, "He's *always* like this whenever I go away. We argue like hell for the last week, and then I get a text message telling me how much he loves me and how proud he is of me." I take her arm and draw her in to a half hug,

"Don't worry babe, he'll get used to it eventually." We both smile, "But I bloody won't!" Her smile widens and she suggests lunch, my stomach growls approval, "Let's go and eat it in the castle grounds," I suggest, so we make our way to the market to buy ham and tomato cobs. I imagine I'm a vampire looking at the various people in the market, wondering how they would taste. So many flavours for a Cardiff vampire to choose from: Welsh of course, Indian, Chinese, so many East Europeans, redheads, Aryan blondes, dark little Celts, Somali, Sikh, Swansea tastes. A boy couldn't make his mind up which to choose first. I would probably go for a redhead, pale skin and blue/green eyes, golden hair dusted onto icing white skin. I suppress a shudder and pay for my cob and diet coke.

We walk arm in arm back through the market and on to the castle. Rosie shoots a look of disgust at the American tourists paying to get in through the gates,

"I'm not paying to share space with them," she says turning her nose up, but only managing to make herself even more beautiful and elf-like. I laugh and agree, so we sit behind a planter filled with bloody flowers and I am reminded of my t-shirt last night. We sit down on our coats watching as people file on to the Cardiff sightseeing buses, we wave at the people on the top deck, they wave back happily and some Japanese businessmen take our photo. I feel like I'm in a film, just waiting for Barbara Windsor to pop out of a nearby bush, giggling. When she doesn't appear, I offer to roll the fags, Rosie declines and mimes smoking a large cigar. I roll my eyes but still put my tin away.

We have to do some creative rearrangement so Rosie is hidden from people walking past on the pavement as she builds a joint.

"Why did you move to Cardiff?" she asks me, plucking some fragrant green leaves from a little baggie, the smell reminds me of rosemary.

"What do you mean?" I ask.

"Well, why Cardiff? Why not Swansea?" she asks me, I shrug my shoulders,

"It's just the place you move to, isn't it?" I say. The sky is so blue today, and the noises of the city have a happy cheerful tinge to them, even the exhaust fumes take on a pretty violet colour. "Of course, I moved to be nearer you too, honey."

"I was *waitin'* to hear that!" said Rosie, raising her eyebrows in a mock warning."

"Why did *you* move here then?" I ask her as she lights up, the pale blue smoke makes me think of incense.

"Well, after Uni it was logical to stay here. I just had to keep remindin' you to come and stay with me." We stayed silent for a while, each thinking about nothing much in particular. "I was so fed up of Llanelli, the whole small-town thing. Cardiff is the Metropolis of Wales, like." Rosie beamed as if she'd made an excellent discovery.

"It's hardly a Metropolis though, is it?" I asked her, sunshine bleaching everything around us into washed-out colours. I recall Kahu saying something lovely the first night I met him about what he first thought of Cardiff when they moved here from New Zealand: he said it's big enough to be a city, but small enough to feel like a town. I didn't know what he meant at the time, but I get it now. I'm a smalltown boy like Kahu, and London scares me when I go there, but

Cardiff has that town thing where old ladies who live next door to you call round with a parcel that they took off the postman for you that morning. I really love that.

Rosie and I finish our joint and head for home after a few more minutes. We both have to get some real sleep, and I know that she has overtime tomorrow helping out with the stocktaking. On the way back to Roath, we stop at every street corner to look at the street names on the corners of buildings. It's a special font that I suspect was designed for Cardiff County Council, back when they were all put up, shiny and new and forever. I wish someone would turn that font into a downloadable one on the Internet, like they did with the London Underground one – I have it on my computer, it's called Paddington. If I had the Cardiff font, I would use it exclusively: for all my letters, in work, on my website, or even to write my shopping lists.

I've been without Rosie for nearly a week and it's killing me, no exaggeration, I really mean it. I haven't been this serious in God knows how long, she's taken my silliness away to Australia with her. I hope those Aussies are enjoying it.

I'm sitting in the Owain Glyndwr, on the same table Rosie and me used to sit at. Even the table looks less clean now that she's gone, all of Cardiff has suddenly become messier and dirtier, nobody feels that they need to make an effort now that she isn't here to look at them or their tables. I've had one email and no phone call yet, I can't take being here alone so I get up to leave, maybe get a video out tonight and a bottle of wine.

The Slug and Lettuce looks busy, brightly coloured people spilling out onto the street, wearing crisp-packet clothes and pints of frothy beer on their heads, it makes me laugh. By the time I get to the top of Queen Street a clown has followed me and walks behind me pulling the same fed-up frown as I'm wearing. He sticks the tips of his white-gloved hands into the corners of his down turned mouth, and makes a smile. His hand reaches into his coat and brings out a magically produced paper flower, which he presents with a flourish. I accept it, and the smile that it brings to my face, gratefully. Outside Boots, a tall skinny young man plays guitar and sings, his guitar playing is amazing but his voice is terrible. I throw a fifty pence piece into his already quite full guitar bag, and he works the words 'thank you' into the Charlatans song he's singing. I smile at him and raise my hand.

What are you doing? I ask Cardiff, in my head obviously, I don't want people thinking I'm touched. Are you trying to make me smile because you know I'm feeling sad? I'm at Sainsbury's now and there's a tiny man selling the Big Issue. I give him two pounds and tell him to keep the change, it is the guy's last one after all and nobody else was in a hurry to buy it from him. He asks me if I'm sure and I tell him yes of course, I'm happy that such a little, easy gesture can make a person smile like he is now. I sigh, and I'm still sighing past the Mayor's house on Richmond Road, she'll be back in a year.

Don't worry Rosie, I'll keep Cardiff warm for you.

Herbert Williams
Brief Encounter

WHAT IT IS, I'm mindin my own business when this bloke from the paper knocks the door an starts askin me a lorra questions. So I asks im in an makes im a cuppa, I don' like standin on the doorstep, there's too many eyes watchin. He's norra bad bloke either 'cept he's got big teeth an you can't see is eyes proper behind them glasses of is.

He sits there lookin awkward an you can tell he's never been this side of Leo's in is life an it makes you laugh, the ole soddin thing. Anyway, he wants to know all about me, ow many kids I got an what I gets from the Social an even what I thinks of Tony Blair. I'm telling you there int much he don' wanna know. I'm thinkin next minute he's gonna ask me if I'm getting it reglar an there's no way I'm gonna tell im things like that, no way at all.

But no, he goes on to other marrers like the slates offa roof an that damp patch I been goin on about for years without no-one doin' nothin about it an the way everythin round here looks like a tip an the vandalism an that. An I tells im straight, you don' find no councillors down here 'cept at election times an even then they don' stay longer than they as to. They drives round shoutin the odds but where do they live theirselves, up in Cyncoed or Lisvane an places like that. You don' find em down the Ruperra on a Sat'dy night or even the Moorlands. Well that's up to them an I don' blame em livin somewhere nice but that's not to say they gorra pretend the sun shines outa their arse because it don'.

Anyway, this man from the paper sits there takin it all in an lookin real serious like I was Lady Muck or summ'n an I says Here, what's this for, an he says I told you what, we're doin summ'n on social whatsit an to tell you the truth I don' know what he means, it's one of them long words that social worker used to throw out till they gives er a new pitch somewhere else. Well why come to me I says, there's plenny others livin round here an he says I didn', not specially, I just knocks your door opin' someone was in. Thank you very much I says, a bit sarky like, cos though you may not wanna be picked out special it's better than bein just tipped outa the barrel. And just then Debbie comes ome and starts chopsin as usual an givin me funny looks like she thinks I'm up to summ'n with this bloke. I tell you kids today ave got one-track minds and you knows what sorta track I means. So I sends er across the road for some ciggies an then Gary comes in bawlin is head off an I tell you I've ad a gutsful, I've ad it right up to here. So anyway I says, ow about a cuppa an he says that's OK by me an he puts down is biro an starts talkin to Gary, calmin im like. An Gary takes to this bloke, there's summ'n about im, you can tell he's used to kids like, they're not just summ'n that gets under your feet like a loada dirt. An I asks im, ow many you got then, an he says three, two boys an a girl. That's nice I says, ow old they now then, an he says the oldest is eight or nine, to tell you the truth I can't remember now what he did say exactly. But it was real nice talkin to im, it's ages since I talked to anyone like that, well I mean Mick an me don' talk we just fights arf the time an when he's over the wall like he is now we don' talk at all.

Next thing you knows Debbie's back with the ciggies an I opens the pack an offers im one but he says no thanks I give em up las' Frid'y an I says only las *Frid'y* an he says yeh don' tempt me an I laughs cos if it was me I'd be eatin the flamin packet, too right I would. So I lights up an Debbie says can I ave one all cheeky like an I tells er to sod off an she gives me a bitta lip. So I swipes er one, at least I tries to but she's like a whippet that one and outa the ouse before you can say knife. An Gary's just sittin there quiet as a lamb an next thing I know this bloke's got im on is lap an is talkin to im real nice like he was is own father or summ'n.

Anyway, I makes the tea an we sits there drinkin it. Real nice it is. Soothin. An I thinks ow nice it'd be livin like this alla time, just nice an quiet, no fussin or quarrellin. An I wonders what is missus thinks of im bein in a job like that, lookin up strange women an goin into their ouses. I tell you if it was my ole man I'd be givin im the once-over every night of the week. But I suppose you gets used to it. Or maybe you doesn'. An anyway it's no business of mine so I stops thinkin about it, at least I tries to stop thinkin but I can't really cos it's there at the back of my mind, naggin an worryin me like one of them cold sores you gets on your lip inna winter. An I'm thinkin then ow nice it'd be to go upstairs with a bloke like that, yes I knows what you're thinkin but I don' mean that, what I means is jus lie there an stroke each other an talk a bit. Cos he seems so kind. An considerate. Yeh. That's what he seems like then. Kind an considerate.

Then Gary gets restless an wriggles off is lap an this bloke goes on talkin, not making notes or nothin just talkin. An I tells im everythin, I'm not kiddin. Everythin. About our Dad with is rhubarb an our Ernie with is bike an Uncle Tom with is accordion, an ow our Mam used to stuffa turkey at Christmas an the time Auntie Mabel runs off with the man with one arm from the war. Christ I even tells im that, God knows why, I musta been barmy. But I tells him orright an I got the bruises to show for it. Like I says, it was so nice just sittin there talkin. Not doin nothin. Just talkin. Like we was human beings. Not dumb animals like they treats you up at the Social.

But at last he ups an says he as to be goin. Yeh. Goin. An I'm really sorry cos he seems real nice, the sorta bloke you can trust. An I feels lonely when he's gone. Real lonely. An that night I lies awake, thinkin about im. Lyin with is missus in a posh house in Cyncoed or Lanishen or wherever. Lyin with er. Makin love possibly. An then I thinks about Mick, in is stinkin cell in Adamsdown. Stinkin rotten pit you wouldn put the cat in. An I thinks about the judge who put im in there. Sittin there with is stupid wig an is big bum an is pot belly. Sendin im down for five years. An the way the copper grabs old of im, grabs im by the arm as if he's a loada dirt and shoves im down outa sight. An me up there inna gallery cryin my art out.

Oh yes I thinks about that. An I cries again, honest. I cries till there's no cryin left in me. All because of this bloke from the paper. An I goes to sleep at last clutchin the pillow. Like a flamin kid aye. Clutchin the pillow pretendin it's Mick. God what a night. I'm glad to see mornin.

An the next thing I knows, it's a day or two later an Sadie from over the road's wavin the paper in fronta my face. Hey kid you seen this she says, you're famous, you're all over the paper. An I looks at it an there I am, my name an all, even the kids, everythin I flamin said is there in black and white. God elp I says, I'm not avin this, I'll ave their guts for garters you see if I don'. You will too says Sadie, I knows you will, they got no right. You show em kid she says, stirrin it up like. An

I tells er to bog off an leave me to it, an she gets all uffy an grabs er paper back off me, an I as to go out an buy another but I don' mind cos she gets on my nerves. An I think everyone's lookin at me, honest to God I does, cos the things they puts in there int fit to print, I tell you no word of a lie. An I sees is name over it, an I thinks you rotten stinkin swine, comin to my ouse an sittin there takin it all in an puttin it down like I'm a loada dirt, some animal or summ'n. Cos that's what it means. He thinks I don' count. Just cos I int got the brains he as. Just cos I lives where I does. Just cos my boyfriend's over the wall. Just cos of everythin. An I don' care what he is, Labour or Conservative or anythin, what he did's a rotten mean trick an I don' care who knows it. Cos he didn' care for me at all. He couldn ave. He didn think nothin of me. Nor of Gary. Nor Debbie. Nor any of us in the ole soddin' street. Because he did it to the lot of us. Not just to me. The ole lot of us. Even mouthy Sadie, if she only knew it. An I thinks of goin up to the paper an givin them a mouthful, but I doesn. Cos you can't win with the likes of them. I knows it. An don' tell me you can cos I knows better. I wasn born yes'dy. Nor the day before for that marrer.

So I just stays where I am. Opin' it'll all blow over. Puttin up with the nasty looks an the remarks. You knows the sorta thing. *Some people'll do anythin to get their names inna paper.* Not sayin it to me straight out like but I knows what they're sayin about me orright. God ow I ates 'em. You finds out who your friends are at a time like that, I can tell you that for nothin.

Of course it dies down, after a week or two. They can't go on talkin about me for ever like, can they? Even Sadie can't do that. But I don' forget. Oh no. You don' forget a thing like that.

But I keeps the paper. You bet. I keeps the bleedin paper, with is name in big letters. An is photo an all. An one day I sees im in St Mary Street, walkin with is missus. I sees im a mile off an I knows im straight off. I tell you I'd know im if I seen im in the pitch dark in the middle of the desert. An I goes up to im an says, ullo I says, ow are you this long time? An he looks at me blank. Honest to God he does. An is missus gives im a queer look an the devil gets into me. An I says, when you comin back then love, didn you like it the first time? An he goes all red an catches is missus's arm an tries to urry er on, but she pulls back an stares at me an says, what you talkin about? An I says, he knows, you ask im. Real evil like. An he starts coughin an splutterin an says, I never seen er before in my life, I don' know er, I never met er. An I laughs like a drain an says, shoutin it out so all the soddin street can hear me, Twenny quid everythin off! Twenny quid! God elp me love, I says, he wasn worth twenny pence. An everyone's starin. An she goes white as a sheet, is missus. An suddenly it clicks with im – he knows who I am. An is missus looks at im an she sees it in is face, she knows he knows who I am. An she puts er ands over er face. An I scarpers. Jus scarpers. Because of the crowd. Because of what I've done. Because I'm scared. Jesus I'm scared. An I practically runs. I goes up the arcade like a whippet, pushin an shovin, thinkin the fuzz is gonna catch up with me any minute. I just keeps goin like the clappers, not seein nothin or no-one, just keeps goin cos I'm scared of what I done. An I gets on the first bus I sees an before I knows it I'm up by Roath Park, an I gets out an walks round an round till suddenly my legs give way an I as to sit down. An I wonder what the ell got into me, to do a thing like that.

But I'm not sorry. Oh no, I'm norra bit sorry. Cos he ad it comin, din he? He took advantage of me. He took advantage somethin rotten.

But er? Well... I gotta tell you, I do feel sorry for *er*. Cos she looked quite nice, far as I could see any road. Yeh. Very nice. But I keeps thinkin about er... the way she looked at me... an ow she put er ands up over er face...

But she ad to be warned. Cos I meanta say, a bloke who does a thing like that will do anythin, won' he? Well, won' he?

John Williams
The Legend of Tiger Bay

TIGER BAY was the original pirate town. The way I heard it as a child, the real old-time pirates, Captain Morgan and his crew, used this promontory off the then small town of Cardiff as a base: a little piece of Britain that was beyond the law. God knows whether it's true or whether my addled memory has simply cobbled together a new myth out of two or three old ones, but still, it's a legend that suits the wild side of the Welsh.

What we know for sure is that Butetown, not yet Tiger Bay, came out of the Industrial Revolution: in the 1840s the Marquis of Bute ran a railway from the new mines of the south Wales valleys to the Bristol Channel, coming out at Cardiff, by the mouth of the River Taff. Huge new docks were built at the end of the promontory, and the nascent city spread south to meet them. They called this settlement between the docks and the town Butetown, after the man whose coffers it was filling. And from the beginning the arrangement of railway lines, Bristol Channel and river was such that there was a natural division between Butetown and the rest of Cardiff.

In those early days, though, Butetown was the heart of Cardiff. Mount Stuart Square, at the entrance to the docks, was the city's commercial hub and Loudoun Square, in the heart of Butetown, was among the city's smartest addresses, boasting a Young Ladies' Seminary as well as providing a home for the shipwrights, builders, master mariners and merchants, the new aristocrats of a seafaring city.

The second half of the nineteenth century saw Cardiff expand at a breathtaking rate. By the end of the century it was one of the world's biggest, busiest ports. The sheer number of ordinary seamen using the port forced changes in the area's make up. The smart houses of Loudoun Square were converted into seamen' s lodging houses, the merchant classes retreated into the main body of the city which soon sprouted smart northern suburbs, and the seafaring supremos, the ships' captains and so on, congregated around the southern tip of the island, in smart streets like Windsor Esplanade.

By now Butetown was home to a fair cross-section of the world's seafaring peoples – Chinese, Lascars, Levantines, Norwegians, Maltese, Spaniards and all. A wild and licentious community was emerging, finding worldwide fame as 'Tiger Bay'. Black seamen too, both from East Africa and the West Indies, were a part of this cosmopolitan mix, the first of them arriving as early as 1870, and by 1881 being numerous enough to have their own Seamen's Rest. By the time of the beginning of the First World War, there were around seven hundred coloured seamen in Cardiff, though this was still a mostly transient population of men without families.

The war changed everything. Many of Tiger Bay's citizens joined the war effort. Seamen went into the Navy and Merchant Navy. The *Western Mail* reported, in 1919, that fourteen hundred black seamen from Cardiff lost their lives in the war (which also demonstrates the somewhat unreliable statistics nature of the era's statistics – there having allegedly been only seven hundred black people in Cardiff). Others joined the Army, the West Indian regiments or the Cardiff City Battalion. A Mr Rees recalled, in the *South Wales Echo*, that: "All the boys of military age joined up and most of them paid the penalty, some at the Dardanelles, and a lot with the Cardiff City Battalion at Mametz Wood."

Conscription into the army also left a huge gap in the domestic labour force and, at the same time, East African trading ships were being requisitioned for the Navy, leaving a pool of unemployed sailors. So in Cardiff, as also happened in Liverpool, factory jobs were opened up to the seamen. Unsurprisingly, now that they were based in Cardiff for a substantial period of time, the sailors began to put down roots and to make the first moves towards an integration into the wider community – one aspect of which was the forging of relationships with local women. This last development foreshadowed the GI bride phenomenon of the Second World War, except for the crucial distinction that this time the exotic suitors were not intending to whisk their brides across the ocean, but were planning to stay put in Butetown.

Trouble came with the war's end. The soldiers returned, unemployment loomed. Black workers were thrown out of their factory jobs, and seafaring work was likewise in high demand. Black unemployment rapidly became chronic and meanwhile general white unemployment became one of the key issues of the day. In some cities, notably Glasgow where John MacLean, 'the British Lenin', held sway, the whiff of communist revolution was in the air, and the government was briefly terrified. In seafaring cities like Cardiff and Liverpool, however, the racial minority was fitted up for the role of scapegoat.

Racial tensions first began to appear among the returning soldiers. Peter Fryer in his remarkable and ground-breaking history of the black presence in Britain, *Staying Power*, tells the awful tale of an incident in a veterans' hospital in Liverpool in which five hundred white soldiers set upon the fifty black inmates, many of whom were missing at least one limb. A pitched battle was fought with crutches and walking sticks as the principal weapons (though not all the white soldiers sided with the racists: a contemporary account, in the *African Telegraph*, records that 'When the (military police) arrived on the scene to restore order, there were many white soldiers seen standing over crippled black limbless soldiers, and protecting them with their sticks and crutches from the furious onslaught of the other white soldiers until order was restored'.)

If the Belmont Hospital affair had an element of cruel farce, much of what followed was tragic. In the summer of 1919, in South Shields and Liverpool and Cardiff, Britain's first race riots of the modern era broke out. The post-war slump provided the conditions for these mass outbreaks of racist violence – and Fryer clearly demonstrates that these riots consisted of white mobs randomly attacking blacks –

but it was generally sex that provided the flash point. The returning troops could easily be goaded into believing that 'their' women were being stolen. Whites would repeatedly claim, as justification for assault, that blacks had been 'making suggestive remarks to our women' or some such. And the newspapers were swift to follow this line. Fryer records a *Liverpool Courier* editorial pontificating that:

> One of the chief reasons of popular anger behind the present disturbances lies in the fact that the average Negro is nearer the animal than is the average white man, and that there are women in Liverpool who have no self-respect.

The 1919 race riots were not simply regrettable occurrences from the far-off days but rather the crucible in which Britain's subsequent racial pathology was formed. The cry for tribal solidarity to protect their jobs from these 'outsiders' was overlaid with sexual hysteria; not simply 'they're taking our women' but 'they're taking our women because they're sex-beasts'. This hysteria presumably arose from a combination of black people having long been caricatured as apelike or bestial, and the legacy of Victorian prudery that regarded sex as a bestial activity. Certainly what emerged was the potent construction of blackness as both an economic and a sexual threat.

According to Fryer the flash point of the Cardiff riot on 11 June 1919 was, ironically enough, 'A brake containing black men and their white wives, returning from an excursion, attracted a large and hostile crowd'. However, a recently unearthed account, written by a policeman present at the time, gives a rather less genteel and more detailed account. According to PC Albert Allen (as reprinted in the *South Wales Echo*):

> I was the only PC on duty at the Wharf when it started and I was on duty the whole time it lasted in the Docks area. First of all I would like to point out the cause. In

Cardiff there were quite a number of prostitutes and quite a number of pimps who lived on their earnings. When conscription came into force these pimps were called up. Then a number of prostitutes went to the Docks district and lived with these coloured people who treated them very well. When the war finished the pimps found their source of income gone as the prostitutes refused to go back to them. The night the trouble started, about 8.30 p.m., a person who I knew told me to expect some trouble. I asked him why and he explained that the coloured men had taken the prostitutes on an outing to Newport in two horse wagons and that a number of pimps were waiting for their return.

Next, by Allen's account, the pimps attacked the wagons near the Monument – at the edge of the city centre and fifty yards or so from the Bute Street bridge which signals the beginning of Butetown – and a pitched battle ensued before police reinforcements dispersed the crowd and attempted to cordon off Butetown. What was by now an angry white mob, among them many armed demobilised soldiers, then proceeded to rampage around the town looking for blacks to assault. Some managed to get past the police lines and into Butetown, where they smashed the windows of Arab boarding houses.

This initial disturbance petered out around midnight, but the rioting was to continue for several more days. On the second day a Somali boarding house in the centre of town was burnt down and its inhabitants badly beaten. More boarding houses were then burnt down in Bute Street, and an Arab beaten to death. On the third day, a white mob gathered once more in the centre of town and prepared for another assault on Butetown.

This time, however, Butetown was ready for them. If its position on an isthmus at the bottom of the city made Butetown a convenient ghetto, it also made it a fortress. There was only one easy way in from the town centre, via

Bute Street itself, and the other approaches, from East Moors and Grangetown, could be easily watched, so armed sentries were posted – the blacks too having brought their weapons home from the war – and the community waited. As a South Wales News reporter saw it on 14 June 1919:

> The coloured men, while calm and collected, were well prepared for any attack, and had the mob from the city broken through the police cordon there would have been bloodshed on a big scale... Hundreds of Negroes were collected, but these were very peaceful, and were amicably discussing the situation amongst themselves. Nevertheless, they were in a determined mood and ready to defend 'our quarter of the city' at all costs... Long-term black residents said: It will be hell let loose if the mob comes into our streets... if we are unprotected from hooligan rioters who can blame us for trying to protect ourselves?

Their defence was successful and the rioting died away over the next few days, leaving in its wake three dead and many more injured, but a decisive corner had been turned. The authorities' only response to the troubles was to offer to repatriate the black community. Around six hundred black men took up the offer within the next few months, though many of the returning West Indians went back with the express intention of citing anti-British feeling. And, indeed, within days of some of the Cardiff seamen returning to Trinidad, fighting against white sailors broke out, followed by a major dock strike.

The majority, however, decided to stay on, to make a permanent home on this ground they'd fought for. But from this point on Butetown was not simply a conventional ghetto or a colourful adjunct to the city's maritime life, but effectively an island. It was not simply a black island: the area had always had a white Welsh population and continued to do so. There was an Irish presence too, as well as Chinese, Arab and European sailors, and refugees from successive

European conflicts as well. And as the black or coloured population was initially almost exclusively male, Butetown rapidly became a predominantly mixed-race community, almost unique in Britain, the New Orleans of the Taff delta, home of the Creole Celts. But this integration was firmly confined to Tiger Bay: above the Bute bridge you were back in the same hidebound old Britain.

The following twenty years before the next great war did nothing but further entrench the racial segregation. What soon became known as the 'colour bar' came down to deal with black immigration. Industry was almost entirely closed to blacks and seafaring jobs were made ever harder to obtain by cynical manipulation of nationality laws. In Cardiff the police arbitrarily interpreted the Aliens Order of 1920 to mean that any coloured person was *de facto* an alien. If they produced a British passport to prove otherwise, it would simply be seized and thrown away. And, as if times were not hard enough already, the slump of 1929 simply saw economic matters go from bad to worse.

So trapped as they were between the bigots and the murky green sea, the people of Butetown had to construct their own economy, based on catering to the traditional desires of men who have spent the last few months on the ocean wave. The community that emerged, though economically deprived and rife with disease, was possessed of a vitality that is remembered with great fondness by virtually all those who lived there in the inter-war period. Harold Fowler was born in Butetown in 1905, the son of a West Indian seaman and a Welsh ship captain's daughter. Talking to the South Wales Echo in 1970 he recalled that "Bute Road used to be like St Mary Street. It had jewellers' shops, restaurants, big poultry stores, laundries, music shops… There was always lots of music in Tiger Bay. The sailors and the prostitutes used to drink and dance in the pubs and cafes. And there was Louis Facitto's barber shop. He had an automatic piano with bells and drums attached to it. You put a penny in and it played to you."

Noise was always one of the community's defining characteristics. Mrs Bahia Johnson remembers in her unpublished memoir of living in Tiger Bay in the thirties, "On almost every door there were cages with screaming parrots and cockatoos. Were they able to talk! Believe me, they put many a seaman's language in the shade. Many people were forbidden to put them outside their homes. Tiny canaries sang in their little cages. There were men with little monkeys on their shoulders. They wore little red hats and gloves. Often a barrel organ would be wheeled around the streets with a little monkey on top. In the Roaring Twenties, Bute Street was like a Persian market..."

Tiger Bay's landmarks were its pubs. Eleven of them crammed into the neighbourhood: The Freemason's Arms (better known to one and all as the Bucket of Blood), the Rothesay Castle (or House of Blazes), the Adelphi Hotel, the Loudoun Hotel, the Glamorgan Hotel, the Bute Tavern, the Peel Hotel, the Cardigan Hotel, the Bute Castle Hotel, the Marchioness of Bute and the Westgate Hotel.

Wally Towner, long-time landlord of the Freemason's, admitted that its nickname was not undeserved:

> We had some tough times down there all right. It was nothing for a couple of pounds worth of glasses to go in one night. I had a shillelagh behind the bar and I used to use it now and then. There was a big coloured girl there. She could knock a man out and think nothing of it. She came to my rescue many times. One night there was a brawl in the smoke room. One chap was out on the floor. She'd given him one. I got a siphon and squirted it in his face.
>
> That was a general occurrence. If they fought in the pub you just had to wade in and take a chance. Once one of the prostitutes saved my life. She took off her stiletto shoe and hit them over the head while I got up. There were the girls there of course.
>
> They lived for the day, they would make a lot of money and live it up, but some mornings they'd come

in with black eyes, the pimps had given them those if they hadn't made enough.

The girls used to quarrel sometimes. One day I saw some of them fighting, clawing at each other. I put two in the gents' toilet, two in the ladies' toilet and I told them not to come out till they'd finished scrapping. "I'll give a bottle of wine to the winner," I said. My pub was a great one for the vino, 6d a glass. The police were marvellous down there. They didn't always lock them up. They just used to take them round the back and give them a damn good hiding. They can't do that today, poor fellows. And of course the boys used to come down from the valleys to see the place and see the girls. They were looking for trouble.

One of those Valleys boys, 'Charlie' as he called himself in the *Echo*, remembers his first visits to Tiger Bay:

I went down there first because it was such a contrast with my home town of Merthyr. Merthyr was very drab at the time. It was a distressed area. I joined the army in 1926 to get away from the place and they sent me to Maindy Barracks in Cardiff. On our nights out the more adventurous of us dodged the military police and went down Tiger Bay. There were honky-tonks from one end of Bute Street to the other. It was great, so gay and colourful. We were 'seeing life', as we called it. We went in the back rooms and danced with the girls... The inevitable happened. I got caught and had a dose of detention. When I came out I decided to join with some of the real boys of the bay. I thought, "This is the life for me", and I sold my uniform to a docker. So I'd burned my boats good and proper. (A career in petty crime ensued until) two of us got caught in a tobacconist's shop in Pontypridd and were remanded to await trial at the assizes. The girls visited us with cigarettes and tobacco. I got three months and naturally returned to my friends in the Bay. I was met at the nick gate and given a few bob and a good booze-up in the Freemason's, the haunt of pimps, prostitutes, wide boys and queers.

But, like Wally Towner, Charlie had scarcely a bad word to say for the police of the time. "There was a comradeship. They were out to get us and we were out to get them. We had very great respect for each other. In those days we believed that if a copper and another fellow were having a go, let them have a go. But if three or four boys were beating up a policeman we'd go to his aid. And if three or four cops set on one man, we'd help him."

And it's the same story from old-time Bay cops like William Rees, who started out as a Tiger Bay copper in 1921, stayed there till 1941, and finally retired as Chief Constable of Stockport. "I made more friends down there than anywhere else, real genuine friends", he recalls. "The great thing was knowing how to speak to them. If you spoke officiously you could expect trouble. But if you treated them like a pal you got your evidence. Of course there was trouble now and then, but there was far more violence in other parts of Cardiff, such as Caroline Street and Wood Street."

Butetown even had more flamboyant cops than the rest of Cardiff. Mr Rees remembers a detective called Gerry Brobell: "He was a famous figure in his khaki breeches, leggings and trilby hat. And he always had a pipe. He used to walk around in uniform with a pipe in his mouth. Time was of no consequence to him. He used to roll up at half past ten or eleven in the morning but nobody knew when he went off duty. Maybe two or three in the morning. He was a fount of information. He always knew where to get it. He was always behind the curtains, so to speak."

Butetown's most celebrated curtains were those of the Chinese community. "From 190 to 198 Bute Street was all Chinese houses," recalls Harold Fowler. "The Chinese were great gamblers – and many of them used to travel down from their laundries in the Valleys to Tiger Bay to play paka pu, a kind of lottery game with numbers, and fan tan, played with shells.

"At the back of one or two of those houses were opium dens. There used to be bunks in those rooms with curtains around and several opium pipes. A man sitting at the table would put a ball in the pipe and light it for them and then they used to be down on a bunk and dream their dreams."

Well respected though the police may have been, it was within the community that the real arbiters of right and wrong were found. Community leaders of real authority emerged. Chief among them were a West Indian boarding-house master and a man noted for his diligence in fighting for the rights of black seamen.

In the late 1930s Tiger Bay was graced with the presence of a more celebrated black leader. Paul Robeson, the great American singer, actor and communist who came to Britain to appear in two films – Hollywood of course having little use for black men at the time, except as eyeball-rolling Stepin Fetchits – *The Proud Valley* and *Sanders of the River*. In Butetown actor/writer Neil Sinclair's wonderful memoir-cum-history 'The Tiger Bay Story' he remembers that "Robeson found a welcome in Tiger Bay, where he made several visits to the Jason home on the west side of Loudoun Square. There he used to visit the African-American activist Aaron Mossell who lodged there."

The film that brought Robeson to South Wales was *The Proud Valley*, a charming if unsurprisingly sentimental tale of a black seaman landing up in a Valleys mining village, over-coming prejudice to become a stalwart of the choir (Robeson remains an enduring favourite with the still mighty choirs of the Valleys) and ending up with the immortal line, "we're all black down the pit".

Robeson was the only black face in *The Proud Valley*, but *Sanders of the River* called for two hundred and fifty black extras, and Tiger Bay provided many of them – including among them, remarkably enough, the future Kenyan revolutionary leader Jomo Kenyatta, then a penniless anthropology student living in London. Sinclair recalls, 'Everyone knew the witchdoctor dancing wildly in the African village was Mr Graham from Sophia Street. And that was Uncle Willy Needham in the loincloth that he kept for years after. The little black baby Robeson held in his arms was Deara Williams. Deara went on to become an exotic dancer with an act including a boa constrictor. And we all waited for the 'River Boat Song' to begin so we could all join in. "Iyee a ko, I yi ge de," we would chant in unison with Paul and all the African boatmen. Some twenty years later you could often see a gang of Bay boys on a separated timber log, singing the 'River Boat Song', rowing across the lake of the timber float, a little south of west Canal Wharf."

And then there was another great upheaval. The Second World War rolled around and once again black faces were grudgingly invited into the factories. Meanwhile Tiger Bay's reputation was such that black American GIs would converge on Cardiff from all over Britain when they had some leave. So throughout the hostilities it was business as usual in the world of illicit leisure.

After the war, the decline of the shipping industry was a devastating blow to the community. It deprived residents of both seafaring jobs and the money brought in by visiting sailors. But still, for a while Butetown continued to flourish. Mass immigration from the West Indies began, and at first Cardiff was one of the major destinations, a place where newcomers could be sure of a friendly welcome – to this day Cardiff remains a haven for Somali refugees.

In the fifties a new arrival could stroll down Bute Street and find, in rapid succession, the Cuban Cafe, the Ghana Club, Send Lee's Laundry, the Somali People's restaurant and Hamed Hamed's grocers. The House of Blazes and the Bucket of Blood were still open for business. And, for a place to stay, there was, for instance, the Cairo Hotel, run by Arab ex-seaman Ali Salaiman and his wife Olive, a valleys Methodist who converted to Islam and whose five daughters, in true Butetown style married an Arab, a Welshman, a Maltese, an Englishman and Dutch Muslim.

One of the new arrivals was a young Trinidadian called Michael de Freitas, who was later to achieve brief fame as Britain's apostle of Black Power, Michael X, and later still was to be hung for murder, back home in Trinidad, under the name of Michael Abdul Malik. His autobiography, published in 1968, is unsurprisingly self-justifying and generally economical with the truth, but it contains this fond reminiscence of life in Tiger Bay in the fifties:

The Bay was a world of its own, cut off from the rest of the city. A black world. It swarmed with West Indians, Arabs, Somalis, Pakistanis and a legion of half-caste children. In its food stores you could buy cassavas and red peppers and in the restaurants you could eat curries and rice dishes just like those in the West Indies.

The city's black people, who mostly worked in the docks, were the sweetest people I've ever met in Britain. They had a real friendliness. Everyone seemed to be married to everyone else's sister and they'd all sit on the doorsteps of their elegant, dilapidated old houses chatting and exchanging greetings... I usually lived with a half-caste family who cooked Trinidadian food and I would spend my time talking, going to the Friday night dance at the solitary dance hall, and watching the street gambling. This was illegal of course, but even the policemen had grown up in Tiger Bay, and when they saw a crowd standing in a circle they'd know a couple of men were in the middle shooting dice and they'd stroll in the other direction. They very rarely broke up a game.

There were a lot of old timers, old sea salts, in the Bay and when I sat around chatting with them they'd always tell me the same thing – to stay with the Norwegians and not get mixed up with the British ships because there was no future on them for a black man; he couldn't get anywhere.

For the same reason they seldom crossed the canal which formed a frontier between Tiger Bay and the rest of Cardiff. They preferred to stay in the family atmosphere away from the cold prejudice they met in the white world beyond... Like many other black people from Tiger Bay, I've had the experience of going up into the white town, standing in a bar and calling for a half pint and having the barman look straight through me and serve everyone else until there was nothing to do but leave.

Not that white people ever left Tiger Bay alone. They were always driving across the canal bridge at night and slumming it along Bute Street. They had the idea that the Bay was a den of vice and violence and they wanted to add a little spice to their lives. I don't think I ever saw a fight in Tiger Bay. All I remember are the smiling families on the doorsteps and the beautiful black children playing everywhere.

By the late fifties, slum clearance was the watchword in town planning, and Butetown was sure enough a slum, with its TB rate seven times that of the rest of the city. In 1957 the South African priest Trevor Huddlestone visited Butetown and found it to be a slum indeed but racially speaking, "a wonderful community".

Plans were drawn up for Butetown's redevelopment and Tiger Bay enjoyed a first flush of celebrity even as it was under sentence of extinction. A film called *Tiger Bay* was made, directed by J. Lee Thompson and based on the Howard Spring novel set around the turn of the century, with Hayley Mills as the plucky heroine. The filmmakers, however, took one look at the real *Tiger Bay* and opted to shoot most of the film in the genteel Edwardian seaside resort of Penarth instead. The real Tiger Bay did provide a host of extras and bit part actors, though, among them Neil Sinclair.

He recalls, "I was the boy that fought with Hayley in the film and prevented her from playing with us down at the Pier head. "Get back to London, Gilly Evans. You don't belong here!" I said. *Tiger Bay* is loved by the local inhabitants not so much for its story, although it is quite enthralling, as for its scenery. Everyone knew that Herbert Street was not actually in Tiger Bay, but we still thrill to see our Junie Fettah calypsoing down that street in the wedding celebration, to the strains of 'Never Make a Pretty Woman Your Wife'."

Meanwhile the real Tiger Bay gave its most celebrated protege to the world – the most histrionic of UK chanteuses, Miss Shirley Bassey. No matter that Bassey, though born in the Bay, actually grew up in another less romantically named neighbourhood, she made her name there, and 'the girl from Tiger Bay' had a rather better ring to it than "the superstar from Splott".

And then the axe came down. In the sixties, virtually all of the old Tiger Bay, the central portion of Butetown, was torn down and replaced with a combination of high- and low-rise council housing, leavened with a new community centre and a new mosque. Meanwhile Cardiff had dwindled to nothing as a port, and Butetown residents of whatever colour were lucky to get the most menial of jobs, faced as they were with blanket discrimination (as detailed by Dilip Hiro in his 1967 report for *New Society*). The community was henceforth simply ignored by the rest of the city, with just a couple of clubs left to attract the occasional intrepid outsider. When the *Echo* published its 1970 tribute to Tiger Bay all the interviewees seemed to take it for granted that the era was over. Betty Anderson, of the Adelphi, was typical in her lament: "There's no Tiger Bay now. The Tiger's dead. The life has gone, hasn't it?"

As was Harold Fowler when he said, "It was alive. It's gone, never to return, but it brings back memories. There used to be dancing and jollification. People made their own amusement then. Today they watch television. You can go down there now and it's like going into an estate like

Llanrumney." Mr Fowler was one of the many docks people who were moved to the new estates of Llanrumney and Llanederyn following the redevelopment.

But still there would be the occasional public reminder of times gone by. Butetown had always been known for its funerals – most celebrated of all being that of Peerless Jim Driscoll, the legendary Cardiff boxer, with a mile-long procession and a model boxing ring on top of the coffin. And all the stops were pulled out one more time for the 1978 funeral of Vic Parker, the Bay's very own jazz and blues guitarist, who was given a full New Orleans marching band send-off.

Butetown's decline ran slowly on into the eighties. The depleted community quietly endured massive unemployment, apparently cut off from the rest of the world, barely flickering during the riot 1981, evolving a Welsh Creole community out of time and out of town, notice, only when it came to the annual carnival and secure at least in the knowledge that it had little else to lose.

At least not until the prospect of Docklands redevelopment, long a rumour, at last became a reality.

That's how I left things twelve years ago, when I wrote the above. Back then Docklands redevelopment was still in the knocking things down phase and had barely begun on the rebuilding. Though at least it had been decided that there was to be rebuilding. Which was an improvement on the early eighties when swathes of the commercial heart of Docks were knocked down to make way for a flyover.

By the early nineties, though, waterfront development had become a buzzword for all the former ports of the west, and Cardiff had decided not to miss out. The Cardiff Bay Development Corporation was set up and a billion pounds spent on turning derelict dockland into born again marina. Much of the money was spent on the Bay Barrage, the vast structure that converted a tidal basin into a placid lake. The rest has been spent, in a rather stop go fashion, on land.

The County Council offices on Atlantic Wharf were the

outriders of progress, soon followed, in the mid 90s, by the Wharf pub and its stillborn environs. Next came the UCI cinema complex which, for the first time in a generation, did succeed in luring ordinary Cardiffians down to the Bay.

Then, as the barrage was finally completed at the turn of the millennium, the new lake was decorated with new structures like the St David's Hotel and the Mermaid Quay restaurant and bar complex, as well as rejuvenated docks buildings finding new life as yet more restaurants and bars. Just now they've been joined by the hulking structure of the Millennium Centre and one fine day, no doubt, there will be a brand new Assembly building too, more or less designed by Sir Richard Rogers.

And as for the Butetown community itself – how has it fared during these extraordinary changes? Well for starters it's shrunk. It has been shrinking for years, of course, ever since the sixties clearances, and the process has accelerated of late.

People wishing to move to larger council accommodation are invariably offered properties out of the area; the only new arrivals have been a new wave of immigrants from Somalia who have set up camp in the northern part of Butetown.

As for the pubs and nightspots that gave the community its reputation, they are now almost all gone. The Casablanca is now a parking lot. The Big Windsor now an upmarket Indian restaurant. The Docks Non-Political was fitted out with some striking murals and renamed the Baltimore and flourished for a while – especially the Friday night karaoke sessions – but at the time of writing its doors are closed. The Custom House and the North Star, of fond infamy, have both been bulldozed; the New Sea Lock likewise. The Dowlais has opened, closed, opened with bewildering rapidity. One evening I walked past it and saw a sign declaring it was soon to open as a theme bar called Ally McBeal's. The Hollywood copyright lawyers must have intervened because next time I passed it was a rock venue called the MS1. At time of writing it's still a rock venue but called the Engine Rooms, while, just up the road, The Coal Exchange has become, intermittently, another rock venue, used by the likes of Van Morrison and Southside Johnny.

So all is not dead. It's not time to write the funeral notices. the light goes out in one place but flickers back into life somewhere else. But what is surely the case is that Butetown is no longer a hidden quarter of the city, it no longer stands apart to anything like the degree it once did. It's now essentially just another run down inner city suburb with a few slightly iffy venues of its own, and an eating & drinking mall stuck on the end of it.

Butetown, then, is still here (and shows no sign of going anywhere), it is simply not what it was. And in many ways this is a good thing because what underpins it is another truth, that racism is not what it was either. The black and mixed-race people of Cardiff do not have to live below the bridge any longer, between the railway and the sea. And that is progress. In fact it is all undeniably progress, this transformation of the Bay. Where there was dereliction there is life, where there were no jobs there are some jobs, where there was mud there are sailing boats, where there were wading birds there are now, on sunny days at least, tourists. So what if much of the development is banal, off the peg, no different to every other waterfront development from here to Hartlepool? So what if the unique culture of the area is erased from the new development – with the single shining exception of Glen Jordan's wonderful Butetown History & Arts Centre. So what that Tiger Bay is now remembered only as history – replaced by something new and shiny, and determinedly without history, called Cardiff Bay?

Well so quite a lot – without memory and history we lack community and we lack soul. Community is something Cardiff has always been good at. But Tiger Bay gave it its soul. So let us remember it for sure, but let us also try to preserve something of its anarchistic tolerant, cosmopolitan soul in this new place that we have learned to call Cardiff Bay.

Nia Williams
The Great Bay Bridge

TWO SEAGULLS wheel and yodel outside the window as the rain begins again.

"Tell me stories."

My granddaughter presses herself deeper into the sofa, one leg swallowed into the cleft behind the cushion.

"What about?"

But I know what about. It's always the same.

"About before."

Eight years old and fascinated with the passage of time. She can spend hours scrutinising pictures of me as a child, as a teenager, a young woman – monitoring progress, comparing features, hair, similarities and changes. If we stop and talk to anyone on the street, anyone older than me, she'll gaze at their cracked faces and trace the curve of the shoulders, her mouth hanging softly open, her neat, miniature lower teeth revealed. And then, when they're out of earshot, the questions will start: who was she? What did she used to look like? What was it like in her day, Before?

Hammocks of grey cloud are bulging over the Bay. The windows mist over as the temperature drops. I hoik my sleeve over my hand and smear a space on the glass, though the weather is already veiling the spectacular view.

"Once upon a time" I say, peering through the murk, "Cardiff was a rich and important city".

Behind me, I can hear Meinir settling herself more comfortably.

"It had gardens and parks and grand, white buildings. It had a castle, where peacocks roamed the grounds." I dig beneath the decades to unearth memories of a school visit.

"In this castle there were rooms of marble and gold, and there were secret panels and levers, and people were carved into the walls – people who looked so real that you thought they might break out when no one was there and gallop through the halls on their horses…"

There's a snuffle of impatience and Meinir prompts me: "And the Bay…"

The old city centre holds little interest for my granddaughter. She's never been there – to her it's an item on the news, a blasted place of casualty figures and jagged ruins, barred windows and barricades. I return to familiar territory.

"And the Bay, oh, the Bay defied belief. Visitors came from all over the world to see it. There were great towers of silver and crystal, that caught the sun and dazzled for miles around. There were buildings shaped like stars and moons, and buildings shaped like birds with roofs like wings…"

"How high?" asks my granddaughter, as if she's never been told.

"So high that when you reached the top and looked down through the glass, you could see the real birds flying far below. And of course the most wonderful part of all was the Great Bay Bridge."

We bought this house because of the bridge. In those days we couldn't see the whole vista, as you could from some of the pricier places further up the hill, but the bridge swooped above the opposite roofline like a frozen rocket, sparkling at noon, glowing in the sunset with enamel shades of violet, azure and deep sea green. Even on dull days like this, when the tubular lights flicked on and the glass walls lost their colour and vanished into cool transparency, the Great Bay Bridge had magic. Frank and I would stand here, at the first-floor window of our new house, and watch people emerge on the see-through elevator to walk across the upper bow, apparently treading on nothing but air and light, some stopping to gawp at the sky or squeal at the pewter sea beneath them, some groping their way along the curved sides, some striding across with the proud complacency of locals. We could spend hours following their course up one side, down the other, mapping and redefining its elegant, elongated curve. That's why we made this our living room and had the bedrooms and bathroom moved downstairs. It was a hell of a job – took months of hole-digging and pipe-laying and furniture banked against walls and builders and plumbers swearing at unforeseen problems. But we never regretted it. One summer evening, as the towers began lighting up and the fainter illuminations of the city appeared on the horizon, Frank pointed out his office – his own yellow rectangle flickering into life – on the 23rd floor of Capital Tower.

"Is someone in your office?" I said, indignantly.

"No, they always have the upper floors lit up for aircraft" said Frank. He kept his voice level and matter-of-fact, making an effort not to sound condescending. Frank was used to accusation: don't patronise. Don't be a prig. Don't be so pompous. I didn't say these things to hurt him, although they were often true. It was Rhian who borrowed the phrases at an early age and injected them with venom; Rhian who made her father feel besieged in his own home.

She was born reluctantly, emerging after 18 hours with a raw scream of fury, and her anger stretched and developed with her skin and bones. We moved here just before her 10th birthday and she took the upheaval as a personal affront. She refused to open her presents here or to have a party. She hated the Bay, hated the water and the chink of moored boats and the cinemas and ice-cream parlours and the restaurant customers who sat outside to eat, and most of all she hated the Great Bay Bridge. To Rhian the bridge represented everything about our new home that was useless and sterile. What was wrong with our old place anyway? she fumed. What was wrong with trees and cars and proper gardens and corner shops? But look, we said, look at the view, look how far you can see from here – kings of the castle! She locked herself into her room. She wanted houses, not towers. Houses that sat eye-to-eye, not lording it over the terrace below or cowering under the next row up. As she grew older her loathing of the bridge grew too. It became an indictment of the wider world, a symbol of human arrogance. A flying leap, destined to fall.

Frank loved his job in Capital Tower. He loved the whole ritual of office life, the collar and studs of it, the trouser-crease, the takeaway latte. He never would have said so, but I always knew what a relief it was for him to retreat from domestic havoc and Rhian's temper to his work station's neon tranquillity. Diary, stapler, computer screen, memo pad, all in place, all quiet, serene and ordered. He loved to lose himself in the abstraction of finance and figures, their logic and sudden moods, the hilly contours of calculation and prediction.

When Rhian was a student she organised a protest at the base of the tower. There was a piece about it that evening on Wales Today. They showed Tower employees avoiding the crowd at the entrance, picking their way to the side doors across corporate pebbles and bark chippings. Then the camera panned along a line of demonstrators, travelling from face to face: one bellowing hearty slogans, one smirking self-consciously and then Rhian, glossy with distress, roaring at global injustice, mouth wide with grief for the crushed lives and dashed hopes of strangers.

Frank had gone in early that day. He sat in his high room by the floor-to-ceiling window and craned sideways to see the dots below. He couldn't make out which one of them was his daughter.

After dropping out of college Rhian calmed down. Her rage didn't exactly diminish: it set hard. She hitched round Europe, made her way to India, Latin America... we lost track. Occasionally she came home. When she did she treated us with polite reserve, on guard against any tricks of affection. She'd come for a couple of nights, maybe, or a meal, and would sit in the kitchen, or on the floor in the living room, as far away as possible from the view. She always turned up unannounced, and it always took me a few seconds to recognise her. Her hair might be black or white or green or a combination of colours. It might be long and twisted into cords, sprouting little coloured rags and wooden beads, or it might have been shaved off, so that the curve of her skull and neck were outlined with fuzzy bristles. She might be wearing layers of long, draping material that dragged on the ground, or army fatigues, or (one hot summer) what looked to me like vest and pants. On the last occasion I opened the door and saw a plump, pink-cheeked young woman with auburn hair scraped back into a pony-tail. She was wearing an old-fashioned floral dress and a mack that strained by one button over her swollen belly.

"Hello, Mum" she said. "Surprise, surprise."

Rhian had never told me about boyfriends or lovers or any other intimacies, and I knew better than to ask, even about the father of her child. She said, "Can I stay for a few days? It should all be over by then."

She was businesslike and brusque. She thought she'd disguised her fear.

"When you were my age" says Meinir, following her usual script, "what was the Bay like then?"

"Oh, when I was your age it was only just beginning."

She likes this story, too. She likes to hear about beginnings, about the first stone laid, the rising of floor above floor. She doesn't ask about endings yet. Perhaps some marrow-deep instinct of self-defence wards them off.

"When I was your age, there was no bridge at all. There were smaller buildings – a wooden church, where you could have tea, and a strange silver tube, a bit like a hot dog. In fact there was only one building that I could see then, and you can still see now. You know which one?"

"The red one" she says, absently. I turn and see her concentrating on a mental image, chewing the side of her thumbnail, trying to see a familiar landmark through my unfamiliar, eight-year-old eyes.

"That's right."

"Pierhead stands forever" sings Meinir, waggling her head from side to side, "Pierhead never falls…"

They've been teaching them that song from the nursery, ever since the Outbreak. During the worst years it was broadcast three times a day, always the same tuneless, defiant recording by a community youth choir. Since hostilities died down we've heard less of it, thank god.

Rhian left when Meinir was six months old. I knew she was leaving, though of course she said nothing about it. There was something about her – a change in her bearing, an intensity, a gathering-in, even as she went about ordinary tasks, tucking in Meinir's bib, spooning mush into her mouth. Actually, that was fairly unusual. Ever since Meinir's birth most of the daily baby-work had been left to me, while Rhian stood apart like an awkward house-guest. Frank asked me (in a whisper, in the safety of our own room) whether it might be post-natal depression, but I never thought so. Sometimes I caught her watching Meinir twitch and chirrup in her sleep, or stooping to let her clamp a fist around her hair. She seemed to battle against the urge to delight in her child.

But that day, the day of the Outbreak, Rhian fed and changed her daughter, stroked the hot downy head, twiddled the tiny toes, hummed a song I'd never heard. When Frank left for work that morning she said,

"Bye, Dad." Said it quite clearly, looking directly at him so that his colour rose. And then I knew she was leaving.

She'd gone by mid-afternoon. Meinir was having her nap and the day had subsided into a languid pause. Rhian appeared at the living-room door in her mack, with her hair pulled back as it had been the day she'd come home.

"What time does Dad normally get back?" she asked.

About six, I told her. She nodded once, efficiently, and said, "Right. I'm off out. Bye, Mum."

And I said goodbye, and sat there with my hand resting on the bar of Meinir's cot, and heard hurried footsteps down the stairs, and the click and clutch of the front door. I didn't call out, or ask where she was going and why. As I've tried to explain to so many people so many times, I knew there'd be no point. I just stayed where I was, listening to the backwash of silence and my granddaughter's quick, soft breaths.

At 7 o'clock that evening Frank called me in from the kitchen to see a newsflash. Meinir was restless, twisting and whining in my arms, and I had trouble following the gist of the report. Warning issued. Declaration made. Police evacuating area. The Great Bay Bridge appeared in a library shot, taken at another time of day in another season, showing children parading across it, sticking their tongues out for the cameras. Frank and I moved over to the window, Meinir still wriggling in protest. The bridge lights were on, and other lights around the Bay had started to needle the dusk. We couldn't see what was going on at ground level, but a number of boats had sailed into formation on the horizon, necklacing the entrance to the Bay. And it must be my imagination, but I could swear I saw Rhian, in vivid, close-range detail, standing at the apex of the emptied bridge, her mack buttoned over some new bulk, hands pressed against the glass, staring straight into the centres of my eyes. Then the sky erupted, a gash of red and black. The walls of the house bowed and trembled. Meinir jolted and for a split second was quiet, gazing at a snowstorm of glass. Shards and crumbs and shavings and specks. We heard it spatter into the water and rattle over the roof before Meinir could draw breath for a terrified howl.

"Rain, rain, go away…"

Meinir drags out every syllable. She's studying a scab on her knee, losing interest in my tales of 'before'. She wants to be outside, now, exploring the bombsites and skeletons of office blocks with her friends. I curse the rain and I curse the authorities for imposing this extra holiday. It's meant to be in celebration of peace, but distinctions such as peace and war have little meaning nowadays. No treaties, no signatures on dotted lines, no cut-off points for the convenience of future historians. No enemies we can name. For a few weeks after the Outbreak and the bombardment that followed, nobody could identify our assailants. Theories buzzed around. It was a worldwide alliance of anti-Western terrorists; a militant wing of the movement against globalisation; something to do with nationalism, something to do with anarchy... In the end they made them up: The Anti-System Coalition. That became the Antis, which was handy for cartoonists, who could show Anti with her Pantis Down, or Anti's Head on the Block, for the sake of public morale. The Antis themselves, as far as I'm aware, never offered any clues or explanations. What did we expect? If they were all like Rhian, they were simply playing a different game. All the same, I have a theory of my own: that Rhian was like a black hole, sucking in the wrath of every radical, every victim's despair, fuelling her power until she could engulf us all.

'Mum, I'm bored' Meinir moans. I squint towards the shattered stub of Capital Tower and the pocked harbour wall, but all I can see through the drizzle are the dim crane lights swinging over marshy ground.

'Let me see...' I try and sound as if I've got something up my sleeve. 'What can we do to entertain you...'

Strategies and stories – I dredge through them all, searching for a way to deflect her curiosity, to fend off the questions that are bound to come, about why cities fall and have to be built again.

Biographical Notes

Dannie Abse was born in Cardiff in 1923. Last year Hutchinson published his *New and Collected Poems* and Enitharmon brought out *The Two Roads Taken* which includes autobiographical essays touching on his two vocations – literature and medicine.

Ifor ap Glyn is London born and bred, but has lived in Caernarfon for many years. A noted performance poet, he has toured extensively. His sequence *Golau yn y Gwyll* (*Light in the Twilight*) which won the National Eisteddfod Crown in 1999, deals partly with the experience of people learning Welsh in Cardiff.

Trezza Azzopardi was born in Cardiff and has published two novels, *The Hiding Place* (2000) and *Remember Me* (2004). She lives in Norwich.

Leonora Brito was born in Cardiff and educated mainly in Cardiff Central Library. Her book of short stories *Dat's Love* was published by Seren in 1995. She has also written for TV and radio.

J. Brookes was born in south east London in 1951 and now lives in Cardiff where he edits the little poetry magazine, *The Yellow Crane*. He has published a number of booklets including *Dusting the Bin* (Red Sharks Press, 1994), *43 Poems* (The Profitless Press, 2000) and *The Deafening Nose* (The Profitless Press, 2001)

Sean Burke was born in Cardiff in 1961 and studied at the universities of Kent and Edinburgh. His books include *The Death and Return of the Author and Authorship: From Plato to the Postmodern*. His first novel, *Deadwater*, was published by Serpent's Tail in 2002. He currently lives in the North East and teaches English at the University of Durham.

Duncan Bush was born in Cardiff and educated there, then at Warwick University, Duke University (USA) and Wadham College, Oxford. He has published several prize-winning volumes of poetry, among which *Masks* was chosen as Welsh

Arts Council Book of the Year in 1995. His novels include *Glass Shot* and *The Genre of Silence*. He is a founding editor of *The Amsterdam Review*.

Gillian Clarke was born in Cardiff in 1937, and lived in or close to the city until 1984 when she moved to Ceredigion. She read English at Cardiff University. Poet, playwright and tutor on the M.Phil in Creative Writing at the University of Glamorgan, she is President of Ty Newydd, the Writers Centre in Gwynedd which she co-founded in 1990. Her last five collections of poetry, all published by Carcanet, have been Poetry Book Society recommendations, including *Making the Beds for the Dead*, April 2004.

Grahame Davies was born in Wrexham in 1964, has lived in south Wales since 1986 and in Cardiff since 1996. A poet, editor, literary critic and novelist, his *Cadwyni Rhyddid* won the Welsh Book of the Year Award in 2002. His web site is www.grahamedavies.com

Lewis Davies moved to Cardiff in 1990 to avoid law school. He is a founding member of Parthian, the independent publisher set up at 53, Colum Road, Cathays, Cardiff in 1993. His play and novel *My Piece of Happiness* is set in the city. After several attempts he finally escaped in 2002. His collection of essays *As I Was A Boy Fishing* also features the city.

Tom Davies grew up in Cardiff and now lives in the Bay. 'How Jack London Got me my First Berth' is an excerpt from *Mirror Man*, a memoir in which he traces how he was crucially affected by artists and writers in his youth. He is the author of sixteen books including four novels set in Wales, the latest of which is *One Winter*. His *Merlyn the Magician and the Pacific Coast Highway* was shortlisted for the Thomas Cook Travel prize and was hailed by Bono, the U2 singer, as the one book which changed his life.

Anna Davis grew up in Cardiff, studied at Manchester University and lives in London with her husband and baby daughter. She is the author of three novels: *The Dinner*, *Melting* and *Cheet*, all published by Sceptre. A fourth, *The Shoe Queen*, is currently in progress.

Sonia Edwards won the main prose prize at the National Eisteddfod in 1999, and she is a prolific author of both prose and poetry. Her *Merch Noeth* (*Nude Girl*) was longlisted for the 2003 Welsh Book of the Year prize.

Mari Emlyn was born in Cardiff in 1964. She studied Theatre in London before moving to Felinheli in north Wales. She is an actress, television scriptwriter, dramatist and novelist. Her second novel *Traed Oer* (*Cold Feet*) was published in October 2004.

Peter Finch was born in Cardiff where he still lives. He is a poet, critic and occasional historian. He ran the Oriel bookshop for more than twenty years and is now Chief Executive of Academi, the Welsh National Literature Promotion Agency and Society of Writers. He is author of *Real Cardiff* and *Real Cardiff Two* from Seren. His *New and Selected Later Poems* is due from Seren in 2007. His web site is www.peterfinch.co.uk.

Mari George was born in Bridgend in 1973 and has lived in Cardiff for five years. A poet and television script writer, she has won the Literary Medal and the Chair at the Urdd Eisteddfod. In 2003 she travelled to Mexico for six months to work with street children. She has received a Welsh Academi grant to write a book on her experiences.

Niall Griffiths was born in Liverpool in 1966 and has now been a mid-Wales resident for over ten years. He is the author of five novels. The latest, *Wreckage*, was published early 2005. His work has been translated into several languages and two of his novels are being filmed. A novella, *Runt*, will be published early next year.

Tessa Hadley was born in Bristol, has lived in Cardiff since 1982, and teaches at Bath Spa University College. She has written two novels. *Everything Will Be All Right*, was published by Jonathan Cape in January 2004 and was shortlisted for the Encore Award for second novels. She has had short stories published in the *New Yorker* and *Granta*, and has also written a book on Henry James.

Graham Hartill lived in Cardiff for ten years in the seventies and eighties working on community projects. He got involved in the poetry scene and did many readings and performances. He now lives near Abergavenny where his selected poems, *Cennau's Bell* was published in 2005 by The Collective.

James Hawes lives in Cardiff. His novels include *White Merc With Fins*, *Rancid Aluminium* (which was turned into what Hawes admits was 'the worst film ever made in the UK'), *Dead Long Enough* and his skit on the eccentricities of Welsh media life *White Powder, Green Light*. *Dead Long Enough* is in film development.

Viki Holmes is a Cardiff-based writer and performer who first entered the city's poetry scene as part of the Happy Demon poetry collective. Her poetry has been published in the Parthian anthology *Pterodactyl's Wing:Welsh World Writing*, and magazines including *Poetry Wales*, *The Yellow Crane* and *The New Welsh Review*.

Mererid Hopwood was born in Cardiff; and in 2001 became the first woman to win the Chair of the National Eisteddfod, which is reserved for strict-metre poetry. In 2003 she added the Eisteddfod Crown to her trophies. An expert in German literature, she is also a translator and freelance writer. She now lives in Carmarthenshire.

Anthony Howell was born in 1945. By 1995 he was a dancer in the Royal Ballet, but soon after he left the ballet to concentrate on writing. In 1973, he was invited to join the program for International Writers at the University of Iowa. Since then his output has included many collections of poetry, mainly published by Anvil, the most recent being his *Selected Poems* and *Dancers in Daylight*. His novel, *In the Company of Others*, was published by Marion Boyars in 1986. He has just been awarded a £6,000 Live Art Development Fund Bursary to study the tango.

Bill James was born and educated in Cardiff and now lives just outside. He is author of the *Harpur and Iles* crime novels. The latest is number twenty-one, *Easy Streets*. He has also written several crime novels set around Cardiff docks – where he grew up – most recently, *Hear Me Talking to You*. He has published a critical study of the British novelist with Welsh roots, Anthony Powell.

T. James Jones was born in Newcastle Emlyn, but is more recently resident in Cardiff. He was an Independent minister, drama lecturer and script editor, and won the Eisteddfod Crown in Fishguard in 1986 and Newport in 1988.

Emyr Lewis was born in London in 1957 and brought up in Cardiff. An expert in Welsh strict-metre cynghanedd poetry, he has won both the Crown and the Chair of the National Eisteddfod. His Crown poem for 1998, 'Rhyddid' (Freedom) was set in Cardiff.

Geraint Lewis is from Tregaron but now lives in Cardiff. A full-time writer for 20 years, he is a scriptwriter, dramatist and novelist. His Cardiff-located novel *Daw Eto Haul* (*Sun Will Come*) was on the long list for the Welsh Book of the Year in 2003.

Phil Maillard was born in London in 1948, and has lived (mostly) in south Wales since 1975. He currently works in Cardiff as an NHS speech therapist. He has published five poetry collections and a paperback of stories.

Owen Martell lives in Cardiff, although he was brought up at Pont Nedd Fechan in the Neath valley. His first novel *Cadw dy Ffydd Brawd* (*Keep the Faith, Brother*) won the Novel 2000 and Welsh Book of the Year prize in 2000, and his second novel *Dyn yr Eiliad* (*Man of the Moment*) was shortlisted for the 2003 Book of the Year prize.

Owain Meredith was born in Cardiff in 1969 and moved to the Llanuwchllyn area when he was 10. He edited the pop magazine *Sothach* between 1992 and 1995, and was a rapper with the group *Pregethwr III* before joining HTV in Cardiff. He is now a film historian and producer.

Twm Miall, real name Llion Williams, was born in Trawsfynydd, Meirionnydd, in 1956. He lived in Cardiff for 16 years. He's the author of two novels and has written extensively for Theatr Bara Caws and S4C. He now lives in Caernarfon.

Gareth Miles is a prolific novelist, dramatist and television writer as well as being an influential radical political activist. Born in Caernarfon in 1938, he now lives in Pontypridd.

Tôpher Mills lives in Cardiff two doors away from the house he was born in. He has published several books of poetry and had his writing published and performed in many magazines, anthologies and on radio and television. He's written regular review columns in the *Western Mail* and *New Welsh Review*. He is currently stringing sentences together in the vain hope that a novel will appear.

Sheenagh Pugh was born in 1950 and has lived in Wales, mainly Cardiff, since 1971. She read German and Russian at Bristol and teaches creative writing at the University of Glamorgan. Her collection of poems, *The Beautiful Lie,* was shortlisted for the 2003 Whitbread Prize. Her most recent collection is *The Movement of Bodies.*

Elinor Wyn Reynolds, was born in Treorchy in 1970, and brought up in Carmarthen, lived in Cardiff for a while and is now back in Carmarthen. She is a poet, broadcaster and dramatist, and is a popular performer of her own work on tours.

Lloyd Robson is a poet and prose writer whose texts spillover into typography, photography, visual art and performance. His poetry/prose collection *bbboing! & associated weirdness* and his novel/prose-poem *cardiff cut* are both published by Parthian.

Penny Simpson moved to Cardiff in 1989, initially to work for the *Western Mail* and *Echo.* She's still not left. *DOGdays,* her debut collection of short stories, is published by Gomer Press (www.dogfiction.co.uk) and her play *Knuckle Down* will premiere at the Edinburgh Fringe Festival in 2005.

Iain Sinclair was born in Cardiff but left almost immediately for Maesteg. He visited Hackney for a weekend in 1968 and has been there ever since, writing novels that lean heavily on cullings from newsprint (*Downriver, Dining on Stones*) and polemics of walking and stalking (*Lights out for the Territory, London Orbital*) that aspire to the condition of myth. His solitary attempt at a Welsh book, *Landor's Tower,* was judged, by metropolitans, to be a career suicide note.

Ifor Thomas has lived in Cardiff since 1973. A veteran of the performance poetry groups Cabaret 246, Horses Mouth and Working Title Writers he has published five books of poetry and one book of short stories. In 1999 he won the John Tripp award for spoken poetry. His work has featured on radio and television.

Chris Torrance was born in Edinburgh and helped start *Origins Diversions* magazine in the early 1960s. Based in the Neath valley for 30 years now, Chris is a founder member of poetry and music band HEAT POETS (formerly POETHEAT).

Anna Wigley is Cardiff born and bred. She studied English at the University, and wrote a Ph.D. on the novels of Iris Murdoch. Her first collection of poems, *The Bird Hospital*, was published by Gomer in 2002, and a book of short stories, *Footprints*, has recently appeared.

Andrew Craig Williams was born in 1977, and lives with his partner in Cardiff. He has previously been published in *The Yellow Crane*, *Poetry Wales* and *The New Welsh Review*. His web site address is www.andrewcraigwilliams.co.uk.

Herbert Williams was born in Aberystwyth but has spent most of his life in Cardiff. He has written 16 books including poetry and short story collections, novels, biography and history. His novels include *Punters*, set in Cardiff, *The Woman in Back Row*, and *A Severe Case of Dandruff*, based on his time in a TB sanatorium.

John Williams lives with his family in his hometown of Cardiff. He is the author of seven books including four works of fiction set in his hometown of Cardiff, the most recent of which is *Temperance Town* (Bloomsbury, 2004).

Nia Williams was born in Cardiff in 1961 and studied History at Exeter and European Studies at Reading. Her short stories have been published in a number of anthologies and in *Cambrensis* magazine, and have been broadcast on BBC Radio 4 and Radio Wales. Her first novel, *The Pier Glass*, was published by Honno in 2001, and the second, *Persons Living or Dead*, is due for publication in September 2005. She currently lives in Oxford, where she works as a freelance writer, editor and pianist.

Acknowledgements

Return Ticket to Cardiff (Dannie Abse) appeared in *A Strong Dose of Myself*, Hutchinson 1983; 'The Story of Lazarus' was Dannie Abse's contribution to The Great Cardiff Poem; it is included in his *New and Collected Poems*, Hutchinson 2003; *Light in the Twilight* (Ifor ap Glyn), was first published in Welsh as *Golau yn y Gwyll* in the compositions and adjudications of the National Eisteddfod of Wales in 1999, and then appeared in *Cerddi Map yr Underground* (Gwasg Carreg Gwalch, 2001), translated extracts first appeared in *Oxygen*, Seren, 2000; 'The Three Disastrous Poetry Readings of the Island of Britain' (Ifor ap Glyn) first appeared in *Golchi Llestri mewn Bar Mitzvah*, Gwasg Carreg Gwalch, 1998 as '*Tri Darlleniad Trychinebus Ynys Prydain*', and the translation first appeared in *Oxygen*, Seren 2000; 'Warning, Welsh Assembly' (Ifor ap Glyn) first appeared in *Cerddi Map yr Underground*, Gwasg Carreg Gwalch, 2001, and the translation appears here for the first time; 'Cardiff Glowed' (Trezza Azzopardi) is from *The Hiding Place*, Picador 2000; *Digging For Victory* (Leonora Brito) is from *Dat's Love*, Seren 1995; 'St. Fagans', 'Caravan Site', 'St Mary's Well Bay', and 'Lisvane' (J. Brookes) are previously unpublished; 'Europe's Most Exciting Waterfront' (Sean Burke) is from *Deadwater*, Serpent's Tail, 2002; 'Hayes Island' and 'Butcher's Window' (Duncan Bush) are from *Glass Shot*, Secker & Warburg, 1991; 'Letting the Light In' (Gillian Clarke) is previously unpublished; 'You Alright?' (Lewis Davies) is from *As I Was A Boy Fishing*, Parthian, 2003; 'Red' (Grahame Davies) was first published in Welsh as 'Coch' in *Barddas*, and the English translation first appeared in *Oxygen*, Seren 2000; 'Grey' (Grahame Davies) was commissioned by the Wales Millennium Centre in 2003, together with a Welsh companion piece, 'Llwyd', to commemorate the laying of the foundation stone of the building; 'Number 62 Bus' (Grahame Davies) first appeared in Welsh as 'Bws Rhif 62' in *Taliesin*. The translation is previously unpublished; 'How Jack London Got Me My First Berth' (Tom Davies) is previously unpublished; 'Tequila-Bonkers' (Anna Davis) is previously unpublished; 'Nude Girl' (Sonia Edwards) is taken from the novel *Merch Noeth*, Gwasg Gwynedd 2003, which was on the longlist for the Book of the Year Award, the translated extract is previously unpublished; 'Step by Step' (Mari Emlyn) is an extract from the Welsh-language novel *Cam Wrth Gam*, Gomer, 2002, the translated extract is previously unpublished; 'The Entry of Christ Into Cardiff' (Peter Finch, 2004) is previously unpublished; a version of 'St Mary Street' (Peter Finch) appeared in *Real Cardiff Two*, Seren, 2004; 'Wales From the Air' (Mari George) was commissioned by S4C for a series of films screened in 2003, in which Welsh-language poets responded to aerial films of Wales (translation previously unpublished); 'A Kind Of Liverpool/Cardiff Thing' (Niall Griffiths) is previously unpublished; 'The Trouble Is With Summer' (Tessa Hadley) is previously unpublished; 'Cardiff Ghosts' (Graham Hartill) is previously unpublished; 'Artichokes' (James Hawes) is taken from *White Powder, Green Light*, Jonathan Cape, 2002; *post card #1 (winter wonderland)* (Viki Holmes) is previously unpublished; 'A Walker On The Wall' first appeared in *Howell's Law*, Anvil, 1990 (Anthony Howell); 'Beneath the Shadow of John Bachelor The Friend of Freedom' and 'Cardiff Born' (Mererid Hopwood) both appeared first in *Cerddi Caerdydd*, Gomer, 2004. 'Big City' (Bill James) first appeared in *Ellery Queen* magazine; 'Robert Croft' and 'Question' (T. James Jones) first appeared in Welsh in *Diwrnod i'r Brenin*, Barddas, 2002 (translations previously unpublished); 'Freedom' (Emyr Lewis) first appeared in Welsh as '*Rhyddid*' in the compositions and adjudications of the National Eisteddfod of Wales in 1998, the translated extracts first appeared in *Oxygen*, Seren, 2000; 'Sun Will Come' (Geraint Lewis) is extracted from the novel *Daw Eto Haul*, Gwasg Carreg Gwalch, 2003, which was on the long list for the Book of the Year award (translated extract previously unpublished); 'The Arm' (Phil Maillard) is previously unpublished; 'Man of the Moment' (Owen Martell) is from the novel *Dyn yr Eiliad*, Gomer, 2003, which was shortlisted for the Book of the Year Prize (translation previously unpublished); 'Totally Mindblowing Day Today' (Owain Meredith) is extracted from the novel '*Diwrnod Hollol Mindblowing Heddiw*', Lolfa, 1997 (translated extract previously unpublished); 'Dole Queue'

(Twm Miall) is an extract from the novel *Cyw Dôl*, Lolfa, 1990 (translated extract previously unpublished); 'Fireworks Party' (Gareth Miles) is an extract from the novel *Cwmtec*, Carreg Gwalch 2002 (translated extract previously unpublished); 'Nevuh Fuhget Yuh Kaairdiff' (Tôpher Mills) is from *The Bicycle is an Easy Pancake*, Red Sharks Press, 1987; 'Dis Is Jest Tuh Say Like' (Tôpher Mills) is from *Swimming In The Living Room*, Red Sharks Press, 1995; 'Toast' (Sheenagh Pugh) was a runner-up in the Academi's Cardiff International Poetry Competition, first published in *New Welsh Review* and then collected in *The Beautiful Lie*, Seren, 2002; 'Nye' (Elinor Wyn Reynolds) is a translation of a previously unpublished poem; 'a curious place' (Lloyd Robson) is previously unpublished; 'Something For The Weekend' (Penny Simpson) is previously unpublished; 'Crackerjack' (Iain Sinclair) appeared in an earlier version in *Brought to Book*, edited by Ian Breakwell and Paul Hammond, Penguin, 1994; 'I Told Her I Loved Her A Lot In Splott' (Ifor Thomas) first appeared in *Giving Blood 2*, Red Sharks Press, 1987; 'Caroline Street' (Ifor Thomas) is previously unpublished; a short section from 'The Loneliness of the Long Distance Writing Tutor' (Chris Torrance), 'Haibun – Road Rage', appeared in *Wobbly Chair*, Canna Press 2003; 'Carnival' (Chris Torrance) first appeared in *Poetry Wales*; 'In The Castle Grounds' (Anna Wigley) first appeared in *The Bird Hospital*, Gomer, 2001; 'Rosie's Last Week' (Andrew Craig Williams) is previously unpublished; 'Brief Encounter' (Herbert Williams) first appeared in *The Stars In Their Courses*, Alun Books, 1992; 'The Legend of Tiger Bay' is copyright John Williams, 2004, and is largely based on a chapter from his *Bloody Valentine*, HarperCollins 1994; 'The Great Bay Bridge' (Nia Williams) is previously unpublished.

A Note on the Translations

Around a quarter of the items in this book were written originally in Welsh, and appear here in English translation. In two
cases – those of Ifor ap Glyn and Elinor Wyn Reynolds – the
translations were done by the original authors. In all other cases
they were done by Grahame Davies, although in consultation
with the original authors. A couple of points about the translations are worth mentioning. The first is from a prose work. In
the extract from Twm Miall's novel *Cyw Dol*, (*Dole Queue*)
when the main character speaks English, his speech is spelt as
though the words were Welsh, e.g. "ddy" for "the". This is how
the English-language speech was represented in the original
novel, where it is intended to convey the character's strong
accent and his discomfort in speaking the English language.
This spelling has been retained in the translation to represent
those parts of the narrative where the character is speaking
English. Where, in the original, he speaks Welsh, in which he is
comfortable, normal English spelling is used.

The second point relates to poetry. The work of two of the
Welsh-language poets, T. James Jones and Mererid Hopwood,
whose original work was written in the Welsh strict metres
known as cynghanedd. These are very ancient metrical forms in
which an intricate and complex system of internal rhyme and
alliteration is used, in conjunction with a strict system of metre,
stress and end-rhymes. It is notoriously difficult to translate
cynghanedd, and in the case of the four examples here, no
attempt has been made to represent the internal rhyme and alliteration. However, an attempt has been made to represent the
end-rhyme pattern of couplets which rhyme alternately on
stressed and unstressed syllables. It has also been attempted to
try to convey something of the syllabic structure of the original
verse together with the sometimes incantatory quality which is
often an essential part of the effect of these ancient metres.
Other poems which do use rhyme and metre, but which are not
in cynghanedd, such as those by Emyr Lewis and Grahame
Davies himself, are represented with rhyme and metre structures much closer to those of the original poems.

Real Cardiff and Real Cardiff Two

Jan Morris hailed *Real Cardiff* as "...a marvellous book – one of the very best books about a city I have ever read." In it Peter Finch discovers the real Cardiff – lost rivers, Roman forts, holy wells, Arthurian knights, itinerant poets, the old race course, the revitalised city centre, the redeveloped Bay – as he travels the city from east to west and north to south. This is offbeat topographical writing, guaranteed to enthrall the native, the visitor and the armchair traveller alike. It's celebratory, it's subversive, it's Real Cardiff.

And in *Real Cardiff Two*, Finch explores the city further, visiting the parts the tourist guides don't tell you about, exploring the far reaches and even crossing the Atlantic in search of the Cardiff Giant. He traces the original route of the River Canna, plots the ancient town walls, views the city from the roof of the Millennium Centre and meets Billy the Seal in the National Museum.

Other anthologies from Seren

The Chosen People: Wales and the Jews
ed. Grahame Davies

The histories of the Welsh people and the Jewish people have entwined in a number of ways over the centuries. Grahame Davies' illuminating anthology draws on poetry, drama, novels, short stories and memoirs to reveal the variety of Welsh responses to the Jewish people from the sixth century to the present day: from conversionism to comradeship, and from scepticism to solidarity. Among the topics covered are the curious tale of the Welsh Calvinistic Methodists' mission to convert the Jews; the sensational Cardiff Jewess abduction case; the dramatic Welsh role in the recapture of Jerusalem from the Turks; the shameful anti-semitic riots in the Valleys; the parallels drawn between Welsh and Hebrew; and the crucial part played by Wales in the establishment of the State of Israel. Contributors include Dannie Abse, Aneurin Bevan, Richard Burton, George Eliot, David Lloyd George, Gwenallt, Josef Herman, TE Lawrence, Saunders Lewis, Bernice Rubens, WG Sebald and Lewis Valentine.

Birdsong ed. Dewi Roberts

From the epic mythologies of the *Mabinogion* through to the present day, birds have exerted a powerful influence on the literature of Wales. This unique anthology brings together a remarkable range of poetry and prose, illustrating the varied and multi-layered responses of writers across the centuries. Fragile, yet marvellously enduring, birds are the spark for powerful writing, a cause of wonder, reverence and joyous celebration. Includes RS Thomas, Gerard Manley Hopkins, Gillian Clarke, Gwyneth Lewis and Dafydd ap Gwilym.

Christmas in Wales ed. Dewi Roberts

Celebrate Christmas the Welsh way, in the company of some of the country's leading writers, past and present. Among the many subjects drawn from stories, poems, diaries and letters are Christmas Mass, the Nativity Play, plum pudding and turkey, folk customs such as the Mari Lwyd, shopping, presents, frost and snow, and the post-Christmas blues. *Christmas in Wales* is the perfect literary companion to the festive season, a present that will be opened again and again...

Childhood: An Anthology for Grown-ups
ed. Dewi Roberts

Childhood has always been a source of particular fascination for writers. This hugely entertaining and wide-ranging anthology surveys the pleasures and pains of growing up. Here are our shared experiences of childhood – the everyday and the extraordinary – in poems, stories, novels and memoirs. These pieces are sure to strike a chord with grown-ups everywhere – and put them in touch with the child within.

Love from Wales ed. Tony Curtis & Siân James

The passionate nature of the Welsh finds full expression in *Love From Wales*, a selection of poetry and prose on the theme of love in a Celtic climate. Poet Tony Curtis and novelist Siân James have chosen from the works of Wales' most intense and romantic writers in an anthology ranging from the eleventh century to the present, including translations from the original Welsh. Writers include Jean Earle, David Lloyd George, Dafydd ap Gwilym, Richard Llewellyn, Edward Thomas, Jean Rhys, Emyr Humphreys, Alexander Cordell and many more.